*Millay at* 100

*Ad Feminam: Women and Literature*
Edited by Sandra M. Gilbert

*Christina Rossetti*
The Poetry of Endurance
By Dolores Rosenblum

*Lunacy of Light*
Emily Dickinson and the Experience of Metaphor
By Wendy Barker

*The Literary Existence of Germaine de Staël*
By Charlotte Hogsett

*Margaret Atwood*
Vision and Forms
Edited by Kathryn VanSpanckeren and Jan Garden Castro

*He Knew She Was Right*
The Independent Woman in the Novels of Anthony Trollope
By Jane Nardin

*The Woman and the Lyre*
Women Writers in Classical Greece and Rome
By Jane McIntosh Snyder

*Refiguring the Father*
New Feminist Readings of Patriarchy
Edited by Patricia Yaeger and Beth Kowaleski-Wallace

*Writing in the Feminine*
Feminism and Experimental Writing in Quebec
By Karen Gould

*Rape and Writing in the* Heptaméron *of Marguerite de Navarre*
By Patricia Francis Cholakian

*Writing Love: Letters, Women, and the Novel in France, 1605–1776*
By Katharine Ann Jensen

*The Body and the Song*
Elizabeth Bishop's Poetics
By Marilyn May Lombardi

# *Millay at* 100
## *A Critical Reappraisal*

### *Edited by Diane P. Freedman*

*Southern Illinois University Press*
*Carbondale and Edwardsville*

*For my sisters, supportive always*

Illustration on title page, portrait of Edna St. Vincent Millay, photograph by Mishkin. Used by permission of Elizabeth Barnett, literary executor.

Quotations from the work of Edna St. Vincent Millay appearing in this volume are protected by the copyright laws of the United States of America and are reprinted by permission of Elizabeth Barnett, literary executor. All rights to these quotations are strictly reserved.

The lines from "Twenty-One Love Poems" are reprinted from THE DREAM OF A COMMON LANGUAGE, Poems 1974–1977, by Adrienne Rich, by permission of the author and W. W. Norton & Company, Inc. Copyright © 1978 by W. W. Norton & Company, Inc.

**Library of Congress Cataloging-in-Publication Data**

Millay at 100 : a critical reappraisal / edited by Diane P. Freedman.
    p.  cm. — (Ad feminam)
    Includes bibliographical references and index.
    1. Millay, Edna St. Vincent, 1892–1950—Criticism and interpretation.
2. Women and literature—United States—History—20th century.  I. Freedman, Diane P.  II. Title: Millay at one hundred.  III. Series.
PS3525.I495Z73  1995
811'.52—dc20                      94-12823
   ISBN 0-8093-1973-X             CIP

# Contents

# Ad Feminam:
# Women and Literature

Ad Hominem: to the man; appealing to personal interests, prejudices, or emotions rather than to reason; *an argument ad hominem.*

*—American Heritage Dictionary*

Until quite recently, much literary criticism, like most humanistic studies, has been in some sense constituted out of arguments *ad hominem.* Not only have examinations of literary history tended to address themselves "to the man"—that is, to the identity of what was presumed to be the *man* of letters who created our culture's monuments of unaging intellect—but many aesthetic analyses and evaluations have consciously or unconsciously appealed to the "personal interests, prejudices, or emotions" of male critics and readers. As the title of this series is meant to indicate, the intellectual project called "feminist criticism" has sought to counter the limitations of *ad hominem* thinking about literature by asking a series of questions addressed *ad feminam:* to the woman as both writer and reader of texts.

First, and most crucially, feminist critics ask, What is the relationship between gender and genre, between sexuality and textuality? But in meditating on these issues they raise a number of more specific questions. Does a woman of letters have a literature—a language, a history, a tradition—of her own? Have conventional methods of canon-formation tended to exclude or marginalize female achievements? More generally, do men and women have different modes of literary representation, different definitions of literary production? Do such differences mean that distinctive male- (or female-) authored images of women (or men), as well as distinctly male and female genres, are part of our intellectual heritage? Perhaps most important, are literary differences between men and women essential or accidental, biologically determined or culturally constructed?

Feminist critics have addressed themselves to these problems with increasing sophistication during the last two decades, as they sought to revise, or at times replace, *ad hominem* arguments with *ad feminam* speculations. Whether explicating individual texts, studying the oeuvre of a single author, examining the permutations of a major theme, or charting the contours of a tradition, these theorists and scholars have consistently sought to define literary manifestations of difference and to understand the dynamics that have shaped the accomplishments of literary women.

As a consequence of such work, feminist critics, often employing new modes of analysis, have begun to uncover a neglected female tradition along with a heretofore hidden history of the literary dialogue between men and women. This series is dedicated to publishing books that will use innovative as well as traditional interpretive methods in order to help readers of both sexes achieve a clearer consciousness of that neglected but powerful tradition and a better understanding of that hidden history. Reason tells us, after all, that if, transcending prejudice and special pleading, we speak to, and focus on, the woman as well as the man—if we think *ad feminam* as well as *ad hominem*—we will have a better chance of understanding what constitutes the human.

Sandra M. Gilbert

# Acknowledgments

In 1992, for three days surrounding the one hundredth anniversary of the birth of Edna St. Vincent Millay, Skidmore College hosted its third and most ambitious conference devoted to the life and work of Millay. "Millay at 100: A Critical Reappraisal," like the two conferences preceding it, was the creative result of the affection, hard work, and generosity of a great many persons. The conference, which featured five of Millay's poems set to music by Deems Taylor, book and art exhibits, along with critical reappraisals, served as source and springboard for this critical collection, and its supporters should be mentioned here.

Foremost among enthusiasts and supporters are Frank Crohn, Chairman of the Board of Trustees of the Edna St. Vincent Millay Society, and his wife Helene. The Crohns supplied the impetus for the conference series at Skidmore with their extensive donation of Millay materials ranging from correspondence to autographed first and rare editions, and they provided a generous grant towards the 1992 conference. Several administrative and academic units at Skidmore College, chief among them the Office of the Dean of Faculty, the Office of the President, the Lucy Scribner Library, and the Departments of English, Women's Studies, and Music, also provided financial and personnel support. Guidance and inspiration were provided throughout by several other board members of the Millay Society: Elizabeth Barnett, Vice President and Literary Executor of the Millay Estate, to whom this collection is especially and additionally indebted; Holly Peppe, President of the Society and a contributor to the volume; and Nancy Milford, biographer, also our keynote speaker at the conference. I thank as well all the other conference participants whose work, whether or not directly included in this volume, helped shape and sustain it. I especially wish to thank contributor and conference speaker Sandra M. Gilbert for encouraging me to produce a volume for the Ad Feminam series at Southern Illinois University Press.

Although I have compiled and edited this volume while at the University of New Hampshire, and with its assistance, I could neither have organized the 1992 conference nor committed myself to this collection were it not for the invitation, support, and diligence of my former Skidmore colleagues, several of whom—Terence Diggory, Susan Kress, Barry Goldensohn, Alan Wheelock, Carolyn Anderson, Phil West, Charlotte Goodman, Sarah Webster Goodwin, and Phyllis Roth—deserve special mention.

At the University of New Hampshire, the Department of English and Michael DePorte have supported the publication project in countless ways small and large. The Dean of Faculty of the College of Liberal Arts, Stuart Palmer, has very generously supported my work in the form of both a summer research fellowship and a grant for research and editorial assistants, without whom this project could not have been completed. The research, editorial, and technical support of former University of New Hampshire students Vicki Beaudoin, Justin Tussing, and, especially, Daniel Huston is greatly appreciated.

# Editor's Introduction

Edna St. Vincent Millay has long enjoyed popular and biographical attention, if not always critical respect. In 1920, she was what Sandra M. Gilbert terms the "It-girl" of poetry following the publication of *A Few Figs from Thistles*.[1] Not quite the Anne Sexton or Tama Janowitz of her generation, Millay was nonetheless an actress performing—"more like a diva than like the gray-suited male poets," writes Suzanne Clark. With her feminine beauty, youth, and large collection of trailing gowns for readings, Millay, America's foremost sonneteer and important verse dramatist,[2] was beloved in the popular imagination for the personal and poetic performative emotion for which some critics soon condemned her.

Her history is fairly well known. Raised in Union, Rockland, and Camden, Maine, Millay lived with her mother, Cora, and her younger sisters, Norma and Kathleen, her parents having divorced when Edna was eight. (Both Cora and Kathleen wrote poetry; Norma was an actress and a singer and served as Millay's editor and literary executor following her death.) At nineteen, Millay won recognition for her poetry, especially "Renascence," appearing in the anthology *The Lyric Year*. She attended Vassar College from 1913 to 1917, lived and loved in Greenwich Village through 1920 (the period in which she also appeared as an actress at the Provincetown Playhouse), traveled abroad (bringing her mother to Europe for

---

1. Gilbert borrows from Elizabeth Atkins's assessment of Millay as "the It-girl of the hour, the Miss America of 1920" (qtd. in Gilbert, "Female Female Impersonator").

2. See, for example, Patton, "Edna St. Vincent Millay" and "Edna St. Vincent Millay as a Verse Dramatist" or Tate, "Miss Millay's Sonnets."

several months) from 1921 to 1923, and in 1923, married Eugen Boissevain and became the first woman poet to win the Pulitzer Prize in poetry.

Though she left New York City to live with Eugen at Steepletop, a seven-hundred-acre farm they purchased in Austerlitz, New York,[3] often summering on Ragged Island in Maine, Millay followed and wrote on behalf of political causes. In 1949, Eugen died, and a little more than a year later in October 1950, Millay also died. She had been working on poems for another book. The volume *Mine the Harvest* was published posthumously.

Millay was a prolific author. Her published volumes include *Renascence and Other Poems* (1917); *A Few Figs from Thistles* (1920; enlarged ed., 1922); *Aria da Capo* (1920); *Two Slatterns and a King* (1921); *The Lamp and the Bell* (1921); *Second April* (1921); *The Harp-Weaver and Other Poems* (1923); *Distressing Dialogues* (1924, published under "Nancy Boyd"); *Three Plays* (1926); *The King's Henchman* (1927); *The Buck in the Snow and Other Poems* (1928); *Poems Selected for Young People* (1929); *Fatal Interview* (1931); *The Princess Marries the Page* (1932); *Wine from These Grapes* (1934); *Flowers of Evil* (1936, a translation from the French of Charles Baudelaire by Millay and George Dillon); *Conversation at Midnight* (1937); *Huntsman, What Quarry?* (1939); *Make Bright the Arrows* (1940); *1940 Notebook* (1940); *Collected Sonnets* (1941); *The Murder of Lidice* (1942); *Collected Lyrics* (1943); *Letters of Edna St. Vincent Millay* (1952); *Mine the Harvest* (1954, edited by Norma Millay Ellis); *Collected Poems* (1956, edited by Norma Millay Ellis); *Collected Sonnets* (1988, revised and expanded edition with an introduction by Norma Millay coedited by Elizabeth Barnett and Holly Peppe); and *Edna St. Vincent Millay: Selected Poems*, the Centenary edition (1991, edited and with a critical introduction by Colin Falck).

The intensity of Millay's popularity started to wane in the late

---

3. The Millay Society is based at Steepletop, now a repository of Millay materials and the site of the Millay Colony for the Arts. The Society hopes to restore Millay's former home to serve as a library and a museum, further documenting the poet's life and work for scholars and the general public the world over.

1930s, when her critical reputation and the attention paid her declined under the reign of high modernism and its critics, as several essays here detail. Jo Ellen Green Kaiser reminds us, for example, that a popularity due to the force of her personality was not exactly the modernist formula for art and the artist. Kaiser goes on to say that like others of her generation, Millay wrote some modernist-imagist verse, viewed literature as a profession, and perceived a crisis in meaning but that she rejected modernist elitism and its lack of "faith in the political present . . . and in the general public's ability to recognize and reform its world." Instead, Millay used her powerful public voice to plead for an end to the Sacco and Vanzetti trials or for U.S. entry into World War II. She was condemned both for her politicizing and her political poetry. She was denigrated by John Ciardi for her posturing and melodrama, by John Crowe Ransom for being insufficiently masculine (intellectual, unemotional), and by M. L. Rosenthal for sentimentality and spontaneous emotionality. She herself confessed that she and her poetry suffered in the service of public causes.

But the wide range of the accomplishments of Edna St. Vincent Millay deserves and is finally receiving renewed public and critical praise—beginning with feminist critical attention in the late 1970s and continuing through the 1992 celebrations in honor of the one hundredth anniversary of her birth on 22 February 1892: poetry readings, theatrical performances, art and book exhibits, a spate of new manuscripts and books, and the three-day conference held at Skidmore College in Saratoga Springs, New York. "Millay at 100: A Critical Reappraisal," brought together renowned experts in Millay and modern poetry and resulted in this volume.

Also in 1992, Suzanne Clark and Cheryl Walker, whose essays are included here, published chapters on Millay in their books, *Sentimental Modernism: Women Writers and the Revolution of the Word* and *Masks Outrageous and Austere: Culture, Psyche, and Persona in Modern Women Poets*, respectively. Colin Falck, a conference speaker, drew many to Millay with the centenary edition of *Edna St. Vincent Millay: Selected Poems*. Nancy Milford, keynote speaker, wrote "The Final Chapter" in her forthcoming biography of Millay, from which she spoke at the conference. William Thesing, a conference speaker, sent to press *Critical Essays on Edna St. Vincent Millay*, his edited collection of older, recent, and newly commissioned critical responses to Millay. Enid Mark of ELM Press published an illustrated volume of fifteen poems by Millay in a limited edition entitled *Grace from Simple Stone*, exhibited at the conference. Elizabeth Barnett brought out an illustrated *Ballad of the Harp-Weaver*, also in the exhibit. And an unusual number of Ph.D. students produced dissertations, represented here by the essays of Susan Gilmore, Lisa Myers, and Deborah Woodard, with significant attention paid not only to Millay's poetry but also to her verse drama, private letters, novel, and "potboiler" magazine fiction. Clearly the recent critical activity culminating in *Millay at 100: A Critical Reappraisal* marks a definitive revival of interest in all of Millay from an array of new perspectives predicated on a reexamination of the old.

Part One of this collection, "Music, Memory, Modernism," directly takes up the paradox of why Millay continued to allure even while she was critically obscure. It addresses an array of questions also engaged elsewhere in the volume: Where is Millay's place in the literary histories of modern writing and in our hearts? How are we to value, interpret, and map the various forms and genres in which she wrote? What is the cultural work Millay achieves and reflects? What do her great gifts enable us to see about ourselves and her life and writing?

In "Uncanny Millay," Suzanne Clark reminds us that the "work of Millay impacts literary studies more unconsciously than most" not only because Millay continues to be popular in the public domain, but because the music of her poetry is uncannily at hand in the body of memories of academics across the United States. Clark asks, What is the cultural work that Millay does? Besides inspiring feminist students today with her progressive politics and feminist defiance, Millay, by refusing to separate life from art and by using masquerade (addressed also in essays by Walker, Gilmore, Woodard, and Gilbert), problematizes modernist notions, the tradition of its criticism, and the very institution of literature as a separate aesthetic.

In "Displaced Modernism: Millay and the Triumph of Sentimentality," Jo Ellen Green Kaiser argues against what she calls the old critical consensus that Millay, although living in the modernist period, did not participate in modernism. Instead, asserts Kaiser, Millay "attempted to negotiate a modernist as well as a sentimental aesthetic," actively choosing to reject the modernism of Eliot and Pound in favor of political engagement. Further, Millay's position in what contemporary critic Debra Fried has called the rearguard of the literary world allows the critic "to observe the ways in which sentimentality and modernism, pop and high culture, and feminine and masculine writing intersected and diverged during this period."

Part Two, "Love (and) Connection," focuses on Millay's revisionary perspectives on women in love and children beloved. Ernest J. Smith, in " 'How the Speaking Pen Has Been Impeded': The Rhetoric of Love and Selfhood in Millay and Rich," sees that Millay's *Fatal Interview* anticipates Rich's "Twenty-One Love Poems" in its engagement with the themes of love, separation, and emerging self in the language of heterosexual love and the convention of the sonnet sequence. Like Rich, Millay "works within, yet works to subvert, established poetic forms and conventions," struggling to overcome the "forces that would impede poetic and personal [female] freedom." Smith finds that Millay is in many ways a modernist in her treatment of love and selfhood, arguing that "Millay, like Rich, deals extensively with the struggle to overcome the forces which would impede poetic, personal, female freedom."

In "Rewriting the Myth of the Woman in Love: Millay's *Fatal Interview*," Holly Peppe demonstrates how Millay importantly challenges the male romantic tradition of the beautiful, cruel, shallow, manipulative, fickle, and vulnerable love object with a female speaker who draws strength from female elements in nature and who, "uninterested in deception, exercises her capacity for rigorous self-examination and takes a critical, realistic view of her male partner." In so doing, argues Peppe, Millay presents an unprecedented, extensive psychological portrait of the woman lover who, unlike the struggling woman artist, is no longer " 'Hell's mistress' but her 'own.' "

Using recent revisions of classic psychoanalytic theories of the role of the mother in sexual development and language acquisition, Lisa Myers's "Her Mother's Voice" reexamines Millay's writing in Europe during 1921 and 1922. Through Millay's letters, "The Ballad of the Harp-Weaver," and the novel *Hardigut*, Myers explores the impact of heterosexual models of erotic investment on notions of poetic vocation—of Millay's sense of herself as both a woman and a poet.

Where the essays in Part Two seem to argue for Millay's capacity to construct and repose faith in her own identity, the essays in Part Three, "Time's Body," are a bit less optimistic, revealing Time has had its way with Millay as much as she with it. Cheryl Walker, in "The Female Body as Icon: Edna Millay Wears a Plaid Dress," argues in part what she has in *Masks Outrageous and Austere*: that Millay's work is "contemporary and tragic" because it both aptly describes, and shows Millay a victim of, the modernist and contemporary proposition that nothing is stable, that everything and everyone is replaceable, a commodity. While Walker acknowledges Millay's cultural effectiveness as a spokesperson for the rights of women and pleasurable and courageous living, she demonstrates how the 1939 volume *Huntsman, What Quarry?* contrastingly underscores "the lack of control one has over the semiotics of the female flesh."

In "Love's 'Little Day': Time and the Sexual Body in Millay's Sonnets," Stacy Carson Hubbard finds some feminist misgivings about Millay misdirected and wishes to point critical attention "away from Millay's individual experience and 'inner'. . . self toward . . . literary history and its role in the rhetorical and cultural construction of sex and gender." She attributes Millay's gestures and postures—what other writers here examine as masquerade—to "the instabilities of both gender and poetic authority," a situation revealed or performed by language and the discourse of *carpe diem* love poetry in particular.

In "A Moment's Monument: Millay's Sonnet and Modern Time," Robert Johnson observes that despite her affinity for Renaissance models of time and the sonnet, Millay clearly evokes the modernist model of the flow of time in such sonnets as "Only until this cigarette is ended" and those of *Fatal Interview*. Her sonnets finally "stand as monuments to the very attempt of the mind to erect a stable insight of words, while experience seems ever to be slipping away."

In "Vampirism and Translation: Millay, Baudelaire, and the Erotics of Poetic Transfusion," Marilyn May Lombardi suggests that

Millay's covert theme of vampirism in her preface to her translation of Baudelaire challenges the male modernist view of translation: offering one's life blood to resuscitate the past. Millay instead achieves a bodily and textual transcendence over "the most influential poet of modernity," reversing what Lombardi deems "the dynamic of power so often reinforced in her own verse."

Part Four, "Millay's Drama of Impersonation," explores some of the most overt examples of Millay's penchant for masquerade or multiple constructions of identity. In " 'I Could Do a Woman Better Than That': Masquerade in Millay's Potboilers," Deborah Woodard analyzes the "unresolved dilemma of the masquerade." Woodard explores some of Millay's alter egos—her fiction-writing pseudonymous self Nancy Boyd, whose stories were published in *Ainslee's* and *Vanity Fair* and brought out by Harper as *Distressing Dialogues*, and the characters themselves, who Woodard claims often share much with Millay the poet.

Moving from Joan Riviere, Simone de Beauvoir, Luce Irigaray, Marilyn Monroe, and Dorothy Parker to Millay, Sandra M. Gilbert argues in " 'Directions for Using the Empress': Millay's Supreme Fiction(s)" that Millay as "female female impersonator" was aware that Edna St. Vincent Millay was a fictive construct. Like Woodard and Peppe, respectively, Gilbert asserts that Millay attests to the distance between person and poet in her Nancy Boyd stories—especially those mentioning Millay—and critiques the ideology of romance in poems featuring speakers who are not traditional femmes fatales. "Millay-as-poetic-speaker," Gilbert concludes, "surmounts the plots that would wound her. For her, it is never fatal to be a femme fatale because she can always . . . deploy the vengeful arts of linguistic 'making-up.' " But, citing Millay's use of baby talk in her letters throughout her life, Gilbert suggests that Millay nonetheless, as John Crowe Ransom commented, " 'found it difficult . . . to come of age,' " persistently struggling, in Gilbert's words, "toward a maturity in which she could use the artifice of 'femininity' without being used by it."

Unlike Gilbert and Woodard, who explore the danger and confusion associated with female masquerade as aesthetic practice, Susan Gilmore finds Millay's use of a male cast of characters aesthetically and politically subversive and successful. In " 'Posies of Sophistry': Impersonation and Authority in Millay's *Conversation at Midnight*," Gilmore argues that by eliminating the female speakers with whom Millay is typically (and too intimately) identified, "Millay finds one solution to the problem of the modernist persona" and its too-reductive criticism. Millay also succeeds in suggesting that " 'maleness,' because imitable, is neither fixed nor natural," but supported by such privilege and homosocial relations as the play's setting in a men's salon reveals. Moreover, Gilmore observes, the "modernist experiment" *Conversation at Midnight* "expresses a transitional moment in Millay's personal politics and in America's political consciousness," poised as it is "between Millay's pacifist allegory, *Aria da Capo* (1920), and her pro-intervention, antifascism piece, *The Murder of Lidice* (1942)."

Thus, Part Four returns us to the issues with which the volume begins: Millay's role in American poetic, social, and political history; the definition of modernism; Millay's long exclusion from both academia and the modernist canon; and both the duration of her popular appeal and the renovation of Millay's critical reputation— as a modernist after all, or postmodernist, or self-conscious and successful alternative modern, or musical lyricist, ironic sentimentalist, female female impersonator, feminist, psychologist, cultural icon, and cultural critic.

Part I  *Music, Memory, Modernism*

# I  *Uncanny Millay*
## Suzanne Clark

Writing sonnets in the era of high modernism, popular though she was, Edna St. Vincent Millay courted oblivion. She has not, as it turns out, been forgotten. But as we remember her, I want to account for her endurance in terms that acknowledge, as she said: "Beauty is not enough" ("Spring"). I want to point out the difficult cultural work her poetry has done. The work of Millay impacts literary studies more unconsciously than most, if my experience is any marker. This is not because continuing interest exists only in the popular domain, outside the university. Academics across the country—male as well as female academics—can quote Millay for you when you walk past in the hall, at the drop of a hat, at the slightest mention that you might be working on her. What they quote probably depends on their generation, but the memorability of her lines persists. She is not forgotten; she is very much remembered, on the tip of so many tongues. But this is more like a memory of the body than of the mind, the repetition of a kind of unconscious evoked by her words, in the mnemonics of sound.

By speaking of the "uncanny," I mean to suggest the work of the unconscious, the ghostly reappearance analyzed by Freud, and the special functioning of women's fiction discussed by Hélène Cixous. Though the body of her work has made its ghostly reappearance, Millay was dismissed from the literary by a generation of critics. There were good reasons for keeping Millay's impact out of mind, because her work challenges the gendered identity assumed by the modernist aesthetic.

Millay criticized gender roles and sexuality explicitly, in defiant lines that made her notorious in 1923 and that once again delight feminist students today. "I, Being Born a Woman and Distressed" is a love sonnet that concludes: "I find this frenzy insufficient reason / For conversation when we meet again." The poem is made especially notable for this generation by being included in Sandra M. Gilbert and Susan Gubar's edition of the *Norton Anthology of Literature by Women* (1555–56). Millay also positioned herself firmly on the side of progressive politics, not only in her public life, but in poems like "Justice Denied in Massachusetts," on the Sacco-Vanzetti case. But such poems are not typical of her work; it cannot be said that most of her poetry thematizes a political feminism. I am interested, rather, in how she engages in a *poetic* politics as well. Within the modernist aesthetic, the speaker of a poem may be theatrical, figurative, and ironic without upsetting cultural assumptions about personal identity. The male poet (Wallace Stevens, for example) may write like a lady, but the rigorous separation of impersonal literary complexity from the reductiveness of ordinary life keeps the gender distinctions clear.

The modernist aesthetic separated literary language from ordinary language and, in particular, from the personal.[1] Millay's poetry, however, does not acknowledge this separation of life from art. Modernist critics including Cleanth Brooks, Allan Tate, and John Crowe Ransom claimed that Millay's poetry was not only too susceptible to the conventional but also too easily overwhelmed by sensibility.[2] Conversely, I wonder, doesn't Millay's poetry take the figurative, parodic—*conventional*—character of literary language and extend that rhetoricity to life, denaturalizing the personal? Her poems make visible through a theater of the personal how identity functions in culturally determined ways. If the social construction of male and female and the narrative of their sexual fates is produced by discourse, including literary discourse, this productivity is nevertheless hidden by the closure of identity. This cultural unconscious may therefore be exposed through doubling and parody—and, in Millay's case, in particular, masquerade. Literary techniques enable her to critique cultural ideology from inside its technology, at the level of producing subjects, that is, at the level of figuring through form certain possibilities for desire. In the displacement of the lyric subject from its singularity, Millay's poetry is "novelized," in Bakhtin's sense, moved away from the monologic.

Think about the performative context of Millay's work as America's best-known poetess. She would appear in a long gown for readings, her voice dramatic, her form girlish and attractive, more like a diva than like the gray-suited male poets. The self in her work is an actress performing, at once embodiment and interpretation. There is no separation of artist and person. She is neither inside nor outside the communal order because from inside she delineates the trying on of identities that might work a remedy to alienation at the same time that she denaturalizes this identity-making project and exposes its unconscious webbing as art. Masquerade functions as critique. Furthermore, allegorizing the forms of the imaginary, Millay tropes identity through personification, and the figures of personification define a specific poetics for her work. In other words, while the figure of masquerade may suggest a multiplicity of roles for a single person without really challenging the notion of a core identity, the figure of personification suggests that personhood itself is a trope. This is not to say that I see Millay in a new guise as a postmodern writer, because this play on the figures of identity takes place in the context of a historic body of language. The uncanny specters of a bardic tradition are evoked and embodied in this materiality of a voice. Or of a lyric *song*.

So Millay's poetry does not simply participate in the social construction of the personal, reinscribing love stories: her work troubles the process, sounding repetition in a new voice. Millay interrupts the closure of womanhood by her necessarily failed attempts to speak like a man, the equivalent on the level of sound of a cross-dressing. Without this kind of troublemaking, both the sounds of language and the familiarity of conventional stories and characters can work to reproduce and limit the possibilities for individual identity. Millay represents an unconscious that is at once of musicality and of cultural repetitions: a cultural unconscious. Millay's writing, even though it participates in the symbolic order, opens up a space for difference, for the uncanny return of the repressed, through disturbances of that order.[3] She makes the traditional resources of a male literary tradition uncanny, strange. The resurrections of literary traditions inhering in forms like the sonnet, in figure and phrase, extend to influence the cultural politics that depend on their keeping their place.

A reader might assume that any repetition of traditional forms would serve a traditional or conservative purpose, at least at the level of the unconscious, but Millay mobilizes their power to her own ends. Literature, in Millay's work, is not kept separate from the political questions of gender. The ideology of the aesthetic, as Terry Eagleton argues, has provided for capitalism and the middle class a way to produce self-governing subjects. Millay's poetry reveals the way the ideology of the aesthetic works, through the imaginary, as a cultural unconscious that is exposed in the critical discomfort she provokes.

It is the masquerade of personal identity that distinguishes Millay from modernist poets. T. S. Eliot said, in "Tradition and the Individual Talent," that

> we shall often find that not only the best, but the most individual parts of [a poet's] work may be those in which the dead poets, his ancestors, assert their immortality most vigorously. And I do not mean the impressionable period of adolescence, but the period of full maturity. (4)

Millay, too, writes with the sense of those poetic ancestors in her bones, and her style testifies to their influence. But Millay's poetry is not what Eliot had in mind. "The existing monuments form an ideal order among themselves, which is modified by the introduction of the new (the really new) work of art among them" (5). Millay threatens to introduce something new that unsettles the ideal order profoundly; she speaks among the poets as a woman.

Even though we encounter again and again in Millay the resurrected speech of dead poets, it is not with the effect of impersonality Eliot insisted upon. It is not in the form of an aesthetic influence, which leaves the person aside, intact. Rather, in Millay, the unassimilated speech of poetic history enters into an intertextuality that detaches the personal from its aura. Shortly, I will look closely at some examples of this—of appearances by Yeats and Ronsard in Millay's poems. Here what I want to make clear is how speaking as a woman while she speaks men's words might unsettle modernist impersonality. To retain the marker of gender is to resist that complete surrender of the ordinary embodied self that Eliot was advocating. Millay's poetry does not appear to practice "a continual self-sacrifice, a continual extinction of personality" ("Tradition and the Individual Talent" 7). The memorability of the poetic word involves effects of transference and identification that depend on personality. Poetry that mobilizes response like Millay's (the shared memories) discloses for us the uncanny powers that may account for the hold of ideology upon us and may offer a way to hold out *against* ideology.

Feminist criticism has often characterized its work as restoring the unconscious to consciousness, using writing to reorganize psychic space. In a related sense, Millay's poetry can be read as a restorative project that would propel the woman's uneasy figure into juxtaposition with the figure of the writer, shadowing the traditionally male-gendered creativity of the poet with another gender, another sexuality, another creativity. Millay's rhetoric of personification, her attentiveness to the question of Beauty, her violation of the modernist poem's autonomous objectivity raises a gendered poetic into view. When modernist critics such as John Crowe Ransom (of whom more later) called this a woman's poetic, however, they did not mean to be complimentary.

A ghostly body inhabits the poetry of Millay, a haunting image hovering between the fantasy and the impossible real, like poetry itself. It is the very figure of language and beauty, animated within the folded space of anamnesis or unforgetting where the past both is and is not recovered as the trace of embodied and sensuous experience. This figure invokes us as the subjects of the long book of literature, the realm where the apples are, Millay says, "half Baldwin, half Hesperides" ("To whom the house of Montagu was neighbor"). Readers, we are invited not to revere the poetic object but, as Millay writes in her sonnet to the feminist Inez Milholland, to "take up the song." The invitation to transference or identification makes a strong bond and opens literature out into the imaginary. The uncanny in Millay is the ghost of a cultural unconscious, the forgotten woman, but also the forgotten power of poetry. This imaginary power is forgotten by the most critical among us because it has seemed regressive, the mere slave of ideology—because identities have seemed to contemporary feminist and other critics either essentialist or fragmented and the politics of identity no question for poetry.

With the help of Millay, however, we can explore the role of literature in making identities and the difficult question of how the forgotten might use literary power. Because hers is not a narrowly aesthetic conception of literature, Millay dramatizes in both form and theme the way culture shapes individuals, what Teresa de Lauretis has characterized as the technology of subjects, beginning with herself. Does Millay know that she is problematizing the very idea of an identity by asserting the oxymoron of the woman poet? She seems to know that gender makes the cultural construction of selves as free, autonomous individuals questionable, that with gender we are plunged into the problem of the social, of empathy, of the love story, and of our entanglements with others, from mother to lover. What Millay may not know is that her challenge to the gendered identity of the poet might also problematize the very institution of literature as a separate aesthetic. As Cheryl Walker demonstrates, Millay cannot construct a space outside the commodification of culture, and indeed, by making the identity of the self the subject and the object of her poem, she enters that identity into the reifying forces of the culture around her.

The various appearances of a poetic avant-garde in the past two centuries have signaled a historical crisis in the personal and the literary alike. The school of Eliot, which led to the school of new criticism, tried to stabilize the crisis by insisting on separating the poem from the person. This formalist ideal of impersonal poetry had the virtue of calling attention to language, but at the cost of disavowing any connection between the situation of poems and of persons. The practice of an impersonal poetics kept the poetic/personal identity separate, away from the disruptive effects of an avant-garde discourse. Defamiliarization might call attention to literature without disrupting the family. The school of Eliot enlisted avant-garde poetics against a progressive politics, denying any rhetorical purpose for literature, denying especially that literature might have any connection with the way culture disciplines the body's emotions and desires.

Edna St. Vincent Millay's poems refuse to function within this aesthetic. Millay uses the traditional forms of poetry in a productive and radical challenge to the hierarchies of modernism. Millay's poems involve a different rhetorical situation for poetics, not based on self-contained symbols, but rather on figures—embodiments— that point outside themselves in an allegorical gesture. Millay's allegorical storytelling reproduces literature itself as a figure of re- production. Her poems require a different view of literature alto- gether, and of language too, a view of literature that is interested in exploring the imaginative possibilities for different identities offered by the heterogeneity of language. There is an admitted doubleness to this productivity, an inevitable complicity with com- modification and vulnerability to cultural definitions of self. Millay's work differs from the school of Eliot precisely because it does not deny the complicity of art with seduction or the way that beauty can betray. As Millay says: "Beauty is not enough."

If Millay was a public, contemporary figure who came to repre- sent the new woman and who came to seem the voice of a rebellious generation, that image must be informed by how very seriously she took the historical and literary powers of language. This notion of literature as a public, not a private or separate art, contravened the dominant critical movement of her time. Are we, postmoderns, more receptive to such a sense of responsibility? Most especially, she challenged the critical agreements of the moderns not just by seeing herself as a public poet but by writing a poetry that moves the problem of female identity into the public domain. Though she used the leverage of all the history of literature, that very history carried with it the supposition of male authorship. Does Millay fully acknowledge the closure of poetry's high traditions against female authorship?

"Reader, do not let me die," she wrote in "The Poet and His Book." Death and grief is a frequent subject in Millay's poems. But is it her own death she fears? More often than the familiar poetic search for immortality in verse, death is associated in her texts with the pain of losing someone else. This other may be the beloved but is also the person she addresses, the reader, and the very possibility of re-membering a community of readers. Precariously, Millay has constructed a body of work that might mediate the relationship of self and other and inscribe the woman as writer in a poem—and in a culture—where she might address empathetic readers. These repeated confrontations with death gesture toward a certain abyss, a black melancholy that does not believe in the power of poetry to resurrect intimate presence or the power of beauty to connect individuals. That abyss is both private and public for a woman poet. The authentic experience is not real, but uncanny, written, bringing the unconscious into contact with style, bringing the self through language into contact with another. The authentic experience is, in this sense, always only remembered, in the anamnesis that reverses the displacement of desire. Experience and identity are transitory, brought into being—or not—as the fate of the book will allow:

> Search the fading letters, finding
> Steadfast in the broken binding
> All that once was I!
>
> ("The Poet and His Book")

The transference from writer to reader operates according to an uncanny logic.

I am especially struck by the way personification tropes poetry as one of Millay's chief devices of style. This personifying impulse is rhetorical and melodramatic, not modernist. The persona or speaker, the interlocutor or the *you* to whom the poem is addressed, and the third party all may be figured forth as Love or Death or Beauty or Silence. These are figures of identity in Millay, embodiments that make evident the linguistic body that subtends persons and shadows forth the symbolic identity of all subjects as a kind of personification. Naming the person in the text would not make it more personal than the abstraction if self is an uncanny between-the-lines, not located in the word.[4] Even in the early poems, such as "The Suicide," "Kin to Sorrow", "The Dream," and "Indifference," personification often dramatizes the theme so that a word like *love* is a character more than a representation:

I said,—for Love was laggard, oh, Love was slow to come,—
"I'll hear his step and know his step when I am warm in bed;
But I'll never leave my pillow, though there be some
As would let him in—and take him in with tears!" I said.

("Indifference")

The "him" of this poem balances between abstraction—"Love"—
and a bodied and specific version of the lover.

Poetry is the act of love, and lovers its effect. Poetry tells the
tales that bind us together because it is the persona we speak or
write or draw or paint that represents the person for the other.
This seems to be the theme of a sonnet from *The Harp-Weaver* that
contrasts "the outward you" and the artist. The poem describes
that recurring moment in a relationship when there is no exchange
of desire or when the audience simply is tired of listening. The loss,
the poem says, is redeemed in this failure of a desire to connect with
the once-loved other, the memory entailed by art. The rhetorical
situation has lost its force: "And my gaze wanders ere your tale is
through" ("Sometimes when I am wearied suddenly"). What makes
the promise of love into an act? It becomes a performance that
recurs as performance through the good offices of art: "So are we
bound till broken is the throat / Of Song, and Art no more leads
out the Nine." The history and tradition of literary language guaran-
tees a kind of renewal of human bonds in the allegory of emotional
figures: "Then I recall, 'Yet *Sorrow* thus he drew'; / Then I consider,
'*Pride* thus painted he.' " This reliance upon the constructed subject
of art—as compared to a constructed object—is precisely what
critics of Millay would challenge. Such rhetoricity is something
even Eliot was willing to consider as more than just bad writing
in certain cases of dramatic character—in " 'Rhetoric' and Poetic
Drama," he cites Cyrano's "nose" speech—but Millay's critics do
not read her as participating in theater. If the reader identifies with
the impersonal speaker of modernist poetry, it is with the ironic
indifference that frames emotional expression and not with the
attachments of emotion.

Inviting the identification of the reader with emotion, Millay
situates poetic speech between the mundane and the eternal, in the
figures of Sorrow and Pride. It is not the moment when such

sympathetic identifications would be easy that she portrays, but the moment of distraction when the tale loses its audience: "... when I am wearied suddenly / Of all the things that are the outward you." What song prompts is memory, and it is the memory of Art: "How first you loved me for a written line."

I myself first loved Millay when I was fourteen: my father read me "Oh World, I cannot hold thee close enough." His gesture of reading expected that I would understand how this poem spoke something my adolescent exuberance could move into, a capacious frame for that mobile excess of feeling. But when I learned how early Millay had begun to publish, how young she was when she wrote "Renascence," I despaired of becoming a poet myself, of ever being able to catch up to the poetic genius of Millay. At fourteen, I was already too late. Like so many, I never stopped loving her poems. Yet I, like so many, also associated her with adolescence and the identity crises of adolescence.

John Crowe Ransom promoted a critical tradition of characterizing her work as immature. Even sympathetic readers, including myself, thought of the figure of the girl in her poems as a mark of immaturity; Elizabeth Frank critiqued the girl in Millay as if all her poetry figured forth a single subject. The mistake here was to read her work as if the trying on of identity associated with the adolescent were something to give up with maturity and as if the multiple identities dramatized by her poems could be coalesced into the figure of a girl and labeled immature by their very multiplicity. I would like to suggest that Millay has more to do with the way literature, and especially the novel, is the locus of such a trying on of identities. Julia Kristeva has argued that the novel arises as adolescence comes into being, as just such a discourse, concerned with the "problematic incompleteness of young page-boys, picaros, delinquents, or terrorists—from Casanova to Milos Forman to Mad Max" ("Adolescent Novel" 8). The question of adolescence, she says, allows us to interrogate ourselves on the role of the imaginary and the "open psychic system" that echoes "the fluidity, i.e., the inconsistency, of a mass media society." Such an open structure we grant to the adolescent, but "the adult will have the right to this only as a reader or spectator of novels, films, painting . . . or as artist. I do not see, moreover," Kristeva adds, "what would prompt writing if not an 'open structure' " (11).

The narrative structures implicated in Millay's poetry are complex and various, open structures. The close attention to form especially evident in the sonnets could lead us astray if we read Millay's style as if it were an endorsement of conventional poetic hierarchies, especially of a stable, gendered speaking subject. We do her a disservice to read them monologically, as if they all proceeded from a single subject. This is to say that we need to read her outside a certain prematurely mature tradition of poetic reading in order to recover the aesthetic pleasure to which she invites us.

Millay's novelistic quality, signaled by the adolescent shifting of identity and the allegorizing to narratives, connects her not to the old authoritarian modes of poetic reading, which the school of Eliot, in a reactionary movement, resurrected, but to the increasing domination of a novelistic, polylogic discourse that would finally emerge with postmodernism.

Much after my first encounter with Millay, when I was in graduate school, I imagined I might study her verse. "No," advised my critical friends, "Edna St. Vincent Millay is simply not interesting." So I began my study of Millay asking perversely why the critics felt so convinced she was not "interesting." Despite her witty send-offs and her sustained irony about all the elements of literature usually called sentimental, she had been, I thought—along with the whole tradition of the sentimental—consigned to the stigmatized order of women's writing. Eventually, I wrote a book, *Sentimental Modernism*, about modernism and women writers, including Millay, in which I tried to confront those too-easy dismissals.

In the beginning of the twentieth century, as Edna St. Vincent Millay began to write, the ideal of a disinterested aesthetic increasingly dissociated the practices of art from everyday life and especially from the private extremities of domestic passions. Disconnected from sexual bodies, poetry could seem pure, liberated from the struggles of power and desire among males and females; poetry could seem objective, an objective correlative of distanced emotion. Modernist poetics posits an impersonal, ungendered, universal subject of aesthetic judgment, related to Kant's notion of the aesthetic and to the Coleridgean imagination. Disconnected from the history of the cultural aesthetic and its rootedness in gender, aesthetic judgments could seem disinterested at the same time that they discriminated against women.

Feminist criticism has challenged the discrimination imposed by the doctrine of disinterestedness. But the attempt of such criticism to valorize work like Millay's continues to run up against a stubborn appeal to the universal subject. Questions of gender emerge in such a rhetoric as partial, political, interested contingencies. The woman is the marked sex; if we admire Edna St. Vincent Millay as a woman poet, the rhetoric of universality makes it appear that only the woman poet has a gender, to say nothing of a body. Only a woman's poetry has this doubleness of gender and art; only a woman's poetry supplements art with this excess, an unseemly and suggestive sexuality. A woman's poetry violates aesthetic decorum to the extent that it attracts attention to her different sensibility. But this very attention to difference, this violation of a universal aesthetic, is precisely the point of feminist criticism.

This attention to difference was already in Millay's poetics. Millay's allegorizing dramatized the gendering of the imaginative desire that configures beauty, love, and death. Thus, she violated the repression denying the gendering of the aesthetic, the historical production of an aesthetic double bind. Coleridge once argued that the allegory was inferior art, since he conceived of the poem as a "unity in multeity," a self-enclosed system, autotelic. But that is a closure that would guard against the unmaking of subjects, while the allegorical impulse opens itself to external debate. Aesthetic autonomy works against open structures and the narrative impulse.

Millay violated an aesthetic that claimed universality as it struggled to dominate the politics of literary history. In the 1930s, the drive of formalist critics to establish a timeless foundation for modernist poetics had narrowed the field considerably, cutting down whatever work—black, proletarian, feminist—could not be reduced to formal universalism. Allen Tate, one of the poets of the Eliot school who became part of the formalist New Criticism, attacked the troubling presence of Millay, admitting that she was important in the history of radical change but claiming that her generation was past:

Miss Millay is . . . the spokesman of a generation. It does not behoove us to enquire how she came to express the feelings of the literary generation that seized the popular imagination from about 1917 to 1925. It is a fact that she did, and in such a way as to remain as its most typical poet. Her talent, with its diverting mixture of solemnity and levity, won the enthusiasm of a time bewildered intellectually and moving unsteadily towards an emotional attitude of its own. It was the age of The Seven Arts, of the old Masses, of the Provincetown Theatre, of the figure and disciples of Randolph Bourne. It has been called the age of experiment and liberation; there is still experiment, but no one is liberated; and that age is now dead. (335)

This characterization suggests how Millay is connected to a certain activism that Tate wants to separate from the literary tradition and declare a failure.

For the definition of their allegedly nonpolitical aesthetic, formalist critics like John Crowe Ransom reached back to Kant, to his characterization of the aesthetic as a "purposiveness without purpose" and the work of art as an autonomous object, an ontology. Art was distinctly different from everything else and especially from the language that connected it to matters of personal pleasure and taste or to personal qualities like sexuality, class, and race. Millay posed a formidable threat to this project. She was a powerful, well-regarded poet who had a reputation for wit and for bringing together erudition and the popular, but most of all, she did not keep either gender or sexuality out of her poems. She violated poetic impersonality by her figures of the personal. She threatened to blow open the whole cover-up operation that had quietly obscured and lost the telling connection between gender and the rise of the aesthetic manifested in Kant and claiming modernism as its own. In my earlier work on John Crowe Ransom's "Poet as Woman," I read his attack on Millay as a blatant and outrageous example of the mostly hidden sexism in modernist poetics. On second thought, however, I am inclined to think that Ransom's essay represents something less individualized, an important and dangerous turn, a moment when—thanks to Millay—the figure of woman as poet had emerged into consciousness and the old Kantian ghost has to be invoked to reinforce not only the repression of gendering but the authority of a poetic hierarchy, to repress woman and the power of poetry together.

What Ransom did was to resurrect the old categories of the sensible and the intelligible and associate Millay with the sensible, a concept haunted by the feminine, where, as woman, she would naturally belong. If he could do this to Millay, he could silence the woman in women's poetry with the spectral gendering of philosophy's past. Though he does not say so, the position he names for himself would ally him not only with the intelligible, but with the sublime. That is, Ransom is conjuring up the ideology of the aesthetic, now become a kind of political unconscious. The ideology of the aesthetic, as Terry Eagleton traces its course, began to coalesce in the eighteenth century together with the rise of the middle class and a set of cultural institutions that could seem invisible and ungendered as they regulated the body and desire.

In the eighteenth century, Edmund Burke constructed the conservative position around the responsiveness of the body: the beautiful is pleasing and the sublime is painful; the attractiveness of women is connected to the beautiful, to love, to being the object of desire. The capacity to endure the stronger passions of terror is dependent on reason, of course characteristic of men, and sublime. Even though Burke asserts a Lockian universality to the experience of the senses, and so to the basis for taste, the sublime goes beyond the senses, calling on the resources of reason to gain distance from the terror of death.

At first, Immanuel Kant, in his 1764 "Observations on the Feeling of the Beautiful and Sublime," kept the sublime aesthetic embedded in explicitly drawn categories of gender and class: women were identified with the beautiful, men with the sublime. However, by the time he wrote *Critique of Judgment* in 1790 after *Critique of Pure Reason* and following the direction established there, he would define the aesthetic as independent of interest, a disinterested and universal subjective judgment. That does not mean the gendering of the hierarchy vanishes, however; it is simply mystified. The beautiful is inferior to the sublime, and the beautiful remains feminine while the sublime is masculine. In the section called "Of the Distinction of the Beautiful and Sublime in the Interrelations of the Two Sexes," from the "Observations," Kant sets up the binary that Ransom seems to evoke to place Millay as a woman. It is important to see how here Immanuel Kant, later that very avatar of disinterestedness, sounds like Edmund Burke speaking: "Women have a strong inborn feeling for all that is beautiful, elegant, and decorated. Even in childhood they like to be dressed up, and take pleasure when they are adorned" (395). This characterization of the sexes goes on at some length, concluding that women "contain the chief cause in human nature for the contrast of the beautiful qualities with the noble, and they refine even the masculine sex":

> The fair sex has just as much understanding as the male, but it is a *beautiful understanding*, whereas ours should be a *deep understanding*, an expression that signifies identity with the sublime. . . .
> Laborious learning or painful pondering, even if a woman should greatly succeed in it, destroys the merits that are proper to her sex, and because of their rarity they can make of her an object of cold admiration; but at the same time they will weaken the charms with which she exercises her great power over the other sex. A woman who has a head full of Greek . . . or carries on fundamental controversies about mechanics . . . might as well even have a beard. . . . (395)

In the later *Critique of Judgment*, Kant characterizes women as part of the sensible, the domain of the beautiful, but makes clear that the masculine sublime operates in a superior way as a kind of reverberation between the sensible and the intelligible—the sublime calls up the reason before the limitations of imagination. Thus, a disinterested aesthetic will by that very reverberation of the sublime legislate a gendered hierarchy of aesthetic value.

In Kant, and in the aesthetic history that follows, we do not have a simple gendering of cultural institutions with art and beauty identified with the woman while the culture of reason, science, and technology is for the man. Rather, within the aesthetic there may be a hierarchy of the beautiful and the sublime that also asserts the superiority of the masculine. If Millay challenges modernist aesthetics, she also threatens this pervasive cultural hierarchy. This is what Ransom reasserts when he writes "The Poet as Woman." Ransom is drawing on the ghostly authority of Kant here, echoing his language, relegating Millay to the "beautiful" and excluding her from the "sublime":

Man distinguishes himself from woman by intellect, but it should be well feminized. He knows he should not abandon sensibility and tenderness . . . but now that he is so far removed from the world of the simple senses, he does not like to impeach his own integrity and leave his business in order to recover it; going back, as he is often directed, to first objects, the true and tried, like the moon, or the grass, or the dead girl. (784)

Ransom was, if you read between the lines, acknowledging the danger, from his point of view, that readers were, in fact, taking the poet-as-woman seriously, the danger of sensibility as the threat of Millay. But his words suggest threat as well, that if he is directed to go back, the dead girl is the body he will discover.

What Ransom says he cannot quite find significant is a set of commonplaces that suggest not just the sentimental or the sensible but the space of female melancholy: the moon, the grass, the dead girl. Even though the dead girl is not actually so common a theme in Millay, there is a complex of love and grief that she does address. Feminist critics such as Leslie Rabine, writing about the romance, and Catherine Clément, writing about the melodrama of opera, have thought about what all those deaths of women in literature might mean. Rabine suggests that the principle of identity governing discourse since the Renaissance, what Kristeva calls the "ideologeme of the sign," has demanded that difference be erased, under the assertion of a single, governing meaning, the logic feminist critics have discussed as logocentrism. If Millay's poetry refuses to subscribe to such a principle of identity, partly by reaching back to historical literary strategies that did not assume such a logic, we know how difficult a refusal that might be. Clément concludes that the melodramatic scripts of opera continuously reassert patriarchal power but that the sound of the music does something else, transporting us bodily to another order entirely. The women in the operas die, but the music lives. What is Millay doing with her allegorizing and her musicalizing of the melancholy that so threatened Ransom (and that our male colleagues remember)?

Is she not giving us again and again the loss by which we enter into language, separating ourselves from a maternal boundlessness and taking up—as if entering into a masquerade—an identity, the subjectivity bound first by the image of the other and then by words? If I use Julia Kristeva's study, in *Black Sun*, of the connection between melancholy and the acquisition of language, I find a story that seems also to be told by Millay. Again and again she remembers the sensation of claustrophobic dependency and terrible loss, the rebirth into a separate speaking subject; again and again her readers retrace the temptation to refuse inevitable separation and refuse the moment when words replace absence with the conflict of meaning/ not meaning. It is, in this story, a position of danger: a threat of death if the girl does not succeed in integrating loss into language.

Ransom most particularly gestures toward the scene of the dead girl. Is this really because Millay is too much involved with sensibility and not with intelligibility? Or because he does not want to imagine the fate of those whom language wastes in order to make meaning? What, for example, of the woman who does not fit into the story—or perhaps I should say the economy—of marriage and heterosexual love? Millay attacks that plot in particular, not only by stories of death but by taunts and barbs. Doing so, she challenges the very domain of the beautiful, set as it was in the private sphere, in the scenario of domesticity that I think Ransom is at pains to keep intact.

How does the dead girl come to be a tried and true commonplace? What interests Millay about dying for love is how the mundane detail intervenes, how female extremity seems ironically nothing more than a breach in decorum. In "The Pond," for example, "a farmer's daughter, / Jilted by her farmer beau" had fifty years ago drowned herself in a pond near the public highway. The juxtaposition of "farmer" and "beau" already gives us Millay's specific irony, the perspective by incongruity through which she sees, on the one hand, the romantic story of beauty and beau that alone seems to justify the jilted girl's hidden desperation, and on the other, the vernacular placidity of the pond, the farming life, and the wheels passing on the road. The poem's question asks us to imagine the way these two separate domains might be joined in the girl, setting up a terrible irony by the contrasting insignificance of the gesture that defines both her interaction with the public and the deadliness of her private grief:

> Can you not conceive the sly way,—
> Hearing wheels or seeing men
>
> Passing on the road above,—
> With a gesture feigned and silly
> Ere she drowned herself for love,
> She would reach to pluck a lily?

What interests Millay is the "feigned and silly" gesture with which the girl might dissimulate her extremity. What interests Julia Kristeva is to restore our recognition of how extreme the death-in-life of female depression might be. What interests John Crowe Ransom is to assert that woman's melancholy is no more than sensibility, no more than the gesture of plucking the lily, perhaps.

Millay's poems designate a kind of maternal temporality that at once evokes longing and loss and yet also the irony of reproduction for its own sake, reproduction without progress. This storytelling about the personifications of Beauty, Death, and Love is precisely *not* the making-it-new narrative authorized by a modernism that would function as an avant-garde. Take, for example, Millay's "Spring" from *Second April*. In a period when the opening of T. S. Eliot's *Waste Land*, "April is the cruelest month," reverberated everywhere, Millay refuses to take a part in the debate about pessimistic or optimistic attitudes to history (as did, for example, Hart Crane). Instead, she moves the argument out of linear and into monumental time, hinting that the redemptive force of beauty arises ironically, precisely out of its signifying nothing: "To what purpose, April, do you return again? / Beauty is not enough." The force of Beauty's repetition is what I call maternal irony. The eternal return of life is the mortal body's great joke—and its consolation.

"Beauty is not enough" even though it is the symptom of resurrection: "It is apparent that there is no death." Rewriting the iconography of melancholy, Millay gives us an April like Ophelia who enters the stage "like an idiot, babbling and strewing flowers," but playing in something that is not a tragedy, not *Oedipus*, not *Hamlet*, a story in which death is not what provides the horizon of meaning for life. Millay's wit keeps the speaker of this poem located in a doubled space, where the idea that "Beauty is not enough" is both true and ironic. The concrete energy of April's vocabulary invades the discourse of melancholy—"Life in itself / Is nothing"—and makes the speaker appear a kind of Jacques, overtaken by the babbling and the comic as well.

Through personification, Millay again and again dramatizes a relationship of speaker and other that unsettles both subjects of the rhetorical situation: "For I am Nightmare: where I fly, / Terror and rain stand in the sky," she writes in "Some Things Are Dark"; "Desolation dreamed of, though not accomplished, / Set my heart to rocking like a boat in a swell" ("Desolation Dreamed Of"); "Time, doing this to me, may alter too / My anguish, into something I can bear" ("Sonnet"). Does she resurrect the old understanding that art addresses love and the death of love? If "Beauty is not enough," it is nevertheless more than a tale told by an idiot, signifying nothing—or that, signifying nothing, the poem nevertheless enacts a gesture that seizes the day. The poem remembers feeling, which is both female and public, impossible fantasy. This necessarily plunges Millay into the narrative space explored by women novelists where the question of affirming a kind of masculine power of symbol making is always at issue, where identities are imaginary, a work in progress. This narrative space contains the melancholy threat of emptiness and death. Nonetheless, literature offers the aesthetic pleasure of affirmation. If "Beauty is not enough," nevertheless poetry can seize the day, offering the transient but repeated pleasure of imaging experience, inscribing even the self imagining death into the public, imaginary realm.

Ransom invokes the sensible and the intelligible as qualities of gendered subjects, but Millay's ceaseless translation of subjectivity into narrative figure undermines his assertions of value as well as gender. Millay does not simply represent the value of the poet as woman, for where may the woman in the poem speak? Rather, her work shows us how a reversal of the Kantian categories also undoes their universality. The reception of her work suggests much about the operations of the modern aesthetic: how her poems replicate the way ideology dramatizes the subject and how well defended the institution of art is against admitting its politics.

If Millay's poems do not, for the most part, serve an avant-garde project of formal innovation, it is perhaps because they are involved in flagrant violation of another kind, apparently so threatening that critics such as Tate and Ransom had simply to deny the significance of what she was doing. Invoking the long history of love poetry, speaking uncannily with the voices of dead male poets, Millay writes about sexuality without the Freudian norm of reproduction and marriage. Her poems give us love, but it is before identity has been situated within heterosexual norms—not always homoerotic, but always provoking the limits of decorum. Love poetry has never really served the formulas of bourgeois marriage, which wants to install a respectable and stable private domain. Millay reminds us of this incompatibility. She has the shape of a love affair as a repeated cycle, from beginning to inevitable end. The point of rapture is not stability but a memorable break in time. This has some relationship to the nature of poetry. A number of her wittiest poems rework the *carpe diem* theme so that the discourse of the seducer and the poet are both intertwined with her female sensibility. *Fatal Interview* gives us the sonnet sequence and the love story as a dazzling tour de force of poetic reminiscence. In two sonnets, she takes up Ronsard's sonnet to Helen, the old favorite memorized by every child in French schools, which begins: "Quand vous serez bien vieille, au soir à la chandelle" ("When you are old, of an evening by candle-light"). Ronsard goes on to predict that you will marvel, singing his verses, that he celebrated you when you were young and beauti-ful: you will be old, bent over, regretting your disdain for love. Therefore, as the argument goes, "Cueillez dès aujourd'hui les roses de la vie" (line 14); gather the roses today. Yeats tried his hand at the same poem. He began, "When you are old and gray and full of sleep, / And nodding by the fire, take down this book," and concluded predicting that you will

> Murmur, a little sadly, how Love fled
> And paced upon the mountains overhead
> And hid his face amid a crowd of stars.

Yeats and Millay both diverge from Ronsard after taking the opening lines, with their resonance and their appeal to the remembrance evoked by poetry. Yeats, instead of noting how the poet marks his love with enduring fame, marks with irony the poet's changed relationship to the logic of *carpe diem*, his retreat to the heights. Millay re-marks the triumph of eros—with a flippant couplet asserting the lovers' rapture as solace for the passing of time. She begins with the appeal Ronsard makes to the passing of time: "When we are old and these rejoicing veins / Are frosty channels to a muted stream" (XXVIII). The argument concludes with a punning flippancy: "Be not discountenanced if the knowing know / We rose from rapture but an hour ago." Here the *carpe diem* rhetoric serves pleasure, but it also suggests a very modern defiance of propriety. The sexuality connoted by the Renaissance meaning of "knowing" resists the social intercourse of gossip, what the "knowing know." Is this gendered? In one sense, not. The lovers are "we"; the lover addressed could be a man or a woman; the speaker could be a man or a woman. The lover who speaks with the voice of the tradition is male. The more strongly we as readers insist on keeping the female poet in mind, as does Ransom, the more uncanny this male doubling becomes.

Later, another sonnet recalls the Ronsard poem, together with its conclusion: the memory of the poet's love must be a later source of pride. In this poem, Millay's debt is evident and her revision richly subtle. The poem begins: "If in the years to come you should recall, / When faint at heart or fallen on hungry days" (LI). Like Ronsard (who wrote the sonnet in later years), she imagines her love's power through poetry surviving her own death. Ronsard says: "I will be under the earth and a phantom without bones" (line 8). Millay proposes:

> Might not my love—although the curving blade
> From whose wide mowing none may hope to hide,
> Me long ago below the frosts had laid—
> Restore you somewhat to your former pride?

Whereas Ronsard's poem is a kind of open vaunting—"Ronsard celebrated me"—Millay's enacts a more modest recovery: "Indeed

I think this memory, even then, / Must raise you high among the run of men." Nevertheless, the claim is there—and because the sonnet doubles Ronsard, it shadows forth this larger claim from the history of poetry, that Millay's poetry too will make memory powerful. The seductive moral of the *carpe diem* drops away and the implication of "seize the day" is associated not with the moment's sexual pleasure but with the celebration of the poet's victory over death. And here the beloved is clearly gendered ("among the run of men"). Though this does not even so imply that the poet is female, when the reader identifies the persona with a female poet, the claim itself is defamiliarized—the poet's vaunting persona becomes metaphorical, figurative, personification—part of a larger argument about love and poetry.

This poem, sonnet LI, is the next to final poem in *Fatal Interview*. The final poem, "Oh, sleep forever in the Latmian cave," inserts the sequence into the time of immortals. There is no shrinking from the role of the poet here. It is not love that endures but memory, the chain of remembrance uncannily evoked by poetic language. Did Millay understand the risk she was taking, not resisting but rather inviting the language of past poems to take her over? When it is a question of imaginary identity, can a woman enter into male speech?

This is a question about how ideology works to call up subjects in our culture. It is a question that involves not only psychic but also cultural history. Was there a place for the feminist new woman to enter into literature as a woman poet in the 1920s? In the 1950s? What about now? Is there any way to make a place except by writing? What we can clearly see, in retrospect, is how Millay was able to seize the day for a brief while in the 1920s, in a time of historical crisis, and how much of the ground she took was soon retaken by the counter-revolutionary New Critics. We can see that the question of the imaginary identity is a matter for public and political struggle. The double sense of strangeness and familiarity that marks the uncanny should alert us to the struggle over the terrain of the subject taking place in Millay's poetry.

The uncanny in Millay is a public unconscious, and it is bodied forth as the reader takes up the song. In her words, poetry speaks again, with an uncanny resonance precisely because it was a male tradition that would exclude it. Such speech is a kind of activism, a feminism on her part. Something returns not as remembrance but as the enactment of the empathy made possible by imaginary identifications. The death of the woman and the end of love haunt Millay's poetry, and yet she presses the reader past melancholy to the active engagement with text—and other. Does she write a poetry that expresses the kind of sensibility John Crowe Ransom is talking about? No. The melancholy scenario evoked by his list of "first objects"—the moon, the grass, the dead girl—suggests a kind of stasis that her theatrical presentation unsettles. She is not fixed in the attitudes of gender. Hers is neither cry nor epitaph. She seems quite conscious of the political ramifications of her work. She knows that she is writing in a style that is public and that violates the sequestering of the artist. She writes from the left, as a new woman, as a friend of Emma Goldman and Lola Ridge as well as Floyd Dell and Edmund Wilson. She writes as her independent mother's daughter and as the inheritor of feminist Inez Milholland's task. When she was in college, she and her friends greatly admired Milholland. Later, after Milholland's death, she became the second wife of Milholland's husband.

What do we do in memory of the women who came before us, whose places we uncannily occupy, whose work we hope to commemorate? In her sonnet to Inez Milholland, Millay acknowledges the limits of commemoration: "Upon this marble bust that is not I / Lay the round, formal wreath that is not fame." She tells us that the place of the female subject is empty: "I, that was proud and valiant, am no more;— / Save as a dream that wanders wide and late."[5] And she proposes the remedy: "Take up the song; forget the epitaph."

## Notes

1. This discussion of the difference between ordinary language and poetic language appeared in both Anglo-American and continental criticism. I. A. Richards and Philip Wheelwright both proposed a differentiation of conventional language from the figurative, mythical poetic language, a

distinction that owed much to Coleridge's distinctions between fancy and imagination. The Russian formalists and the Prague school linguists developed a more theoretically rigorous analysis of poetic language around the function of defamiliarization. Millay's forms clearly fail to operate like modernist experiments, defamiliarizing at the level of the sentence. However, what I am arguing is that Millay makes the position of the lyric subject strange, and that she therefore does not reinscribe the aesthetic distinction between literature and the personal.

2. I discuss Millay's relationship to sensibility, the sentimental, and middlebrow aesthetics at some length in *Sentimental Modernism*.

3. Julia Kristeva provides an especially helpful theorizing of the interaction of culture and individual through language. Her terms, the *semiotic* and the *symbolic*, point to the dialectic of body and law, the personal and the public, which underlies any subject at a moment of speech. See, in particular, *Revolution* and "Speaking Subject." This question of the subject has, of course, provided one of the central debates in literary theory in the last decade, with theorists from Althusser and Foucault (rewriting the Marxist concept of ideology as discursive formations) to Derrida to Lacan, together with feminists from Gilbert and Gubar to Butler, agreeing only that the individual is not the origin of individual identity. See, for example, Cadava, Connor, and Nancy, *Who Comes after the Subject?*

4. For a discussion of how the uncanny functions as a textual doubling, and not as a "real" referent, see Gardner Lloyd-Smith, *Uncanny American Fiction*.

5. The poem goes on: "Save as a wind that rattles the stout door, / Troubling the ashes in the sheltered grate. / The stone will perish; I shall be twice dust." At the Friday evening meeting of the Millay centennial conference, when we all gathered in the Surrey, Skidmore's Victorian mansion, to hear Nancy Milford read the last chapter of her biography of Millay, lights flickered, there were noises in the fireplace, and we heard a rustling at the open door behind her. Some said, "That was Norma." Others reminded us that the Surrey was said to be haunted. The next day, when I read this paper, its topic and its title seemed indeed twice "uncanny."

# 2   *Displaced Modernism*
## *Millay and the Triumph of Sentimentality*
### Jo Ellen Green Kaiser

## Vanguard or Rearguard?

In November of 1919, William Carlos Williams discovered that Alfred Kreymborg, writer and editor for the experimental little magazine *Others*, had decided not to use his influence with New York's Provincetown Players to arrange for a premier of Williams's new play, *The Apple Tree*. Instead, Kreymborg admitted, he was going to produce an avant-garde, antiwar play by the very newest addition to the Greenwich Village scene, Edna St. Vincent Millay. Although Williams remained angry at Kreymborg, he later confessed that Kreymborg's choice was not altogether unsound; when he "saw the bill" he found that he "really enjoyed it" (140). In fact, as Paul Mariani has noted, Williams later borrowed from Millay's play, *Aria da Capo*, in the fourth section of his long poem *Paterson*.[1]

The Millay of this anecdote has been largely absent from critical accounts. The consensus has been that Millay, although living in the modernist period, did not participate in modernism. Contemporary supporters of Millay like Elizabeth Atkins congratulated the poet for refusing the "devastating logic of nihilism" (93) that was then believed to underpin the modernist project, while contemporary critics of Millay's work argued with John Crowe Ransom that Millay was deficient in "masculinity" and "intellect" and so was incapable of constructing a modernist critique (*The World's Body* 98). More recent critics have concurred, although a bit regretfully. Jan Montefiore, for example, asserts that "the experiments of modernism passed [Millay] by" (115), while Debra Fried categorizes Millay as a "minor poet" whose place was "at the rearguard of the phalanx of modernism" ("Andromeda" 17).

What does it mean to place a poet "at the rearguard of the phalanx of modernism"? Fried's language maps a terrain long familiar to those who have studied the modernist movement. As Sandra M. Gilbert and Susan Gubar have elaborated in the first two volumes of *No Man's Land: The Place of the Woman Writer in the Twentieth Century*, early twentieth-century American literature has often been conceived as a battlefield in which Spartan, masculine modernists took up arms against their soft, sentimental opponents. Until recently, no one has doubted that the modernists won; in Fried's phrase, for example, the enemy army no longer exists. Indeed, once Fried decides that Millay does not belong in the modernist avant-garde, there is no legitimate space left for her to occupy; she ends up in the "rearguard."

In the last five years, however, historicist and feminist critics have been reevaluating the early twentieth-century culture wars. Ostensibly conducted on the grounds of imaginative discipline as a fight for a more authentic representation of the twentieth-century life and mind, this literary battle is now read as an ideological struggle over far more than the development of a new aesthetic. Changing constructions of gender and race, an emergent culture of professionalism, and the growing division between high and pop culture are just a few of the more salient movements now understood to have reshaped American life and the debates over poetry during this period. In turn, this new historicist understanding questions the very advisability of using tropes of war in describing early twentieth-century literary culture. Rather than imagining a battle between men and women, modernism and sentiment, critics like Suzanne Clark, Cheryl Walker, and Susan Schweik demonstrate that writers cannot simply be divided into opposing camps. Instead, this criticism maps the cultural terrain shared by these figures and the conflicting ideological positions that eventually lead them to embark on aggressively different courses.

For such a project, Edna St. Vincent Millay becomes an exemplary figure. Long read as America's last great sentimental poet, Millay also figured importantly in the 1920s as a member of the avant-garde. Because she first attempted to negotiate a modernist as well as a sentimental aesthetic, Millay's early work provides us with unusual access to the currents informing both of these cultural positions. Even more revealing is her later rejection of the modernism represented by Eliot and Pound, a rejection based on her interest in reshaping the contemporary political scene. By actively choosing to inhabit what was already becoming the "rearguard" of the literary world, Millay allows the critic to observe the ways in which sentimentality and modernism, pop and high culture, and feminine and masculine writing intersected and diverged during this period.

## Millay and Modernism

Millay herself eschewed metapoetic statements—that being, as Clark notes, a sign in itself of her embrace of sentimentality (*Sentimental Modernism* 68). Yet, we can chart Millay's literary decisions by examining her poems and their publication history. A look at this history reveals that Millay published in two very different venues. She made most of her money and certainly the better part of her fame by publishing in such popular culture magazines as *Ainslee's*, *Vanity Fair*, and *Literary Digest*. From about 1915 to 1920, most of the poems that Millay published in these journals were written in either ballad or stanza form. Their poetic content might have been, at times, tantalizingly bohemian, but the form was reassuringly regular.

Simultaneously, Millay was writing more experimental poems in less regular meter for such avant-garde publications as *Poetry*, the *Dial*, and *The Chapbook: A Monthly Miscellany*. The contrast between Millay's experimental and traditional work is most apparent in 1920. In that year, Millay began publishing free verse and promoting herself as an international poet. Importantly, part of this effort involved publishing her work in the *Chapbook*, a British monthly "miscellany" edited by Harold Monro. This journal, which is rarely featured in discussions of literary modernism, should receive more attention. Rather than being encumbered with the usual editorial apparatus, Monro's publication was run as a series of chapbooks, each issue consisting either of the work of one writer or an anthology of similar writers. The list of contributors to the *Chapbook* includes many of the most important figures of British modernism: T. S. Eliot, Ford Maddox Hueffer [Ford], Richard Aldington, the Sitwells, D. H. Lawrence, and Aldous Huxley. A special issue edited by Alfred Kreymborg titled "New American Poems" included work by Kreymborg, Frost, Williams, Cummings, Aiken, Stevens, Moore, Toomer, and Millay. Millay's work appears in four issues of the *Chapbook* and her first published poem in free verse, "Spring," first appears in the *Chapbook*.

In "Spring," Millay employs all the conventions of modernist poetry. As Pound had dictated in his famous imagist principles, "Spring" contains no unnecessary words, presents its images directly and visually, and is written in free verse (*Literary Essays* 3). The poem's aesthetic refusal to admit any of the more traditional poetic embellishments is echoed and reinforced by the poem's second line: "Beauty is not enough." In the world of this poem, no beauty, whether it results from the nature of spring itself or from the formal aesthetics of poetry, can lend meaning to life.

The poem begins when the poet raises an objection to the return of spring. She writes: "To what purpose, April, do you return again? / Beauty is not enough." Spring presents us with an unfolding panorama of beauty—"the redness / Of little leaves opening stickily" and "The spikes of the crocus." Reminiscent of Pound's "phallic crocoi" and the labial flowers of H.D.'s poems, these images represent a sexualized nature in which, however, human love is absent. Instead, in this impersonal poem, both nature and sexuality are aestheticized and objectified.

This impersonal "beauty" masks the reality of life's temporality—it is designed to quiet us, to lull us into believing that the cycles of life and death, spring and winter, will not recur. Each year, spring presents itself as a rebirth into a paradise beyond the temporal; it attempts to convince us that "It is apparent that there is no death." The poet asks, however, "what does that signify?" Spring, in seeming to transcend death, appears to create significance for life, just as art, another form of beauty, was understood in the nineteenth century to be an atemporal sign that lent significance to life in the very act of transcending life. If it "is apparent that there is no death," it is not only because spring has replaced winter, but also because the poem's representation of spring's flowers turn them into aestheticized objects that can transcend life, love, and death.

The poet, however, refuses both the sense and sensations of this impersonally aestheticized, transcendental spring. She knows that art, itself a signifier, is also a sign; that is, art itself is always a representation of the life that it simultaneously seeks to transcend. Art can never completely transcend nature, which is its ground, just as spring itself will once again become winter and death become realized in the poem as the ultimate absent ground of signification: " . . . under ground are the brains of men / Eaten by maggots." For this modernist, post–World War I sensibility, nothing remains to lend transient life any permanent significance; without a notion of transcendent art, "Life in itself / Is nothing." Spring and the beauty it brings are merely a cruel hoax, as is revealed in the poem's final lines:

> It is not enough that yearly, down this hill,
> April
> Comes like an idiot, babbling and strewing flowers.

In certain respects, Millay had touched on the theme of "Spring" in earlier poems. Indeed, what Walker has called the "burden of beauty" theme resonates not only in such early Millay poems as "Renascence," in which the young speaker first finds life empty and meaningless, but it constitutes a minor tradition among nineteenth- and early twentieth-century women poets (*Nightingale's Burden*). But in "Renascence" (and in the sentimental version of the "burden of beauty" theme generally), life is redeemed and given meaning through the auspices of the Christian God. The poet can be reborn into signification in these poems as long as she remains faithful:

> The soul can split the sky in two,
> And let the face of God shine through.
> But East and West will pinch the heart
> That can not keep them pushed apart.

A comparison between "Spring" and "Song of a Second April" provides an instructive contrast between the two accounts of meaning Millay struggled with during the period roughly between 1913 and 1924. Millay's third book of poetry, *Second April*, is titled after "Song of a Second April," though "Spring" is the first poem in the volume. "Song of a Second April," like "Spring," also laments the futility of spring to serve as some kind of rebirth into meaning. But "Song of a Second April" functions entirely within a sentimental framework. In this poem, Millay writes that spring is creating its usual bustle:

> There rings a hammering all day,
>     And shingles lie about the doors;
> In orchards near and far away
>     The grey wood-pecker taps and bores.

The poet, however, is unable to participate in this frenzy of renewal because her loved one has gone: " . . . only you are gone, / You that alone I cared to keep." In "Song of a Second April," the poet's dismay at the recurring cycles of the world can be traced directly to her sentimental loss of that lover or friend who can make life meaningful for her.

In American sentimental poetry, the poet usually attempts to stir the emotions of a reader by depicting a scene of absence or loss. While this use of pathos is usually considered indulgent—the *Princeton Encyclopedia of Poetry and Poetics*, to give just one example, includes the word *indulgent* three times in its entry for *sentimentality*—it is importantly employed, as Clark has pointed out, to persuade the reader to sympathize with the poet's moral attitudes and arguments (*Sentimental Modernism* 20). In "Song of a Second April," for example, the poet is making the argument that life is insignificant without love. An important though unspoken corollary to such sentimental poems is the view that acts of individual will create the possibility of a meaningful world. Whether directly, as in the individual's power to love, or more usually, indirectly, in the individual's ability to believe in a God, each person is perceived as an indispensable participant in the creation of meaning. This belief in the presence of meaning and in the individual's ability to grasp it and even provide it contrasts strongly with the modernist meta-physical crisis enacted in works like T. S. Eliot's *Waste Land*, Ezra Pound's *Mauberley*, and Millay's "Spring."

Much of Millay's work of the early 1920s seems on its surface more like the modernist "Spring" than like the sentimental "Song of a Second April." Most strikingly, Millay attacked the sentimental construction of absent love in *A Few Figs from Thistles* and to a lesser extent in *Second April*. Her most famous poem, after all, does not mourn absent love but rejoices in love's impermanence:

> My candle burns at both ends;
> It will not last the night;
> But ah, my foes, and oh, my friends—
> It gives a lovely light!

While this "First Fig" marked Millay's break from traditional senti-mentality, however, it did not necessarily signal her embrace of modernism. In contradistinction to the modernist creed of imper-sonality enunciated by Eliot, Millay's poetry remains personal. Her attitude toward love may not be that shared by her nineteenth-century predecessors, but she does share with them a belief in the centrality of love for poetry.

Millay's sonnet, "Only until this cigarette is ended," functions as a good example of her negotiations with both modernity and sentimentality. As in Eliot's "Love Song of J. Alfred Prufrock," Millay here portrays the meaninglessness of a love dying with a dying "fall." In Millay's poem, however, we hear not the voice of the timid man who fears that the woman he addresses will reject him, but the voice of that woman herself, who declares that her lover's face is one "which I can forget." Where Eliot's Prufrock feels mesmerized by the sensuality of the women who surround him—"Is it perfume from a dress / That makes me so digress?" (lines 65–66)—Millay's speaker controls male sexuality. She in effect renders her lover impotent by smoking her cigarette; if he is reduced to "quiet ashes" (Prufrock's "butt ends"), it is because she has first lit him up, drawn him in, then smoked him out. She controls the phallus, both metaphorically and symbolically. Indeed, if his "broken shadow" extends to a "lance" in the firelight, it is only because she chooses to "permit [her] memory to recall" his former potency.

Within a four-year period, Eliot and Millay both imagine the failure of romantic love and connect that failure to the power and sophistication of bohemian women who smoke cigarettes, listen to jazz, and refuse to answer men's overwhelming questions. Eliot's poem is written in a fragmented lyric form and implies that the failure of male potency signals larger failures—we find ourselves in a decayed urban world of "lonely men in shirt-sleeves, leaning out of windows" (line 72), a world in which Lazarus is ignored and the crucifixion parodied, a world better suited to Polonius than to Hamlet. Millay's poem, on the other hand, is written in the form of a Petrarchan sonnet, an ironic gesture that contributes to our sense that this female speaker has absolute control over her romance and has carefully designed its failure. Where Prufrock's personality is effaced, that possessed by Millay's speaker is asserted; where Prufrock's "sun has set," Millay's speaker looks forward to a new day. While Prufrock's only hope for relief seems to lie in the past, as he attempts to reconstruct himself in Shakespearean or biblical terms, Millay's speaker recalls the past of her affair only in order to dispense with it—she lives not for past or future, but for the present. What we find, in short, is that although both Millay and Eliot are representing one of the key crises of modernity, the disintegration of traditional relations between the sexes, this crisis leads these poets in quite different directions. Eliot assumes what will be called the classic modernist position—he represents a fragmented, impersonal world that can only be redeemed, if at all, by appeals to a mythic past. Millay, on the other hand, revels in the possibilities of the present and assumes the sentimental privilege of personality in order to more fully participate in modernity.

## The Politics of Sentimentality

The differences between "Only until this cigarette is ended" and "The Love Song of J. Alfred Prufrock" have everything to do with their writers' sexual difference. Sentimentality and modernism are gender-inflected ideologies, feminine and masculine respectively, leading their adherents to pursue very different strategies in depicting and defining gender roles. I am not arguing here that the sentimental was women's "proper place." On the contrary, sentimentality, based in an essentialist account of the differences between the sexes, seems in hindsight to be quite problematic in light of the numerous critiques, both feminist and poststructuralist, of the essentialist position. Indeed, those early twentieth-century writers most feminists see as important precursors—Virginia Woolf, H.D., Gertrude Stein—were modernists rather than sentimentalists. However, the very feminine nature of sentimental ideology made it a superior position in the early twentieth century for effecting political change.

According to sentimental ideology, men were rational by nature, while women were the guardians of the emotions and morality. This sentimental gendering was at first tied to domesticity; women, with their superior moral and emotional natures, were considered ideally suited to raise children, while men were given the duty of ordering life outside the home. By the late nineteenth century, however, women began using this ideology to their advantage, arguing that if women were naturally the most excellent caretakers of children, they should be allowed the vote in order that they might become the nation's caretakers. For example, a suffragette in 1884 told a congressional committee that

when you debar from your councils and legislative halls the purity, the spirituality, and the love of woman, then those councils are apt to become coarse and brutal. God gave us to you to help you in this little journey to a better land, and by our love and our intellect to help make our country pure and noble. (Rothman 128)

The argument for suffrage here is based on the sentimental claim that women have greater access than men to the emotions, which makes them both more spiritual and better crusaders for moral causes. We see a similar argument made in Charlotte Perkins Gilman's utopian *Herland*, and it was ultimately this sort of sentimental argument, rather than the more radical suffragettes' demands for equality under the law, that won women the vote (Kraditor).

This use of sentimentality stressed the importance of the moral virtues, which were understood to appear most naturally in women. In the "flapper" age that followed, emotional life became less spiritual and, paradoxically, more private; women were no longer depicted as idealized mothers but as ideal wife-companions (Rothman 5–6). Women still possessed an emotional nature, as opposed to men's rational one, but now, in contrast to the nonsexual family advocated a decade earlier, women were supposed to use their emotions to foster romance and through romance to keep the now-nuclear family together. With this new stress on the women's duty as keeper of the marital flame came a new acknowledgment of women's sexuality and a campaign in some of the more radical circles for birth control. Birth control was seen as a cause of marital happiness, as couples could engage in sex without the fear of pregnancy. While the birth control movement offended the moral propriety of the older suffragettes, both movements grew out of the sentimental belief in women's special role as guardian of the emotions, and both movements used women's difference as a way to promote women's power within their society.

If sentimental ideology enabled women to use private emotions—the force of their personalities—in order to enact social change, modernist ideology functioned in almost exactly the opposite way. Modernist ideology was based in a negative critique that assumed the collapse of a formerly unified world, a collapse based in large part, as Gilbert and Gubar demonstrate, on the very changes in gender roles that sentimentalists were abetting. If one accepts the modernist position that the world lacks any secure metaphysical basis or "ground," then change itself becomes meaningless, and any show of emotion becomes emblematic of a naive optimism modernists believed was no longer available. Instead, the modernists, and here Eliot in "Tradition and the Individual Talent" is paradigmatic, attempted to transmute their emotions into impersonal observations, to record that cultural destruction they deplored but could not remedy. Especially in their first phase from 1912 to 1923, modernists read art itself as an empty sign and embraced art for art's sake because art for them had become merely a process of signification. The text becomes reflexive and, proto-deconstructively, reveals its own lack, as in Marianne Moore's "Poetry," Eliot's *Waste Land*, and Pound's *Mauberley*.

When the modernists do turn to the social world after World War I, they take with them both a desire to effect change and the premonition that such a desire is futile. Their solution, when they turn to writing poems designed to protest some aspect of their contemporary society, is to do so from a mythic remove; a few examples are the Christian and Hellenic mythology of H.D.'s *Trilogy*, the recast history of Pound's *Cantos*, or the new American mythos Williams created for *Paterson*. In her modernist play of 1920, *Aria da Capo*, Millay also uses the mythic pastoral world of the Latin poets for her social commentary. Later, however, she will use myth mainly for private purposes, as in her epic love poem, *Fatal Interview*.

The modernists' move to myth and their general belief in the fragmented nature of the modern world are not disassociated from the economic realities of their culture. Like sentimental ideology, modernist ideology was rooted in changing social phenomena and contributed to them. As I have argued elsewhere, modernist ideology has been closely tied to the emerging ideology of professionalism, which in turn provided the means for intellectuals to redefine their roles in relation to society. Male modernists struggled to professionalize literature and literary study in order to create a gulf between themselves and women writers, whom they then labeled as mere amateurs. Female modernists, desiring the same rights and position as their male colleagues, joined them in seeking professional privileges, Woolf's *Room of One's Own* being only the most famous example. As part of this search for expertise, modernist writers developed not only their own mythologies, but their own limited audience, as only those expert in culture could be considered capable of reading the signs of culture's decay. By the 1930s and 1940s, Moore's reticence, Eliot's pedantry, and Pound's forthright calls for an audience of no more than fifteen readers (Pound, *Selected Letters* 146) become translated by the American New Critics into an authorization for the professionalization and institutionalization of literary study. Though the case is more complex than I can present in this essay, these developments also eased the way for the split between high and low culture that occurred during these decades.

## Sentimentality as a Politics

Like the modernists, Millay also perceived a crisis of meaning, as is clear from such works as "Spring," *Aria da Capo*, and a handful of other free verse lyrics she composed between 1919 and 1921. She also, at key moments, expressed a desire to assert her expertise. Certainly, she maintained strict control over her publications, admonishing her editors not to "do anything to anything that's signed by my own name" (*Letters*, 1952, 160). At the same time, however, and under a pseudonym, Millay did write material that she allowed her editors to revise, and more importantly, she rejected the elitism embraced by the modernists. Her poems were designed not for a handful of disciples or initiates but for the broad public, and she continually expressed her delight in the increasingly large public she had obtained for her work. Though some critics have argued that the modernists fell back on the notion of discipleship to explain their unpopularity, Eliot, the most popular modernist, only intensified his call for a Coleridgean clerisy of the select few after he achieved his fame.

Millay's gradual move away from what could be called a modernist position became clear, paradoxically, during the very years in which she published most of her modernist work. Though she had embarked on a two-year-long trip to Europe in 1921 because she felt her poetry needed "fresh grass to feed on," she expressed no interest in her letters in participating in any of the famous modernist salons, nor did she give any evidence that she had done so (*Letters*, 1952, 106). Aside from a brief dinner with Brancusi and an admiration she developed in Paris for the work of Henri de Regnier, Millay seems to have spent most of her time in Europe focused more on her marriage prospects than on the modernist milieu. At the same time, she increasingly separated her satiric and stylized work from what she thought of as her serious poetry; she printed her satiric prose under the pseudonym Nancy Boyd and published two separate books of poetry in 1921, one for her snappy, contemporary *Figs*, and another, *Second April*, for what she thought of as her serious work (103).

Millay's persistent dismissal of *A Few Figs from Thistles* as a minor work highlights her growing distaste for highly stylized writing. In July of 1919, she read *Bubu of Montparnasse* on the advice of her friend and editor W. Adolphe Roberts and then complained: "I don't like your Charles-Louis Philippe so damned much. He's such a self-conscious cuss—loves to think he's a stylist, makes me sick" (*Letters*, 1952, 89). That very self-consciousness, of course, is what attracted a writer like Eliot to the book. During this period, Millay was quite conscious of the antimodernist direction in which her work was moving. While she kept in touch with her avant-garde circle in New York, she came to realize that their paths were diverging. For example, in March of 1921 she urged her sister not to "let any of the Provincetown Players" see the manuscript of her Vassar play, later to be published as *The Lamp and the Bell*. While Millay thought the play would be "a great hit" and that it had, along with "some pretty ragged spots," "a lot of fine stuff in it," she realized that her friends "would hate it, & make fun of it, & old Djuna Barnes would rag you about it" (116).

Millay was discovering that the modernist representation of the crisis of modernity was not one she shared. Whereas the modernists had little faith in the political present (Williams' present, it should be noted, is one of the imagination) and in the general public's ability to recognize and reform its world, Millay increasingly turned to the public and to local politics to enact immediate change. Taking up a sentimental position, Millay in 1927 used the force of her personal appeal in "Justice Denied in Massachusetts" to protest the Sacco-Vanzetti trials. Erasing the boundaries between life and art, she also participated in the protests of this trial and was imprisoned twice during the proceedings. In 1929, Millay ran for the position of Democratic committeewoman from Austerlitz. Her political concerns of the 1930s gained literary form in *Conversation at Midnight*, a dramatic poem in which seven men of varying class backgrounds argue over politics. Perhaps most famously, however, Millay appealed specifically to the vulnerability of women and children in *The Murder of Lidice* in order to persuade the American public to recognize the German as well as the Japanese threat in the first year after the United States entered World War II. Performed as a radio play that reached hundreds of thousands of listeners, *The Murder of Lidice* and its companion book, *Make Bright the Arrows*, demonstrate Millay's attempts to write from a sentimental position in order to influence a larger public.[2]

Most of Millay's poems are not overtly political. These political poems, however, framed as they are in sentimental terms, illuminate the reasons, already apparent in "Only until this cigarette is ended" for Millay's general return to sentimentality. Given that sentimental discourse not only pervaded American life, but actually had been used effectively to advance women's political goals and given that modernism seemed in the early 1920s to embrace only what she and her contemporaries believed to be a "devastating logic of nihilism," it should not surprise us that Millay, active in women's politics and an important voice of popular culture, should cease her experiments in modernism and return to sentimentality. In some sense, her choice proved highly successful; Millay became an extraordinarily popular poet who could exert noticeable influence in local and national politics. That her failure to accept the growing dominance of modernist ideology led to her exile from the canon, in which she appears only as a footnote to modernist texts like *Paterson*, tells us more about cultural shifts than it does about the value of her poetry.

## Notes

1. Mariani's account differs from Williams' in several respects. Williams writes that Kreymborg lost the manuscript of a "playlet" titled *The Old Apple Tree*, then refused to present "another small play," favoring Millay instead (140). Mariani records that the only play in question was *The Apple Tree*, which Kreymborg first refused to stage and then lost (154–55). I have used Mariani's account.

2. It would be interesting to examine Pound's radio broadcasts as sentimental; my impression, however, is that Pound remains elusively allusive in these political appeals and so fails to achieve his desired effect.

Part II    *Love (and) Connection*

# 3  *"How the Speaking Pen Has Been Impeded"*

The Rhetoric of Love and
Selfhood in Millay and Rich
Ernest J. Smith

Edna St. Vincent Millay's poetic diction may initially seem to belong to a prior century rather than to the revolutionary era of high modernism during which she produced most of her work. But a comparison of Millay's work with that of the major feminist poet of the second half of this century, Adrienne Rich, shows surprising affinities, particularly in poems dealing with the themes of love and selfhood. A central theme for each poet is the struggle toward emergence and assertion of self amidst forces that would impede poetic and personal freedom. In Millay's work, the dialectic between this theme and the conventional form of the sonnet and romantic language of the love lyric is a paradigm of the artistic struggle Rich herself worked through in her early break from formalism. Millay's effort to define the self is acutely displayed in the *Fatal Interview* sonnet sequence, her chronicle of a love affair that shares many characteristics with Rich's bold 1976 sequence "Twenty-One Love Poems."

Millay's attraction to the sonnet has often been seen as a type of retreat into a safe outlet for her more assertive themes, and surely Adrienne Rich's oft-quoted statement on her own early attitude toward form applies equally to Millay: "In those years formalism was part of the strategy—like asbestos gloves, it allowed me to handle materials I couldn't pick up barehanded" (*Lies* 40–41). While Rich breaks from the strict iambs, rhymes, and stanzas of her first two volumes into a more open verse that embodies process and discovery, she has continued to employ and extend the range of more fluid forms such as the love sequence, the meditative ode, and the elegy. Writing of "Twenty-One Love Poems," a sequence that stands clearly in the middle of Rich's career, Kevin McGuirk describes Rich's act of "opening the intimate space of the love lyric to social and literary contexts" (63). More conventional in overt subject matter (heterosexual love) and in strict sonnet-sequence form, Millay's tone, language, and point of view in *Fatal Interview* nevertheless foreground both the social and the literary context of her sequence as well. Rather than a capitulation to a convenient form, it is quite possible to read Millay's choice of the sonnet as a strategic assertion of her right to both work within and redefine the boundaries of one of the most common poetic modes. Debra Fried questions the theory that Millay "submits" to the form of the sonnet, arguing instead that Millay's sonnets

reclaim that genre as her plot of ground, not chiefly by planting it with 'woman's' themes or using it as a mouthpiece for the woman's voice (though she does both these things), but by rethinking the form's historical capacity for silencing her voice. ("Andromeda" 2–3).

The silencing of the speaking voice is a central concern for both Millay and Rich. In one of her late sonnets from *Mine the Harvest* (1954), Millay confronts and excoriates the bounds put on free, creative expression:

> What chores these churls do put upon the great,
> What chains, what harness; the unfettered mind,
> At dawn, in all directions flying blind
> Yet certain, might accomplish, might create
>
> . . . . . . . . . . . . . . . . . . . .
> Oh, how the speaking pen has been impeded,
> To its own cost and to the cost of speech,
> By specious hands that for some thinly-needed
> Answer or autograph, would claw a breach
> In perfect thought. . . .

While one of Millay's angrier poems, the sentiment here is in keeping with the major theme running through all of her work: the ongoing effort to create space for woman's voice. Of course, Rich has spent a distinguished forty-year career eloquently engaging this issue, and in perhaps her best-known essay, "When We Dead Awaken: Writing as Re-Vision," she urges women's poetry to recognize and "go through," rather than conceal, anger. Reading Millay, one senses the anger couched within surface-level conventions of form and content. As Suzanne Clark has noted, the deliberate ambiguity in Millay's positioning of the "I" often forces the reader "to take up the position of the spectator at the drama of character." She continues,

Then Millay's poetry becomes a gesture of definition enacted at the margins of identity, and the self she does and does not define—does and does not seduce us into taking as the *subject* of poetry—is the borderline character of the adolescent, not Woman as Poet but the Girl, whose chief subject is love. (*Sentimental Modernism* 68)

This late sonnet is an exception for Millay, who rarely expresses anger this forcefully. However, even here—where I would contend that the speaking voice *is* "Woman as Poet"—anger is counterpoised by the vision of "unfettered," "perfect thought," an unencumbered space removed from the social context, which both Millay and Rich yearn for. It is the drive of the voice toward a lyric quietude that constitutes Rich's "dream of a common language" and Millay's "harvest."

At the same time, Millay's poetry necessarily engages the world in the same manner as Rich's: through its profound sense of the weight of history and of women's embattled position within history. Rich's poetry and forceful prose is at times a literal road map of "how the speaking pen has been impeded," how the individual and collective voice of women has been suppressed. Millay, meanwhile, as Cheryl Walker has so clearly shown, offers us a figure who both participates in and critiques "the ideology of sexual liberation, which we now see as far from simply 'liberating' " (*Masks Outrageous and Austere* 136). Until recently, Millay's culture critique, if recognized at all, has been seen as subtle and indirect. Most early Millay criticism distinguishes between her life, read as actively feminist, and her poetry, read as coming from a genteel, romantic tradition. The

Norton *Modern Poems* anthology tells us that the "poems which retain an interest are those in which she keeps alive the tradition of the English lyric and of the disciplined sonnet" (309). But critics like Clark, Fried, and Walker have turned attention toward questioning why Millay chose the sonnet form and the dramatic mode and how those choices relate to her major themes.

Citing Gilbert and Gubar's claim that poetry genres have been thoroughly male-dominated, Fried suggests that "only by acknowledging the woman writer's exclusion from this hierarchy of verse genres can we begin to understand what a woman poet may signify when she chooses to write sonnets" ("Andromeda" 6–7). In a similar vein, McGuirk says of Rich's "Twenty-One Love Poems": "The love sequence is on trial because it is a form that has embodied specific gender relations. The very conventions Rich seeks to overcome operate not just in the poem's content but in the very *materia* of her discourse" (72). As to why Millay's theme of emerging, independent selfhood is so often contained within the love lyric, Rich herself offers a clue in her essay on Dickinson: "I suggest that a woman's poetry about her relationship to her daemon—her own active, creative power—has in patriarchal culture used the language of heterosexual love or patriarchal theology" (*Lies* 170). While Millay is not one of those women from history or literature about whom Rich so often writes, it is clear that much of Millay's love poetry concerns this effort to define a powerful, creative self, which, according to Rich, "is [typically] exteriorized in masculine form, much as masculine poets have invoked the female Muse" (165–66).

In *Fatal Interview*, Millay employs the language of heterosexual love, the convention of the sonnet sequence, and simultaneously deals with the theme of love, separation, and emerging self boldly and directly, anticipating Rich's "Twenty-One Love Poems." Each poet works within, yet works to subvert, established poetic forms and conventions. If the choice of a sonnet sequence for Millay and something very close to a free verse sonnet sequence for Rich is a conventional mode for verse-chronicling a love affair, the actual subject matter narrated is anything but conventional. Millay's poems trace, from the woman's point of view, the consummation and decline of an adulterous liaison, while Rich's sequence follows a lesbian affair.

Both *Fatal Interview* and "Twenty-One Love Poems" combine passages of highly romantic language celebrating sexual and spiritual union with passages of direct, unadorned assertion of selfhood. The form of the sequence, with its linked individual lyrics, allows for alternating modes of language as the dialectic of commitment and self-emergence develops. Rich's poems contain some of her most romantic lines:

> Your eyes are everlasting, the green spark
> of the blue-eyed grass of early summer,
> the green-blue wild cress washed by the spring.

(III)

But conventional romantic diction and subject matter, a description of the lover's eyes, cannot bear up for long amidst the knowledge that "they still control the world" (IV), brought home in the very next poem by a hostage's account of being sexually abused while imprisoned, a description that reaches the poet through the mail. The hostage's concluding words—"You know, I think men love wars"—rekindle the poet's "incurable anger, my unmendable wounds." Even language and art confirm the control of the patriarchal society, as the next poem reminds us:

> Once open the books, you have to face
> the underside of everything you've loved—
> the rack and pincers held in readiness, the gag
> even the best voices have had to mumble through,
> the silence burying unwanted children—
> women, deviants, witnesses—in desert sand.

(V)

Although on the surface much more steeped in the conventions of the Elizabethan sonnet sequence, Millay's poems also express an awareness of the impediments to the "speaking pen" and balance the exuberant treatment of her affair with the depiction of the self's struggle to affirm its legitimate voice. Jane Stanbrough has argued that Millay's is a "language of vulnerability" in *Fatal Interview*: "The sequence dramatizes the spiritual disintegration that must occur through the social conditioning that explains woman's nature as essentially emotional and her greatest need as love" (196). But while Millay's high-toned, poetic description of woman's vulnerability in love seems disproportionately to dominate her sequence, her speaker emerges from the affair with much more of a sense of spiritual wholeness than "disintegration." Like Hart Crane's 1926 love sequence "Voyages" and Rich's sequence of fifty years later, *Fatal Interview* ends, despite sorrow, on a note of willed affirmation. Part of that affirmation is constituted by the poem itself, the brave, honest record of love. The language of both Millay and Rich is daring in its directness, celebrating the erotic, at times risking sentimentality. But ultimately to be vulnerable, to be open to love and its language, enables the individual voice to be heard. Millay's speaker tells her lover: "I might have held you for a summer more, / But at the cost of words I value highly" (XLVII).

Throughout *Fatal Interview*, Millay figures herself as a prisoner of love who, early on in the affair and its literary record (V), would not will herself free. But by the time the lovers have parted, late in the sequence, the speaker resists resignation to her fate: " . . . what you cannot do / Is bow me down" (XLV). While the final third of *Fatal Interview* expresses an overall tone of lament, the sense of an emerging, clear-eyed, capable self overrides any grief or bitterness. Paralleling the concluding line of Rich's sequence—"I choose to walk here. And to draw this circle"—Millay asserts that the lovers' breach was not wholly one-sided:

> . . . I lost you fairly;
> In my own way, and with my full consent.
> . . . . . . . . . . . . . . . . . . .
> Day dried my eyes; I was not one for keeping
> Rubbed in a cage a wing that would be free.
>
> (XLVII)

So, one of Millay's strategies for subverting the traditional love lyric is to have the woman-speaker emerge from the affair whole, rather than in a state of disintegration. In this way Millay, as Rich urges in "When We Dead Awaken," "enter[s] an old text from a new critical direction," an act which serves to redefine both the literary tradition and woman's status within it. Rich continues, "And this drive to self-knowledge, for women, is more than a search for identity: it is part of our refusal of the self-destructiveness of male-dominated society" (*Lies* 35).

Millay's sequence was published in 1932 and is one of the few texts in modern American poetry between the wars to deal with what Carolyn Heilbrun discusses as "a female impulse to power, as opposed to the erotic impulse which alone is supposed to impel women" (44). What is particularly interesting in comparing Rich's revolutionary poems with Millay's is that they share the strategy of employing many conventional literary motifs within the very genre that they attempt to redefine. Both poets employ myth, Millay framing her group of fifty-two poems with the legend of Diana and Endymion, moon goddess and mortal, and repeatedly referring to the beloved as a god. Sonnet XII chides the "Olympian gods," whose "sire" now "lies abed with me," ready to help the speaker bear a son "branded with godhead." A few poems later (XV, XVI), from the perspective of the affair's end, the speaker dreams herself "among the Elysian fields" with other "mortal women" who once kept the company of gods.

Rich also uses myth, in portraying her beloved as rescuer-healer. Sonnet VI celebrates the hands of the lover, capable of reconstructing

> the fine, needle-like shards of a great krater-cup
> bearing on its sides
> figures of ecstatic women striding
> to the sibyl's den or the Eleusinian cave.

Two poems later, the speaker figures herself as Philoctetes, noted archer of the Trojan War. Left on the island of Lemnos for ten years because of a festering foot, the bearer of Heracles's arrows was then retrieved when an oracle decreed that Troy could not be taken without him. Rich uses the legend of "Philoctetes / in *woman's* form" (emphasis added) to highlight the theme of spiritual rebirth after long isolation, love providing the newfound ability to resist "the temptation to make a career of pain."

Each sequence also utilizes the familiar *carpe diem* motif, but in differing ways. Millay introduces the note of urgency and temporality as early as the first poem ("What thing is this . . . / That hastening headlong to a dusty end") and in the second poem anticipates the end of the affair and the abiding pain it will cause: "The scar of this encounter like a sword / Will lie between me and my troubled lord." Hovering over the entire sonnet sequence is an acute awareness of the transitory nature of this particular love. Repeatedly, the speaker rues the end of night and the coming of dawn, and by the midpoint of the sequence (XXVII, XXVIII, XXIX) the principle focus seems to be "unreturning time" (XXVIII). "Twenty-One Love Poems," as we have already seen, is very aware of the political aspect of time, the violence of a patriarchal society where "two women together is a work / nothing in civilization has made simple" (XIX). Rich's sense of time's power, to borrow a phrase from a later volume's title, is more consciously political than that of Millay in *Fatal Interview*.

Each group of poems does seek refuge from unrelenting time within the same state, that of dream. But in each case, dream can offer, at best, only momentary removal from the reality of present existence. Millay's sonnet XVI ("I dreamed I moved among the Elysian fields") resembles Rich's sonnet II ("I wake up in your bed. I know I have been dreaming") in evoking postcoital imaginative suspension. But by the end of Rich's poem, after envisioning the beloved as a poem, the dreamer is again conscious of "the pull of gravity, which is not simple." The next poem immediately brings the theme of time into sharp focus: "Since we're not young, weeks have to do time / for years of missing each other." Throughout the remainder of the sequence, we feel the effort of the lovers fighting against time, battling "the forces they had ranged against us" with "the forces we had ranged within us" (XVII). The Elysian dream of *Fatal Interview* is likewise interrupted but more by internal doubt than by social reality. Sonnet XVII ends with the speaker doubting her lover's sincerity, so that by sonnet XXI, she cannot even conjure him in dream. One of the tasks of Millay's speaker is what Paula Bennett, in discussing Rich's erotic floating poem, identifies as the "healing of the mind-body split" (233).

In "When We Dead Awaken," Rich herself, in discussing her

early poetry, speaks of a split between "the girl who wrote poems, who defined herself in writing poems, and the girl who was to define herself by her relationships with men" (*Lies* 40). Part of that self-definition involved learning from the masters Rich was studying as an undergraduate: Frost, Donne, Auden, Stevens, Yeats. But another part of her style may have been formed earlier, she tells us, in memorizations and imitations of Dickinson and Millay, "the older women poets with their peculiar keenness and ambivalence" (39). As Rich and others move the constraints of patriarchal criticism aside, we can now read and learn in the spirit of the sixteen-year-old Rich. We can read Millay anew, both for her own gift and for the gift she passed to a later generation of American women poets.

# 4 Rewriting the Myth of the Woman in Love

## Millay's Fatal Interview

*Holly Peppe*

When I first read *Fatal Interview*, a cyclical sequence of fifty-two Petrarchan sonnets by Edna St. Vincent Millay, I was struck by the poet's sudden shifts in diction—from archaic and classical to colloquial—and by the apparent incongruity of poetic devices and allusions. While a majority of the poems are laced with conceits and love poetry conventions drawn from a lineage of male poets (notably John Donne),[1] others—written in a less adorned style—contain straightforward nature images and references to the poet's own background in Maine.

And who is the speaker in the sonnets? Millay strikes poses throughout the poems: first, she adopts the persona of the mythical moon goddess Selene, then shifts to the outspoken "female counterpart to Donne's sophisticated lover" (Klemans 8), then to a contemporary woman in the throes of accepting her own sexuality who proudly refuses to compromise the integrity she has inherited from the natural world in order to regain her male lover's attention. All this is complicated because, in assuming each of these poses, Millay filters her speaker's feelings through an array of often oblique, usually paradoxical metaphors based upon traditional, male-defined sexual protocols. What finally threads the sequence together for me is the momentum the poet creates as she guides the speaker through a tumultuous healing process—alternately both painful and exhilarating—that culminates in an acknowledgment of female identity.

Reading this turmoil as a reflection of Millay's own ambivalence toward the ultimate success of male-female romantic love relationships, I consider *Fatal Interview* a vehicle for her view of the difficulties such relationships create for women.

In this essay, I consider how the poet uses the mythical frame story of Endymion and Selene to create a context for this view. I look at how the speaker's identification with women in history and with the female elements in nature ultimately redeem her from sharing Selene's fate. I illustrate that the end result of the speaker's "fatal" meeting is a positive one, that she neither—as other critics have suggested—"resigns" herself to her fate (Atkins 231; Brittin 85, 87) nor undergoes "psychological disintegration" (Stanbrough 197) but is instead strengthened by the outcome of her affair. Finally, I present the idea that the speaker's self-conflict reflects not only Millay's experience as a woman but as an artist.

Millay believes in love and considers it a worthy metaphor for passion. Yet in this sequence (as in "Sonnets from an Ungrafted Tree"), she reveals little hope that love can maintain its initial passionate pitch, much less last, given a woman's tendency toward relationship and a man's aversion to it and tendency toward separation. What jeopardizes the success of romantic love, Millay suggests, is less a question of mismatching than the result of the gender-based differences that underlie the dilemma faced by her speaker.[2]

To set this generic dilemma in a timeless context, Millay adapts a myth in which romantic love is portrayed as satisfying for the male partner but destructive and finally psychologically fatal to the female. In the original myth, the cold-hearted moon goddess Selene sees Endymion sleeping on Mt. Latmus, falls hopelessly in love with him, and descends to earth to kiss him and lie beside him. In one version of the story, Endymion wakes to find the goddess gone and begs Zeus to let him sleep on Mt. Latmus forever so that he may continue to experience the "strong and enthralling" dreams Selene brought him (Benet 34). In another version, Selene casts a magic spell of eternal slumber over Endymion so that she may kiss and caress him whenever she wishes (Hamilton 113–14). In both versions, Endymion enjoys a blissful sleep while Selene's unceasing passion and desire for the boy causes her perpetual anguish.

Millay uses the "unconscious man" motif central to the myth to emphasize men's inability to respond to women's needs. Selene's madness is thus the tragic result of a woman's obsession with a love object who first accepts her sexually, then rejects her. Because Selene cannot die physically, as a mortal can, she loses touch with herself and her environment. Both characters are locked into a state beyond consciousness: Endymion at peace with the universe, Selene at war with herself. Like the moon goddess, Millay's speaker is frustrated by her unquenched desire to share her sexual passion with her beloved. The man, on the other hand, is conspicuously out of touch with the natural world and reveals neither passion nor compassion toward the woman who desires him, his self-centeredness bordering on a tedious solipsism.

Just as Endymion sleeps peacefully while Selene suffers, the man falls into an "emotional sleep" that causes the speaker anguish. His "unnatural" stupor, like Endymion's slumber, releases him from having to deal with the speaker's pain. Millay's strategy is to reenact the plot of the Endymion myth and then to reverse its outcome by giving her speaker both the freedom to choose and the components of a choice that are unavailable to Selene, a character trapped within a male myth of romantic love in which women who reveal their sexuality are eventually driven mad by unanswered desire.

An original composite portrait of a "woman in love," Millay's speaker represents an unprecedented departure from the nameless female love object depicted in traditional romantic love poetry. Within this tradition women are usually depicted as generalized rather than unique; according to convention, they are beautiful and shallow, heartless and cruel, fickle and manipulative, or emotionally vulnerable to the point of hysteria. Because most of the poets writing within the love poetry tradition were men, the traits and the myths associated with the woman's role in the romantic love motif have been primarily male-defined.

In *Fatal Interview*, Millay challenges this male tradition by creating a new type of woman lover who, uninterested in deception, exercises her capacity for rigorous self-examination and takes a critical, realistic view of her male partner. This new female persona is motivated not by a secret need or wish to manipulate, but by a desire to express her sexuality and a tendency toward building and sustaining relationships. She values love, art, and the natural world. She is emotionally vulnerable but draws strength from her innate bond with female elements in nature—earth and night— that unlike her lover, accept her unconditionally.

No woman poet before Millay presented as extensive and detailed a psychological portrait of the woman lover. Within the male-dominated sonnet sequence genre,[3] the few woman poets who present the woman in love as persona and protagonist—Elizabeth Barrett Browning, Christina Rossetti, and Elinor Wylie—reverse traditional poetic conventions by using women as their personae, but they assign those personae the conventional poetic role of the unworthy admirer. The personae in Browning's *Sonnets from the Portuguese*, Rossetti's *Monna Innominata*, and Wylie's *One Person* define themselves in terms of their relationships to men rather than as individual women with specific emotional and sexual desires. They also describe the men they love as unequivocally godlike creatures deserving of unlimited praise and unending devotion.

In contrast, though Millay's speaker praises her beloved with traditional zeal, in sonnet VI she also taunts him for ignoring her sexual desire and finally loses patience with him when he insists on rationalizing a relationship that was fated to fail (XXXVIII). Here she addresses the man both lovingly and scornfully; he is exalted, questioned, criticized, and scolded. He is the object of conceits that are, by design, impersonal in their rather bizarre descriptive effect: his "disturbing eyes" with their "stormy lashes" are like "two splendid planets" (IX). He neither takes shape as a distinct personality nor emerges as a character deserving of sympathy or blame.

Yet the speaker is challenged by both her passionate sexual attraction toward him and her desire for a sustained love relationship. At high points in her struggle to reconcile her dual longing, the feelings she interprets as love elevate her to a position far above life's banal, daily problems. From that lofty perspective, she compares herself to queens and goddesses with whom, as a woman in love, she identifies. Love thus carries her from her immediate time and place into the realm of human history, delivering her from this world into a higher sphere where, theoretically at least, emotion rules all. Yet love also works as a stifling, destructive force that threatens to render her helpless. Only when she is finally free from her attachment to her desire for the male beloved can she transform the pain love causes her into resolve: "I know my mind and I have made my choice" (XLV).

H.D. presented the theme of her *Hermetic Definition* as a version of Psyche's quest for Eros: "Women are individually seeking, as one woman, fragments of the Eternal Lover. As the Eternal Lover has been scattered or dissociated, so she [is] in her search for him."[4] The "scattered" aspects of the speaker's "search" for her lover in *Fatal Interview* are manifested in psychological activity, that is, in the alternate clarity and confusion that characterize the speaker's thinking. I read this shifting perspective as Millay's own thinly disguised ambivalence about investing energy in romantic love. In sonnet V, for example, Millay's speaker admits the agonies of being jailed but declares herself content: " . . . my chains throughout their iron length / Make such a golden clank upon my ear." Yet in sonnet XVIII, she scorns the feeling that traps her:

> Shall I be prisoner till my pulses stop
> To hateful Love and drag his noisy chain,
> And bait my need with sugared crusts that drop
> From jeweled fingers neither kind nor clean?—

She understands that suffering is the price of her freedom, yet fears the consequences of escape:

> Perfidious Prince, that keep me here confined,
> Doubt not I know the letters of my doom:
> How many a man has left his blood behind
> To buy his exit from this mournful room
> These evil stains record, these walls that rise
> Carved with his torment, steamy with his sighs.

In short, she cannot decide which is the better alternative, to be in or out of love.[5]

Millay's ambivalence is also apparent as she switches the speaker's role back and forth between victim and romantic heroine.[6] As heroine, the woman's "tragic flaw," her love for a man, precipitates an emotional "fall" from which she eventually rises, still intact. Her role as a tragic figure is more complex in that, paradoxically, her pain both gives her significance and raises her stature. She takes great pride in her anguish: rather than trying to escape it, she wears her suffering as a badge of superiority. She becomes a self-declared martyr to love who can then relate to other women who have been ravaged by gods or godlike lovers.

Millay continues to use the tragic-heroic motif in treating women's sexuality. Allying herself with the archetypal female symbol, the moon, the speaker is able to express her own sexual needs (VI) but is also aware of the vulnerability or even shame such expression causes her. Uniting sexually with her beloved does bring her some satisfaction, but it also makes her susceptible to further sexual desire and the desire for "love," both of which, in turn, make her vulnerable to rejection. The shame resulting from her acknowledgment of her sexual needs underlies the bravado of lines like "Enraptured in his great embrace I lie" (XII).

Avoiding this shame becomes the barely detectable ulterior motive behind her childlike offer of "Love in the open hand, no thing but that" (XI). Before making the offer, she assures her beloved that she does not give her love symbolically or deceptively but instead acts "as children do" (XI), with generosity and honesty. The undertone here, suggested by the moral condemnation of those women who are deceptive, the "other girls," is that she alone is a moral and sexual "innocent" in the realm of love and is therefore blameless. Using this conclusion as a basis for reasoning, the speaker guards herself against feeling guilty about her own sexuality, which in less morality-bound moments, she presents as a source of pride rather than shame.

Not surprisingly, she often speaks of female sexuality by citing references to other women. In sonnet VI, for example, she accuses her beloved of being preoccupied with his reading and ignoring her sexual needs. She chides him for preferring "the dead," such as Cressid, Elaine, and Isolt, to her, a living woman who feels "the rude sea / Of passion pounding all day long" in her. In sonnet XXVI, when she herself becomes engrossed in "lively chronicles of the past," she seeks out other women whose passion may have equaled her own:

> . . . here and there
> Hunting the amorous line, skimming the rest,
> I find some woman bearing as I bear
> Love like a burning city in the breast.

She is certain that "Women have loved before as I love now," that is, that they too experienced sexual desire. She feels alienated from her own sexually constricted society in which the male is accepted as the aggressive partner, the initiator of the sexual act, and thinks that a male monopoly on sexual activity is not only unfair but unnatural. Consequently, she identifies herself with those women in history who, unbound by social and moral restrictions, sought sexual gratification at will:

> I think however that of all alive
> I only in such utter, ancient way
> Do suffer love; in me alone survive
> The unregenerate passions of a day
> When treacherous queens, with death upon the tread,
> Heedless and wilful, took their knights to bed.
>
> (XXVI)

Here Millay's voice resounds clearly behind her persona—a woman who feels the need to trace her sexuality to a source that her social milieu has not provided her and that her social conditioning, given her gender, has denied her.

The speaker dreams that she is granted the company of other women who "had had a god for guest" (XVI) because her beloved, too, is a god. Ostensibly, she is praising the man and awarding him credit for enabling her to communicate "with sweet women long since dead." Yet Millay undermines his high stature with a paradox: by elevating her male beloved to a position of authority, the woman is able to claim superiority over him.

Significantly, "golden Jove," the god she implies is her beloved's equal (in sonnets XII and XVI), is represented in mythology "as falling in love with one woman after another and descending to all manner of tricks to hide his infidelity from his wife" (Hamilton 27). Even more telling are the circumstances surrounding each of

Jove's "visits" to the three women in sonnet XVI: in each case Jove appears in a nonhuman form in order to deceive the woman he proceeds to rape (Danae and Leda) or kidnap (Europa). Thus, the speaker's sexual experience with her beloved places her on common ground with women who are victims of a male's whims and short-lived sexual desire. Having elevated her beloved's position, the speaker can communicate and empathize with her literary foremothers; she notes: "Freely I walked beside them and at ease, / Addressing them, by them again addressed." Ultimately, by affiliating herself with them rather than solely with her beloved, she is able to translate her unfulfilled needs into power.

I agree with Klemans's observation that the speaker's affinity with the women mentioned in the poems is "unusual in any literature but very rare in love poetry where women are usually portrayed as rivals" (16). Yet the fact that the speaker relates only to women who exist in fiction, myth, or history (even the island women in sonnet XXXVI live only in her memory) suggests a degree of at least psychological isolation from her female contemporaries. This isolation makes her problematic relationship with a man seem all the more unsatisfying.

Millay proposes that women can find relief from such isolation in the natural world. Through images of nature and references to the seasons, she gives the speaker's changing state of mind substance and flow. Nature's relatively predictable course of events directly contrasts with the man's "unnatural" refusal to satisfy his lover's needs. The speaker credits her "mother the brown earth / Fervent and full of gifts and free from guile" (III) as the source of her integrity. In one of the most effective and moving sonnets in the sequence, she also acknowledges her sister, the night:

> Night is my sister, and how deep in love,
> How drowned in love and weedily washed ashore,
> There to be fretted by the drag and shove
> At the tide's edge, I lie—these things and more:
> Whose arm alone between me and the sand,
> Whose voice alone, whose pitiful breath brought near,
> Could thaw these nostrils and unlock this hand,
> She could advise you, should you care to hear.

Small chance, however, in a storm so black,
A man will leave his friendly fire and snug
For a drowned woman's sake, and bring her back
To drip and scatter shells upon the rug.
No one but Night, with tears on her dark face,
Watches beside me in this windy place.

(VII)

During moments of great sadness, the speaker recognizes that
only another female presence (a "sister") can empathize with her
anguish. She realizes that the male who could help her is unsympa-
thetic and unwilling to come forward and thus continues to cause
her pain. The marked contrast between her "fatal" suffering and
his oblivious comfort again reflects the gender difference that leaves
the feeling woman and her needs untended by a man who literally
keeps his distance.

Millay names a second female ally, Beauty, as a protector of the
speaker's sexuality:

Whom as a child the night's obscurity
Did not alarm, let him alone remain,
Lanterned but by the longing in the eye,
And warmed but by the fever in the vein,
To lie with me, sentried from wrath and scorn
By sleepless Beauty and her polished thorn.

(XXV)

Now turning to Beauty for protection, the speaker finds the "natural
darkness of the night" and her own femaleness inseparable. She
recognizes that if her beloved finds her desire for him threatening,
he will reject her rather than "lie with" her. However, because she
has entered a female realm where she is flanked by Night and Beauty,
the possibility of this rejection no longer disturbs her, and she
warns the man not to stay unless he can "brave" the natural darkness.
While love is the woman's apparent preoccupation,[7] it is nature—
her female inheritance, her primary bond—that endures for her and
defines her world. When her beloved proves to be an unreliable
source of feeling and stability, it is nature and what she is *by* nature
that enable her to withstand the demise of the relationship.

At the end of the sequence, the speaker assesses her lover's motives with increased clarity. Having gained self-knowledge and self-confidence, she declares that she will "love again." Beginning with sonnet XLVI, when the "winter" of her grief has ended and the vine is "blackened" from "frost," her prediction proves true, and she reflects on the "fatal interview" from a fresh perspective.[8] Now Millay dispenses with the imagery of incarceration, mutilation, and disease and replaces them with simple, clear images of nature—bud, flower, leaf, tree, vine—in describing the woman's recovery from and new perspective on her loss. The potential for loss of love becomes "the dry seed of most unwelcome this," while her former insistent need to keep her beloved beside her (X) is reduced to the "mild hope" for a "fairer summer and a later fall"—the hope, that is, that they could have defied nature and stayed together longer.

The speaker descends from the "mountain peaks" of love to her former life: "Now by the path I climbed, I journey back" (XLVIII). As she nears the plain, she is drawn into a "dusk" that promises her warmth, security, shelter, and a reunion with her "mother the brown earth" (III). She sees how easily she could regress into renewed misery by dwelling on the memories that she considers dangerous: "There is a word I dare not speak again, / A face I never again must call to mind." She refuses to go the way of Selene and risk her sanity by looking into the well of madness for the sake of a man who has disappointed her:

> I was not craven ever nor blenched at pain,
> But pain to such degree and of such kind
> As I must suffer if I think of you,
> Not in my senses will I undergo.
>
> (XLIX)

What she holds important now is that she has kept her dignity intact. In a voice tinged with self-righteousness, she admits that she might have held her beloved "for a summer more" had she loved him less or attempted to manipulate his feelings through carefully chosen words. Her decision not to stall his leaving, she explains, is based in part on her high regard for words: as a poet, she refuses to compromise her art for a man's attentions.

The former dream of her beloved's godhood shatters once she

realizes her own authority. In sonnet LI, in a condescending voice, she confirms the man's place "among mortal-kind" where, "in the years to come," he is bound to feel "faint at heart or fallen on hungry days," or "full of griefs," or depressed by "failing powers or good opinion lost." Then she poses a rhetorical question that resounds with self-importance: might even the memory of her love "restore" him to his "former pride" and elevate him "high among the run of men"? Once again the poet's paradoxical address is a deceptively generous one designed to empower the speaker. By agreeing to accept her help, the man will confirm the worthiness of her love for him. By accepting her legacy of maternal comfort, he will finally acknowledge the importance and value of that love.

In the final sonnet of the sequence (LII), Millay clarifies the distinction between the speaker's fate and that of the moon goddess by relating the outcome of the myth in the third person: the speaker addresses Endymion scornfully, bidding him to "sleep forever" as Selene, filled with "the hot and sorrowful sweetness" of human sexuality, goes mad, "being all unfit / For mortal love, that might not die of it."

In contrast, Millay's "mortal" speaker not only retains her sanity but thrives. She overcomes the death inherent in the sexual act by transforming it into birth: out of her sexual union with her lover she conceives a son[9] who will inherit her human traits as well as the "divine" traits she assigns to the man. She also "outlives" (XLVII) an emotional death by converting her hope for a lasting relationship into self-reliance. Acknowledging her freedom in turn facilitates the rebirth of her own female identity: when at last she leaves the love affair behind, she is not "Hell's mistress" but her "own" (XXIV).

Millay does not disparage male-female love relationships in *Fatal Interview* but instead attempts to clarify the inevitable problems they raise. She suggests that because men, regardless of their intentions, have a resistance to intimacy and relationship, they are simply not emotionally or psychologically equipped to answer the needs of the women who fall in love with them. Yet she also implies that women are not trapped, that regardless of their innate desire to "relate" rather than "separate," they can exercise their will and integrity and make choices about the extent to which romantic love—or the lack of it—affects their lives.

In creating a new version of the "woman in love" in the *Fatal Interview* speaker, Millay claims the authority of the poet whose artistic struggle, here expressed as emotional pain, becomes primary poetic material. The speaker's conflict between accepting her passion and sexuality and perceiving it instead as a source of emotional vulnerability is analogous to Millay's own bind as a woman poet. The poet must somehow balance the discipline needed to write with the passion and sexuality that fuels her creative urge. Not to achieve this balance is to risk, at best, the inability to create, or at worst—according to Millay's symbolic scheme—madness. Because Millay portrays female subjective experience from a woman's point of view in *Fatal Interview*, the work itself appears to redeem her as a sexual being who has overcome her artistic bonds.

## Notes

1. While John Donne's influence is evident in varying degrees throughout the sonnets, it is most obvious in several line parallels, cited by both Atkins (207, 209, 211, 217, 227–28) and Klemans (16–17), and in two sonnets (III and XI), in which Millay refers directly to two Donne poems, "A Valediction: Forbidding Mourning" and "A Token." For a mention of Millay's debt to Donne early in her career, see Deutsch, "Three Women Poets."

2. Theories about women's development and gender-based psychological and socially constructed differences between men and women describe well the contrast between the male's and female's attitudes toward relationships that recur throughout Millay's poetry, particularly in *Fatal Interview* and "Sonnets from an Ungrafted Tree" (a sequence of seventeen sonnets in which a farm wife returns to the home of a man she no longer loves to care for him on his deathbed). See, for example, Gilligan, *In a Different Voice* 8; Chodorow, "Family Structure and Feminine Personality" 44; and Miller, *Toward A New Psychology of Women* 60–73.

3. Among the best-known sonnet sequences by men are Petrarch's *Canzoniere* (fourteenth century), Sir Philip Sidney's *Astrophel and Stella* (1591), Edmund Spenser's *Amoretti* (1595), Shakespeare's sonnets (1609), George Meredith's *Modern Love* (1862), and Dante Gabriel Rossetti's *House of Life* (1881). A lesser-known sequence, *Sonnets of a Portrait Painter* (1914) by Arthur Davison Ficke, includes a sonnet dedicated to Millay entitled "Epitaph for the Poet V (Hymn to Intellectual Beauty) To Edna St. Vincent

Millay." The first known sonnet sequence written in English by a woman poet is *Pamphilia to Amphilanthus* (1621) by Mary Wroth. The sequence consists of eighty-three sonnets that relate the story of a shepherdess and her inconstant lover. Wroth does not use a first-person woman persona; she does, however, reverse poetic love conventions so that the woman, rather than the man, is pierced by Love's arrow. Wroth also wrote a crown of fourteen sonnets in which her persona addresses Love.

4. The protagonist in H.D.'s *Hermetic Definition* is a woman who, like Millay's speaker, is trying to resolve pouring emotional energy into a relationship with an unresponsive man.

5. Millay often uses images of confinement in her poems about love. For a discussion of her uses of this imagery pattern interpreted as an expression of her "personal vulnerability—and ultimately of women's vulnerability—to victimization by uncontrollable conditions in her environment," see Stanbrough, "Language of Vulnerability."

6. For a stimulating discussion of women's unceasing attraction to the role of the "romantic heroine" and the ways the romantic love myth forms the basis for contemporary definitions of romantic love, see Rabine, *Reading the Romantic Heroine*, and Radway, *Reading the Romance*.

7. Judith Nierman, in her bibliography of Millay, refers to an intriguing article by Kiyoaki Nakao, "Edna St. Vincent Millay on Love: A Study in American Poetry," which appears in a periodical published by the School of Education, Waseda University, Tokyo (*The Scientific Researches*, 9 [1960]: 83–92), which I have been unable to locate. According to Nierman, Nakao discusses "Millay's love sonnets in terms of many aspects of love: fidelity, inevitability of love, blindness of love, ardor, self-sacrifice, despair, origin of love, wistfulness, sorrow for dead love, mutability, attainment of maturity through love, immortality, futility of love, timelessness of love, love as a light, deification of the beloved, love overruling the world, blind passion, lost love, beauty, preoccupation with death, and happiness" (Nierman 144).

8. It is possible to read *Fatal Interview* biographically as a partial account of Millay's early relationship with George Dillon (with whom she had an affair beginning in 1928, while she was married to Eugen Boissevain). Millay's continued friendship with Dillon after their initial passionate meeting had "cooled" is evidence that she neither "died" of love nor a broken heart, nor went mad, as did Selene. For documentation of Millay and Dillon's continued friendship, see Millay, *Letters*, 1952, 263–66, 274–75; for letters regarding their translations of Baudelaire's *Fleurs du Mal*, 300–306 for letters regarding Millay's poetry submissions to *Poetry: A Magazine of Verse* after Dillon had been named editor in 1937, and 309 for a letter regarding her doubt about the reception of her wartime book, *Make Bright the Arrows*.

9. It would be interesting to speculate about whether or not Millay was

aware of a third version of the myth's ending. In this version, Endymion "slept on and on, smiling in his sleep. He dreamed that he held the moon in his arms. But it was not a dream after all, for Selene bore her husband fifty daughters, all pale and beautiful as their mother and sleepy as their father" (D'Aulaire and D'Aulaire 86). Robert Graves also mentions that "Endymion . . . fathered fifty daughters on Selene" (210).

# 5  Her Mother's Voice
## Lisa Myers

It is nearly six months now since I saw you. A long time. Mother, do you know, almost all people love their mothers, but I have never met anybody in my life, I think, who loved his mother as much as I love you. I don't believe there ever was anybody who did, quite so much, and quite in so many wonderful ways. . . .

I hope you will write me as soon as you get this. If you only knew what it means to me to get letters from any of you three over there. Because no matter how interesting it all is, and how beautiful, and how happy I am, and how much work I get done, I am nevertheless away from home,—home being somewhere near where you are, mother dear.

If I didn't keep calling you mother, anybody reading this would think I was writing to my sweetheart. And he would be quite right.

—Millay, *Letters*

In her book, *The Acoustic Mirror: The Female Voice in Psychoanalysis and Cinema*, Kaja Silverman reworks two psychoanalytic models for the relationship between mother and daughter. The first is Julia Kristeva's description of what she terms the *chora*, a protective enclosure around the infant created largely by its mother's voice (Silverman 72). The *chora* has been variously described as a "bath," an "envelope," or a "milieu"; in each case, it has much in common with the womb and represents for Kristeva the earliest stage of life, in which the mother not only provides for all of the child's needs but defines its world. Silverman revises this notion by pointing out that it is a fantasy: that the experience of the maternal voice as an enveloping receptacle or container precedes subjectivity, while the conception of the experience can only come later, after the entry into the system of desire and language.

Silverman sees a tendency in Kristeva's recent work to erase maternal influence in children's development (Silverman 118–19). In an attempt to return some sense of agency to the mother and to account more cogently for the little girl's erotic investment in the mother, she invokes a passage from Freud's *Ego and the Id* that suggests that there are two versions of the Oedipus complex. Each child encounters both versions, but one is culturally reinforced while the other is disavowed. The "positive" Oedipus complex is the familiar narrative in which "a boy has . . . an ambivalent attitude towards his father and an affectionate object-choice towards his mother" (Freud 23; Silverman 120). The "negative" version, on the other hand, is culturally disavowed because it "organizes subjectivity in fundamentally 'perverse' and homosexual ways" (Silverman 120): the little boy also "behaves like a girl and displays an affectionate feminine attitude to his father and a corresponding jealousy and hostility towards his mother" (Freud 23). In terms of the little girl's development, the "positive" Oedipus complex is that through which she comes to perceive her mother as her rival in her desire for her father; in the "negative" Oedipus complex, she desires her mother.

The usual account of the girl's attachment to her mother (an account Kristeva shares) locates the source of that attachment in the pre-Oedipal phase. By replacing this more familiar scenario with the negative Oedipus complex, Silverman is placing the desire for the mother firmly within language and subjectivity. This move has a series of implications for feminist psychoanalytic readings. One is the loss of Kristeva's vision of the mother-daughter bond outside of representation, capable of fulfillment and satisfaction in ways that are impossible within the realm of the symbolic. But Silverman argues persuasively that the gains of rejecting this vision outweigh the losses:

To situate the daughter's passion for the mother within the Oedipus complex . . . [is] to make it possible to speak for the first time about a genuinely oppositional desire—to speak about a desire which challenges dominance from within representation and meaning, rather than from the place of a mutely resistant biology or sexual 'essence.' (123–24)

Thus, in addition to providing an explanation that is more economical and internally coherent with respect to Freudian psychoanalytic narratives, Silverman's revision promises greater political efficacy.

While I hope ultimately to situate Millay's passion for her mother within the Oedipus complex, I begin with an examination of her fantasy of the maternal voice, "The Ballad of the Harp-Weaver." First published in 1923, it won Millay the Pulitzer Prize almost single-handedly, and it retains more of its initial popularity than most of her work has.[1] It tells the story of a poor widow and her son. On Christmas Eve, they burn the last of the furniture for fuel and fall asleep in the cold house; all that remains is one chair and a harp with a carving of a woman's head on it. In the middle of the night, the boy wakes up to see his mother playing the harp and singing. As her fingers move among the harp-strings, she seems to be weaving cloth that forms rich, warm clothing just his size. He falls asleep again, to the sound of her voice; when he awakes in the morning, she has frozen to death, but beside her is an enormous pile of beautiful clothing for him.

"The Ballad of the Harp-Weaver" is uncharacteristic of Millay's work in several ways. It is much longer than most of her previous work (which included three published volumes). The speaker is male; I find only four poems in all of those published through *The Harp-Weaver and Other Poems* in which the speaker is definitively marked as male.[2] This is also one of the few narrative poems in her predominantly lyric corpus and her first use of the ballad form. The relation between the two genres is significant for the topic at hand: the ballad, like the lyric, has its roots in the individual performance of song. As such, it focuses attention on the singing voice that predated verse on the page. The title immediately identifies the poem as part of a genre that foregrounds voice and particularly its role in performance, but it does not identify that voice in the poem: depending on whether "of the Harp-Weaver" is subjective or objective genitive, the ballad may belong to (i.e., be sung by) the harp-weaver or may only be about the harp-weaver and sung by someone else. The first line (" 'Son,' said my mother,") resolves the question in favor of the latter reading, if we presume that a boy is not likely to be a harpist or a weaver. The rest of the poem bears this out, of course; the boy tells the tale, and it is his mother who weaves with the harp. But both of them are singers: he of the ballad, and she as she sings him to sleep in stanza 12 and later accompanies herself on the harp in stanza 27.

The central relationship between mother and son is portrayed in complex and contradictory ways. The boy's age is never given explicitly, and the textual indications vary considerably: at one point, he is "knee-high" (stanza 1), at another, "a great boy" whose "long legs" dangle to the floor when he sits in his mother's lap in the rocking-chair (stanzas 12, 10). In this latter scene, he is naked, because he has outgrown all his clothes and there is no money to buy more; the mother has proposed that he sit in her lap to keep warm while he naps, but they get "silly" together instead (stanza 10). He interrupts their play out of a sense that it is unseemly— "what would folks say / To hear my mother singing me / To sleep all day . . . ?" (stanza 12). Certainly if one pictures the scene, it is not difficult to imagine the neighbors having something to say, about the singing or anything else.

When the poem reaches its crisis, the speaker and his mother have gone to sleep on the floor after running out of firewood. They seem to be huddled together, because the boy says that during the night he "felt" his mother get up (stanza 17). Given that he is also presumably still naked, his describing himself as "like a two-year-old" (stanza 16) once again functions to distract the reader from the more transgressive implications of the scene. The speaker's regression to an earlier stage of childhood also parallels and foreshadows his mother's uncanny rejuvenation only a few stanzas later: as she sits with the harp, she looks "nineteen, / And not a day older" (stanza 19). This descriptive note, which is repeated in the final tableau, is clearly privileged: it is the only piece of description that is repeated, and it is repeated verbatim, as two full lines: "Looking nineteen, / And not a day older" (stanzas 19 and 28). The strong end-stopping, the synchronization of the phrase's natural stresses with the stanza form's stresses, give the phrase a formulaic sound; its exact repetition suggests that this is the most striking, the most uncanny aspect of the entire scene. The only further physical description of the mother is that there is "A smile about her lips, / And a light about her head" (stanza 29); if the transformation has made her beautiful, the poem can portray that beauty only in terms of youth and holiness.

This youthful mother is playing the harp and singing, and in the harp, the boy sees threads that are being woven into cloth:

> She sang as she worked,
>     And the harp-strings spoke;
> Her voice never faltered,
>     And the thread never broke.
>
> (stanza 27)

Here the singer and the harp are united in a common project; the parallelism within the stanza suggests that her song does not merely accompany her fingers' weaving, but rather that her voice creates the weft thread. The weft thread is the one that moves back and forth among the stationary, upright warp-strings of the loom (or in this case, the harp) to form the cloth. I emphasize the mechanics of this metaphor because it seems to me important to note that, while this is clearly a poem about magic, it is nonetheless grounded in an accurate depiction of one form of traditional "woman's work," as well as the more culturally privileged, "high art" of music. This is also a representation of the mother's voice literally as text, that is, a weaving or textile—a metaphor as tangibly enveloping as Kristeva's *chora*, but far less organic.

The transformation of song into thread, and ultimately into cloth, is reduplicated at another level of metaphor. The allegorical content of the poem is that the family, though poor in the things of the world, is rich in love; the miracle is that the mother finds a way to convert tenor to vehicle, to make the wealth of her love for the boy into tangible beauty and wealth. The sense of excess, of luxury, that comes from the mother's gift being not just sufficient and useful but lavish and aesthetic (the clothing she weaves is described as fit "for a king's son" [stanza 24]) in turn gives the poem its emotional weight. At the same time, Millay has repeated the poem's act of materialization in her writing: she has transformed her love for her mother into an aesthetic object. But the impact of the gesture is undercut by the reader's knowledge that the mother's love, even in its new form, is not sufficient to the son's needs. The poem focuses initially on three items that the family lacks—food, clothing, and fuel. But by the end, the need for food has been repressed. The speaker says that on Christmas Eve he "cried with the cold" (stanza 16), not with hunger, and his mother freezes to death overnight making clothing for him. The triumphant ending of the poem, in which the mother has supposedly provided for the child's needs through her own sacrifice, ignores his need for food. The "clothes of a king's son" may keep him warm but will not feed him. In fact, if the child wants to survive, he will probably have to sell some or all of the clothing (to a king's son, perhaps) to buy himself food. The voice that issues from the mother's mouth has been transformed into clothing, but it will have to be transformed again before it can in turn enter the child's mouth.

That the need for food should be repressed in a poem about a mother's love for her child is obviously highly suggestive, and in Millay's case, it turns out that the issue is particularly resonant. This poem (and the letter from which the epigraph to this essay is taken) was written while the poet was in Europe, from early 1921 through early 1923. One of the discomforts of the trip was almost constant illness, which Millay attributed to the "strange," "foreign" foods she was eating. In a letter of January 1922, she complains, "I smoke too many cigarettes, and the German food nearly kills me— hot bread and cabbage and grease, when what I want is a bowl of plain rice and an apple," and later in the same letter, she writes, "I shall now issue forth and fodder my bewildered Muse on Wiener schnitzel, Brussels sprouts and beer" (Millay, *Letters*, 1952, 143–45). (Note also here the direct link between food and poetry: if the poet eats German food, so does her Muse.) But the problem seems to have cleared up almost miraculously once her mother, Cora Buzzell Millay, arrived on the scene in April 1922. As another letter says: "I came within an ace of having peritonitis. . . . Thank heaven mother has been with me, and has been getting me straightened out" (168).

But it is difficult to accept the assertion that the food is the problem when one reads a description of the Millays' diet in Paris; her mother's arrival hardly put Millay on a diet of "plain rice and an apple," as this letter to her sister Norma shows:

Mummie & I about live in this here kafe. We feed on *choucroute garnie*, which is fried sauerkraut trimmed with boiled potatoes, a large slice of ham & a fat hot dog,—yum, yum, werry excillint. That's about all they serve here in the cafe—that and onion soup & sandwiches. And mummie & I come here every day & eat the stinkin' stuff, & all our friends hold their noses & pass us by till we've finished. A few of them are getting inured & acquiring a taste for it.—Today they burned it a little, & it was great. (*Letters*, 1952, 152)[3]

There is clearly all the difference in the world between eating "cabbage and grease" alone and lonely in Vienna and eating *choucroute garnie* with one's mother in Paris, but the difference seems to be in the setting and the company, not the food.

Millay seems to associate eating and being nourished with her mother, so that her unhappiness about the food in Europe is connected to her homesickness for her mother. Many months earlier, when she was in England, she had described a scene oddly reminiscent of Proust's *madeleine*:

The tea was poured when we got to the table, and there was milk in it, for everybody, without a question asked. I drank it, of course, and do you know, rather liked it. I remember you used to take it that way, mother, when I was a little child, very hot, and with milk in it, and I used to come to you with a hard, round, "common" cracker, and beg to soak it in your cup, after which I would butter it and eat it. Oh, the butter melted so quickly, and slid all around, usually dripping on me before I could prevent it, I remember, and nothing was ever so good! The next time I see you, you shall have a cup of tea with milk in, and I shall soak my common-cracker in it, and butter it, and eat it, and we shall be very gay. (*Letters*, 1952, 126–27)

The "common" in "common-cracker" tells us that the point of the event is its very dailiness, its familiarity. It is not that the food in itself is meaningful, but rather that the bond with the mother that the activity reinforces makes the food valuable. Nor is this a memory of the mother providing food: the child has the food already, but contact with Mother's food makes it better. And the mother in this memory is, of course, a perfect mother, a fantasy mother. The daughter "beg[s]" to soak the cracker in the tea, but there is no need to tell the mother's reply for this mother would never say no. The sequence of events moves right from the request to its fulfillment. Furthermore, drinking tea the way her mother did and liking it even though it is not the way she usually likes her tea does not make the daughter feel that she is now like her mother. Instead, it reminds her of her childhood and makes her want to replicate her experience as a daughter—when she sees her mother again, they will not drink tea together like two adult women, they will reenact the mother-daughter scene.

It would be a mistake, however, to conclude that food operates in Millay's psychic economy only as an area of intersection between emotional and financial sustenance. To do so would be to elide the more troubling aspects of her attachment to her mother, namely its erotic components. "The Ballad of the Harp-Weaver" seems obviously to have been written with the poet's own mother in mind; it was dedicated to Cora Buzzell Millay on publication, and in a letter to her mother that accompanied the typescript, the poet wrote, "It is dedicated to you of course, as may be seen at a glance" (*Letters*, 1952, 130). Throughout her letters, Millay addresses her mother in the language of heterosexual courtship. For instance, when she first suggests that her mother join her in Europe, she writes, "and then, Best Beloved, you and I will just have ourselves a little honey-moon," followed by a postscript asking, "—Do you suppose, when you & I are dead, dear, they will publish the *Love Letters of Edna St. Vincent Millay & her Mother?*" (120).[4]

Throughout her childhood and adolescence, Millay was known as "Vincent"; she was the eldest of three daughters, and her parents divorced when she was about eight. Mrs. Millay supported the girls by working as a practical nurse. All three of her children remained devoted to her.[5] Overseas for the first time and alone, Vincent seems to have written "The Ballad of the Harp-Weaver" out of a combination of affection and homesickness for her mother. But as the poem demonstrates, the daughter's gratitude is not just for the mother's having provided the material necessities of life, but also for her having been a role model as a singer/artist. In the letter quoted in the epigraph, Millay credits her mother for her own poetic vocation:

I was telling somebody yesterday that the reason I am a poet is entirely because you wanted me to be and intended I would be, even from the very first. You brought me up in the tradition of poetry, and everything I did you encouraged. I can not remember once in my life when you were not interested in what I was working on, or even suggested that I should put it aside for something else. (*Letters*, 1952, 118–19)

Mrs. Millay had by this time begun a modest writing career of her own: the same letter includes congratulations from Vincent on her having had a short story accepted for publication.

In light of the closeness of the relationship between the poet and her mother, what seems notable about "The Ballad of the Harp-Weaver" is not its correspondences with their relationship but its differences, most conspicuously the change in the child's gender. If Cora Millay is represented as the mother in the poem, then the reader would expect the child, who is also the speaker of the poem, to be Vincent. In this case, I think that the identification is ultimately a sound one, particularly if we hear the poem as originating in Silverman's "negative Oedipus complex." For the little girl, this involves relating to the mother as love object and to the father as rival for her affections, and it disappears in favor of the positive Oedipus complex under pressure of cultural disapprobation. In the absence of a father, however, and in a household that was highly idiosyncratic, the daughter's attachment to the mother may never have been displaced.[6] That Millay would choose, in writing a poem for publication, to figure this relationship in heterosexual terms should come as no surprise, as our culture provides no other discourse for erotic desire. Moreover, the heterosexual model for the relationship was to some extent overt within the family: Vincent is, after all, a man's name. It is said to have been given to the eldest Millay baby in gratitude for the recovery of a much-loved maternal uncle at St. Vincent's hospital. This would not explain why the baby, though female, was never called anything else at home, but as a result, Vincent's persona in the system of family nicknames was also masculine. She was " 'Sefe," short for "Josephus"; her sisters Norma and Kathleen were "Hunk" and "Wump," respectively. The nickname carried its gender with it, as a letter to Kathleen from 1922 shows: "Dearest Wumpus: Sefe sends you bad picture of hisself, just for fun, cause he wanted to send youse picture of hisself, and good ones ain't forthcomin' " (*Letters*, 1952, 164). I do not want to imply that Millay's gender identity was confused. Nevertheless, in writing a poem about her relationship with her mother, Millay found that the most applicable cultural paradigms were those of heterosexual desire, and for various reasons, it was not uncomfortable or unfamiliar for her to imagine herself in the subject position of the male lover.

Again, I am not asserting that Millay depicted a mother-son relationship in her poem in order to mask the "true," transgressive nature of her feeling for her mother. On the one hand, I do not think that Millay experienced her affection for her mother as transgressive; on the other hand, the relationship represented in "The Ballad of the Harp-Weaver" is fairly transgressive as is, without any homoerotic aspect. The letters suggest that Millay's ideas about motherhood were intricately bound up with her ideas of erotic love—and of her trip to Europe, from the moment of her embarkation. In her first letter home, written while she was still aboard the Rochambeau, a discussion about seasickness becomes one about childbirth:

I had some sea-sick remedy pills to be taken as soon as the boat started, & I couldn't make up my mind to take them. Whatever it might be—& I was looking forward to something awful, because I had been sick in my stomach for a week from actual excitement—I wanted the whole of it.—I wanted every bit of the experience, & no dope. (Like you, when I was going to be born.)—But it was not for nothing this chile was brought up on the water-front! I have been the marvel even of the ship's doctor, who says I am an extraordinarily good sailor. (*Letters*, 1952, 114)

The voyage to Europe is, in Millay's terms, like giving birth; and somehow, her mother's intrepidity and sense of adventure in bearing and raising Vincent have made the daughter that much stronger and better able to take life "straight."

But to whom, in this metaphor, is Vincent giving birth? The

next time she alludes to her own maternity is in a letter dated 23 September 1921, which she herself marks as nine months after her departure:

I carry my typewriter all over the world with me, the little Corona Jim gave me. He was a sweet boy, mother. I loved him very much. And still do, whenever I think of him, though it was all nonsense, of course, and I wouldn't want him back. Only I like to think about him sometimes. You were wonderful, mother, about him and me. I realized afterwards how terrible it must have been for you. But you never hurt me in any way.

I have a curious feeling that someday I shall marry, and have a son; and that my husband will die; and that you and I and my little boy will all live together on a farm. (*Letters*, 1952, 131)

Nothing more is known of "Jim." Perhaps he was someone with whom she was involved in Maine before she left for Vassar and New York. But whatever it was that made the experience "terrible" for Mrs. Millay, what remains most important to Vincent in recalling the affair is to reassure her mother that the incident did not interfere with *their* relationship. And immediately thereafter, she repeats the gesture by imagining that when she does marry, her husband will be removed from the picture almost immediately, leaving her to reconstitute the nuclear family with her true "Best Beloved."

The comparative importance to Millay of her mother and even the prospect of a marriage is made explicit when the poet feels herself forced to choose between them. In the winter of 1921–22, which she spent in Vienna and Budapest, Millay engaged in a frustrating "exchange" of letters that involved the possibility of a proposal of marriage. *Exchange* is hardly the right word, however, since the proposal itself was lost in the mail for months. The situation was complicated by the fact that not one but two men, Arthur Davison Ficke and H. Witter Bynner, were involved. The three had been good friends for many years. Unfortunately, Bynner's proposal crossed in the mail a letter of Millay's in which she declared her love for Ficke; Bynner opened the letter to Ficke by mistake, compounding the problem. Millay found out about the proposal in a postscript Bynner scribbled on a letter Ficke wrote, which was sent before they received the one from her. She accepted Bynner's proposal, provided the offer still stood, but someone wisely suggested that further negotiations might better take place in person. Bynner and Ficke planned to come to Europe in the spring (without Ficke's wife).[7]

However, Mrs. Millay was also tentatively scheduled to arrive in the spring for the "honeymoon" she and Vincent had by now been planning for half a year. Vincent, anticipating the men's visit, wrote to her mother to suggest that she postpone her trip. Her mother cabled back: "Postponed trip understood happy birthday love mother." But shortly thereafter a letter came from Norma reporting that their mother was more disappointed and upset than she had revealed. Vincent's response was swift and decisive:

Bless you forever and ever for your letter. If ever a girl needed a letter, I was that girl, and yours was that letter. You see, it put some things straight in my mind that had been a little cluttered before. . . . I realize that nothing in the world is important beside getting mother over here with me. . . . A possible marriage, for instance, is not important beside it. Anybody can get married. It happens all the time. But not everybody, after the life we have had, can bring her mother to Europe. . . . [Now] I know what I want, and I want just one thing, and that thing is to get mother over here, and I'm going to do it. (*Letters*, 1952, 146–47)

She had indeed made her choice: she married neither Bynner nor Ficke, then or later, and by 25 April was able to write that she and her mother were sitting together in a cafe in Paris.

But Millay's romantic entanglements were not the only obstacle to her mother's trip. In the previous letter, Millay goes on to discuss her worries about the money her mother would need. And money, not surprisingly, leads to talk of food—though not in the most predictable way:

It seems to me [Mother] should be able to manage with four hundred, unless prices have gone up enormously since I sailed, and I see no reason why they should have done. As for me, I shall be a pretty busy girl from now on, what with writing my novel, and making a lot of money besides to show mother a swell time with when I get her over here. Anyhow, two can live as cheaply as one, I've always heard, and I shall be so happy and excited all the time she's here that I shan't be able to eat, and that will be a saving. (*Letters*, 1952, 149)

Millay never completed the novel she writes of, but here again writing, food, mother, and money are tightly intertwined. Writing makes money; one needs money to eat; Mother's presence is itself as sustaining as food, but one needs money to provide for Mother's presence.

Once the money has been found and Mother is present, however, Millay's letters expose the idea of not needing food as a fantasy. Even before the paean to *choucroute garnie*, her first letter announcing her mother's arrival is full of "food news." To describe how comfortably they have settled into their new lodging, Millay writes, "We found a little grocery store on our way home in the shower this morning, & bought a whole lot of fruit & dates & little crackers, & little cheeses, & had such fun eating in our room" (*Letters*, 1952, 151). The shop is "little," the food is "little," but altogether there is a "whole lot" of it, which they eat like schoolgirls in a dormitory room. The reason they have changed lodgings in the first place is that their previous residence, where Millay had been by herself, was too expensive; the new place is "cheap" but "not . . . very clean." Contrary to the old proverb, two cannot live as cheaply as one, and contrary to her hopes, Millay's love for her mother and vice versa cannot sustain her instead of food.

Nor did the decision to privilege her relationship with her mother over any heterosexual relationship relieve her of all emotional anxiety or conflict, as is shown by the novel *Hardigut*. Millay first conceived the idea for the book, which was the first and last novel she ever attempted to write, while in Europe. Horace Liveright paid her five hundred dollars in advance, which helped to maintain her in the spring of 1922 and covered a good part of the expenses of her mother's visit as well. The novel was never completed: letters Millay wrote in 1922 contain fairly frequent references to the project, but these are almost exclusively about how far behind she is with it. The one exception is a letter to Liveright himself from November 1922, which he planned to use as copy for the book's dust jacket:

Name of the novel, Hardigut. Ready for publication in April. The circumstances of my story are laid in a country where people, otherwise perfectly sane and normal, do not eat in public, or discuss food except in inuendos [*sic*] and with ribald laughter; where for unmarried people to eat anything at all is scandalous; where young boys and girls struggle through a starved adolescence into a hasty and ill-assorted marriage; where the stomach is never mentioned, and if you have a stomach-ache, you tell people you have a head-ache or writer's cramp.

No, the book isn't too highbrow. It is a story and it has a real hero, and a real heroine, and a plot, and its characters are, of course, just the people you and I have known all our lives. The book will be amusing, satiric, ugly, beautiful, poetic, and an unmistakable allegory. (*Letters*, 1952, 167)

Insofar as the "allegory" of the description is "unmistakable," the central metaphor of the novel is a substitution of eating for sexual activity. Most of the first paragraph quoted is a litany of sexual taboos in respectable American society in the early part of the century: speaking about or engaging in sexual activity in public is forbidden; sexual activity is forbidden to those who are young and unmarried; even mentioning those parts of the anatomy involved in sexual activity is improper. Millay's criticism of this system is that it is irrational and unhealthy but also that it tends toward immorality by motivating people to make "hasty and ill-assorted marriage[s]" on the basis of their physical needs rather than their emotional compatibility.

But in addition to the critique of contemporary sexual mores that the novel might have provided, we have the insight into Millay's psyche that the précis affords. Millay herself, though well out of her adolescence (she turned 30 in February 1922), was "starving" in Europe in several senses. On the one hand, there was the shortage of cash that probably impelled her to write the novel in the first place and the illness and loneliness that made it difficult for her to eat well. But the other side of the metaphor applies as well: although initially she had fled from New York with relief at escaping the importunate attentions of John Peale Bishop, Edmund Wilson, Floyd Dell, and others, and looked forward to being "entirely alone" in Paris (*Letters*, 1952, 106), by the time she had been away for a year, both of her younger sisters had gotten married, and her own hopes for an eventual union with Ficke were fading. The letters indicate that there was no shortage of attentive young men to escort her about Paris, but she was very much alone in Hungary, Albania, and through the long miserable winter in Vienna. For a woman who had made her reputation with a poetic persona advocating sexual and romantic freedom for both sexes, the pleasures of being "entirely alone" may have faded quickly.

But in this brief description of the novel, the initial conceit (sex as food) quickly gives way to concerns about health: the final clause of the first paragraph repeats the taboo against discussing sex, adding only the specificity of illness. The illnesses enumerated, however, are highly provocative. First, there is the headache, the cliché of feminine frigidity and deception. The other option is "writer's cramp," another ailment with more than simply physical significance. While writer's cramp is not so likely to be psychosomatically induced as writer's block, it is still the result of mental activity as well as physical (this is what distinguishes it from tennis elbow). It is also a discomfort that one brings upon oneself, unlike, for instance, the flu. And perhaps most obviously, it is the major occupational hazard of Millay's chosen profession. The sentence thus posits a remarkable string of equivalences: stomach trouble, problems of the (female) reproductive system, headaches, and difficulty or inability in writing.

The other writings of this period have made it clear already that Millay's personal concerns about eating were predominantly with the "hardiness" of her own "gut," rather than with the social constraints on eating. The project of writing the novel is bounded on all sides by the pressures and stresses of her sojourn in Europe. The decision to attempt a novel and to accept an advance on it seems to be born of the need for cash, and the gesture appears particularly desperate in light of the fact that it came at a time when Millay was not writing much. The subject matter combines Millay's anxiety about her health with her concerns about her own "love life" and her romantic future. And with her personal life in something of a shambles, the project that financed her mother's coming to join her in Paris also allowed her to think (and write) about eating—the nurturing bond with her mother—in place of sex.

Ultimately, however, the novel proved to be a dead end. Whether the process of writing it was an evasion or a working through of the crucial issues of sex, nurturance, and relationship, it was not sufficiently therapeutic; it did not make her well. Within weeks of her return to the United States, it was announced that Millay had won the Pulitzer Prize for poetry, largely on the strength of "The Ballad of the Harp-Weaver," which was tremendously popular (*New York Times*, 14 May 1923).[8] At about the same time, she became engaged to a man she had known casually before her trip, Eugen Boissevain, who was about twelve years her senior. They were married six weeks later. The same day, Millay entered a hospital and underwent a serious operation for her stomach troubles. The marriage was childless, and both Millay and Boissevain outlived Mrs. Millay, so the poet's vision of sharing a home with her mother and her son never came to pass. After the wedding, however, she began for the first time to sign her letters to her mother "Edna" rather than "Vincent."

## Notes

1. High school students in this country are still on occasion required by their English teachers to memorize the poem in its entirety and recite it in class. (My thanks to Jill Cunningham-Crowther for bringing this to my attention.)

2. They are "Interim" from *Renascence and Other Poems*, "The Bean-Stalk" and "The Poet and His Book" from *Second April*, and the sonnet that begins "Love is not blind. I see with single eye . . ." from *The Harp-Weaver and Other Poems*. In the last case, I am presuming the speaker's heterosexuality, as it is only the love object who is clearly gendered in the poem, but the presumption seems warranted by the poem's immersion in the commonplaces of Petrarchan love lyric.

3. It should be noted that Millay's diction in her letters was often highly influenced by Krazy Kat, of whom she was a great fan. Several other "dialects" as well as a significant amount of "baby talk" also appear, the latter perhaps particularly while she was in Europe. Untangling the different strands of colloquialism would require a more comprehensive analysis than is possible through the published, selected letters. The reader should be aware, however, that labeling this passage childish or regressive is likely to be an oversimplification.

4. This letter probably contained an earlier copy of "The Ballad of the Harp-Weaver"; a second postscript refers to an enclosed poem. Several weeks later, however, fearing that it had been lost in the mail, Millay sent another copy to which she referred more explicitly: "P.S. Another thing, lost in the shuffle of the international post, is a lovely poem of mine, called

*The Ballad of the Harp-Weaver*. I sent a copy of it to you a long time ago, & I think if you had received it you would surely have spoken of it.—I send you another copy of it now. It is practically the only poem I have written since I left America" (*Letters*, 1952, 130). The last sentence both increases the likelihood that this was the poem included with the earlier letter and provides valuable insight into Millay's literary productivity (or lack thereof) during this period.

5. See Gould, *The Poet and Her Book*, and Gurko, *Restless Spirit*, for detailed accounts of Millay's early years.

6. Although her parents were not divorced until she was eight, Millay's father does not seem to have been a constant or significant presence in the household at any point. On this topic and that of the eccentricity of the household during Vincent's adolescence, see Gould, *The Poet and Her Book*, chapters 1 and 2.

7. This narrative can be reconstructed from the published letters and is further elaborated in Ficke's unpublished memoir of Millay, which is among his papers at the Beinecke Library at Yale.

8. Technically, Millay was ineligible for the prize, which was to be given "for the best volume of verse published during the year by an American author" (*New York Times*, 24 January 1923) because she had not published a book of verse in 1922. She had, however, published two the year before (*Second April* and *A Few Figs from Thistles*), when she had been a finalist for the prize that eventually went to E. A. Robinson. In 1922, an expanded edition of *A Few Figs from Thistles* was released. The jury put together a "package" including this edition, a pamphlet publication of "The Ballad of the Harp-Weaver," and eight sonnets published in *American Poetry, 1922: A Miscellany*, and awarded the prize to Millay.

Part III    *Time's Body*

# 6  *The Female Body as Icon*
## *Edna Millay Wears a Plaid Dress*
### *Cheryl Walker*

The female body has never been so prominently displayed or so critically examined as it is today under the dominance of late capitalism. The results of this display, we can now see, have been mostly negative: women regard themselves at best self-consciously, at worst with disgust. Such astute cultural critics as John Berger and Susan Bordo have explored the way capitalism constitutes the language of body image so that women continually attempt to revise their bodily texts in the hope of increasing their exchange value, thus miming the tactics of prostitution. In *Ways of Seeing*, for instance, Berger maintains: "*Men act* and *women appear*. Men look at women. Women watch themselves being looked at. This determines not only most relations between men and women but also the relation of women to themselves" (47). Given this emphasis on self-scrutiny, it comes as no surprise that middle-aged women experience a reduction of self-confidence regarding their physical presences and a concomitant increase in self-dissatisfaction. It is also worth noting that a querulous tone often afflicts them as they grow older, suggesting that they are at odds not only with others but with themselves.

These reflections are useful in considering the work of Edna St. Vincent Millay, especially with regard to the relatively new set of emphases that appear in Millay's 1939 volume *Huntsman, What Quarry?* published when the poet was forty-seven. The tone of these poems vacillates between irate defensiveness and despondency. In

"The Plaid Dress," for instance, the speaker begins by longing for a new self:

> Strong sun, that bleach
> The curtains of my room, can you not render
> Colourless this dress I wear?—
> This violent plaid
> Of purple angers and red shames; the yellow stripe
> Of thin but valid treacheries; the flashy green of kind deeds
>     done
> Through indolence, high judgments given in haste;
> The recurring checker of the serious breach of taste?

Yet we cannot know in our first encounter with this poem exactly how the body itself is going to figure. Will it present itself as an alternative to this discourse of self-hatred or will it melt into the fabric of self-recrimination?

The very substance of the body is in question here. In recent theory concerning the female body, we have come to see that substance is too often deformed toward a compulsive eroticism engendered by the male gaze.[1] And indeed there is a way of reading Millay as a poet who capitalized upon this very mode of self-presentation.[2] But the fact that the female body is vulnerable to the depredations of the meat market may not be the worst aspect of its cultural significance. For if it retains its substantiality, the female body can be reclaimed, and thus there is some ground for hope within the political realm.

A more ominous approach to the female body as icon has appeared under the aegis of postmodernism, suggesting that the endless reproduction of female bodies in public spaces may signify nothing so much as the impossibility of identifying such a substance by connecting the signifier to a signified. In "the society of the spectacle," Guy Debord's term, one image mirrors another in an endless chain, binding even individual "identities" and gestures of political resistance in what Jean Baudrillard has described as a world of *simulacra*—a culture in which everyone and everything is an imitation—and a solicitation—of something else. In such a culture, governed by consumer capitalism, the erotics of seduction have replaced an older, more teleological eroticism. Perhaps one might even say that contemporary sexuality—repeating itself in overtures that never eventuate in lasting commitments but are simply rewound to start over—has made replaceability the erotic narrative of our time.

In the sustained foreplay of his own reflections on this topic, Baudrillard adopts an ambiguous stance toward this theme in *Cool Memories*, at one moment identifying himself with a preference for the seductive because it "liberates the imagination," at another engaging in commentary that seems embittered by post-inchoative disgust. Yet his cultural commentary is sometimes helpfully provocative as in this passage:

The only passion today: the passion for a multiplicity of simultaneous lives, for the metamorphosis and anamorphosis of modes of life, of places, of ways of loving. Every object is unique and should be all that our imaginations require. But there is nothing we can do about it: we have to move on from one to the other. Every landscape is sublime, but there's nothing we can do about it: we have to swap them one for another continually and the sublime today lies in the intercontinental flight which connects them all together. (63)

Baudrillard repeatedly turns to the media for the controlling metaphors of everyday life: "The TV: every image is an ephemeral vanishing act. But art is the same. In its countless contemporary forms, its only magic is the magic of disappearance, and the pleasures it gives are bloodless ones" (67).

As we reflect on the status of the female body in Millay's poetry, Baudrillard's notion of the de-massification of contemporary imagery will be useful, but there is yet one more strain of cultural commentary that we need to put into play here. Novelist and poet Margaret Atwood provides a political dimension to the discussion that helps us to focus on the way power relations determine the reproduction of simulacra. In her fable "The Female Body," Atwood offers a wonderful gloss on current cultural imagery:

The Female Body has many uses. It's been used as a door-knocker, a bottle opener, as a clock with a ticking belly, as something to hold up lampshades, as a nutcracker, just squeeze the brass legs together and out comes your nut. It bears torches, lifts victorious wreaths, grows copper wings and raises aloft a ring of neon stars; whole buildings rest on its marble heads.

It sells cars, beer, shaving lotion, cigarettes, hard liquor; it sells diet plans and diamonds, and desire in tiny crystal bottles. Is this the face that launched a thousand products? You bet it is, but don't get any funny big ideas, honey, that smile is a dime a dozen.

It does not merely sell, it is sold. Money flows into this country or that country, flies in, practically crawls in, suitful after suitful, lured by all those hairless pre-teen legs. Listen, you want to reduce the national debt, don't you? Aren't you patriotic? That's the spirit. That's my girl.

She's a natural resource, a renewable one luckily, because those things wear out so quickly. They don't make 'em like they used to. Shoddy goods. (2–3)

In this mini-essay, Atwood condenses a number of the ideas I've already mentioned: that the female body is the object of capitalist exploitation, that women are themselves solicited to adopt an entrepreneurial attitude toward their bodies through desire packaged in "tiny crystal bottles," that the culture feeds on replaceability and prostitution, and that its images constantly replicate and solicit one another.

But there are other important issues raised here as well. Atwood suggests that women are inevitably drawn into the process of exchange, that they become counters in a socioeconomic board game in which even resistance loses its force. "Aren't you patriotic? That's the spirit. That's my girl." Furthermore, Atwood's extract ends on a hostile note as the image-hawker transforms what in a more compassionate mode might have been guilt into an attack on the female body being so exploited. Nostalgia hides complicity in the process of obsolescence: "Those things wear out so quickly. They don't make 'em like they used to. Shoddy goods."

In *Masks Outrageous and Austere*, I have argued that Edna Millay can be read as a poet who both thematizes many of these concerns and is herself caught in the meshes of the veil she toys with. In this respect, her work comes to seem not dated or puerile, as so many have asserted, but contemporary and tragic. Millay was precisely the poet who made the replaceability of the love object part of her modernist credo. Just as Baudrillard says, "Every landscape is sublime, but there's nothing we can do about it: we have to swap them one for another continually," Millay wrote, "What lips my lips have kissed, and where, and why, / I have forgotten," calling her past lovers "unremembered lads." She so shocked and delighted her readers that she became the figurehead of free love culture, a position she exploited for her own use.

Like any good marketing analyst, Millay was canny about packaging. Her poetry readings were like dances of the seven veils, and though she grumbled about feeling like a prostitute ("If I ever felt like a prostitute it was last night" she wrote in one letter about a reading [*Letters*, 1952, 181]), she was eager to exploit the power of advertising and visual solicitation for projects she approved of, such as her own book sales, the premiere of *The King's Henchman*, or the American Cancer Society.[3] In fact, Edna St. Vincent Millay is the first American woman poet to become a media personality. Her media career was launched in 1920 by *Vanity Fair*, which did a full-page spread on her, including a calculatingly yearning photograph. *Vanity Fair* turned all levels of culture into photo opportunities. In its pages the young T. S. Eliot looked like Rudolph Valentino; Albert Einstein, Jean Cocteau, Jascha Heifetz, and Bertrand Russell came to seem as glamorous as their *Vanity Fair* picture partners, the Ziegfelds and Greta Garbo. Though Elinor Wylie briefly served as an editor, Edna Millay was the magazine's real literary heroine; unlike Wylie, she created a special genre, the Nancy Boyd "distressing dialogues," to suit its demand for controversy, brevity, and sophistication.

In all these ways, we can see Edna St. Vincent Millay as a poet of our time, both spectacular herself and a manipulator of spectacle. Her kitchen was featured in the *Ladies' Home Journal*. Yet Millay was not entirely at home in the slick world of image commodification that magazines like *Vanity Fair* and the *Journal* successfully mined. In one poem of recapitulation, she claims:

> I have learned to fail. And I have had my say.
> Yet shall I sing until my voice crack (this being my leisure,
>     this my holiday)
> That man was a special thing and no commodity, a thing improper to be sold.
>
> ("Lines Written in Recapitulation")

It is significant that this poem was first published in *Huntsman, What Quarry?* in 1939, when her career was already beginning to decline and was about to take a precipitous fall. The voice in this poem presents itself, in failure, as continually speaking against the commodification of the person. Yet, in fact, Millay had herself successfully participated in this process for twenty years. My point here is simply that a conscious intention to defy commodification does not necessarily add up to effective resistance. Millay had both exploited her physical presence as part of her media attraction and insisted that her body was somehow independent of the frames in which others sought to bind its significance. In this she could be compared to Madonna in our own time.[4]

As an example of the way the female body becomes a counter in a sociopolitical board game, one might instance Millay's involvement with the propaganda machine during World War II.[5] Her radio broadcasts and public appearances contributed to her complete breakdown in 1944, which occurred just after the Writers War Board had insisted that she write a poem for their continuous D-Day broadcast. ("Aren't you patriotic? That's the spirit. That's my girl.")

In the 1940s, even those who had once found her charms seductive, such as Edmund Wilson, noted how her "shoddy goods" had worn thin. "She was a travesty of the girl I had once known," wrote Jean Starr Untermeyer after attending an appearance Millay made in support of Czech war relief in 1942:

Her hair, which she wore in a long pageboy cut, was now shades lighter than the red-gold locks of her girlhood. It seems to me now . . . that she was attired in a long, straight gown of dark red velvet, but the face under the thatch of yellow hair had changed, almost unbelievably: it had aged but not ripened. With its flushed cheeks it reminded me of a wizened apple. (qtd. in Dash 215)

This description captures the narrative of the media heroine whose very success enslaves her and whose body eventually becomes the rejected toy of her own audience. As Millay's career illustrates, constant rewinding ultimately erodes the glamorous celluloid image.

In light of these reflections, *Huntsman, What Quarry?* has come to seem to me the most moving and the most telling of Millay's books, the one in which she explores the semiotics of the female body at the very point of its decline. The body had in some way always been Millay's primary theme, even when she had been most insistent on her independence from it (in Suzanne Clark's words, "Millay's poetry celebrates the failure of independence even in its defiance" [*Sentimental Modernism* 71]). In many of her poems in *Huntsman*, Millay is especially defiant, harsh in her excoriation of fascist politics, war, and commercialism, insistent upon fidelity to principle and the claims of her flagrant flesh. "Modern Declaration" asserts:

> I, having loved ever since I was a child a few things, never
>     having wavered
> In these affections; . . . . . . . . . . . . . . . . . . . .
> Never when worked upon by cynics like chiropractors having
>     grunted or clicked a vertebrae to the discredit of these
>     loves.

It is as if the body were somehow a reservoir of resistance, a site under siege but impervious to exterior forces of corruption.

Yet it quickly becomes clear at another level that the persona who dominates this text is by no means invulnerable, either to cultural or to biological incursions. This is the volume in which appear both "Menses," begun in 1928 but best read as a poem about menopause, and "Rendezvous," in which the speaker memorably concludes:

> Your laughter pelts my skin with small delicious blows.
> But I am perverse: I wish you had not scrubbed—with
>     pumice, I suppose—
> The tobacco stains from your beautiful fingers. And I wish I
>     did not feel like your mother.

The persona in this volume is aging and feels herself distanced from the world of youth: "The young are so old, they are born with their fingers crossed; / I shall get no help from them" ("Fontaine, Je ne Boirai pas de ton Eau!").

If there are ominous suggestions in this volume that the female body in middle life cannot expect to figure with the same force it has previously, Millay also implies here her sense that even the domain of the biological is at the mercy of semiotics. Of the two interpretations of the female body with which I began, the one subject to erotic misuse, the other merely a simulacrum among simulacra, the former is the less virulent one. Where the poems suggest that there is a real body, even if it becomes the plaything of an uncaring lover or the target of a destructive world, there is hope. Thus, in the sonnet beginning "I too beneath your moon, almighty Sex, / Go forth at nightfall crying like a cat, / Leaving the lofty tower . . . , Millay's persona pictures her iconic tower as befouled by birds, derided by youthful laughter, and gossiped about by neighbors, but in the sestet, the speaker still believes that it represents a core reality she can claim:

> Such as I am, however, I have brought
> To what it is, this tower; it is my own;
> Though it was reared To Beauty, it was wrought
> From what I had to build with: honest bone
> Is there, and anguish; pride; and burning thought;
> And lust is there, and nights not spent alone.

This seems at first a brave statement of agency and responsibility. Nevertheless, one should not ignore the way this tower elides the distance between body and text. At one moment, the speaker seems to be leaving it behind at the insistence of the desirous body, much as in another poem she speaks of her little boat being "rolled in the trough of thick desire" ("Theme and Variations"). At first, then, the tower is not the body itself but a monument, an opus—a suggestion repeated in the sestet where she speaks of rearing the tower to "Beauty." Yet in other places in the poem, the tower seems to be the body itself, built with "honest bone" and displaying all the iconography of physical experience.[6]

It is this elision, in which the body comes to seem a representation, a text, rather than a substance existing outside of textuality, that brings Millay's work into the world of the simulacra, that second sphere of interpretation where there is no substance beneath or behind the image but only a series of mirrors in which images wink at one another. "The Fitting" is an example of this darker logic:

The fitter said, "*Madame, vous avez maigri*,"
And pinched together a handful of skirt at my hip.
"*Tant mieux*," I said, and looked away slowly, and took my
    under-lip
Softly between my teeth.

Rip—rip!

Out came the seam, and was pinned together in another
    place.
She knelt before me, a hardworking woman with a familiar
    and unknown face,
Dressed in linty black, very tight in the arm's-eye and smell-
    ing of sweat.
She rose, lifting my arm, and set her cold shears against
    me,—snip-snip;
Her knuckles gouged my breast. My drooped eyes lifted to
    my guarded eyes in the glass, and glanced away as from
    someone they had never met.

"*Ah, que madame a maigri!*" cried the *vendeuse*, coming in
    with dresses over her arm.
"*C'est la chaleur*," I said, looking out into the sunny tops of
    the horse-chestnuts—and indeed it was very warm.

I stood for a long time so, looking out into the afternoon,
    thinking of the evening and you. . . .

While they murmured busily in the distance, turning me,
    touching my secret body, doing what they were paid to do.
(Millay's ellipsis)

I have always delighted in this poem because of the density of its physical details. Millay's ability to externalize the language of the body is impressive. But it is also impossible not to recognize that the speaker is performing for us. Here she performs her suffering over a love affair, for instance in the gestures of looking away slowly and taking her under-lip softly between her teeth. We can read the performance precisely because there is no "secret body" but only textualized bodies that regard one another in endless mirrors.

The moment at which drooped eyes meet guarded eyes in the glass is only the most obvious occasion in which we confront the lack of a Real.[7] Both sets of eyes are defined by their capacity for simulation. If they do not recognize each other, it is only because there is no deeper sense of identity to unite them. We are in a world of unanchored echoes: the fitter who says the speaker has lost weight is echoed by the saleswoman, "rip-rip" is echoed in "snip-snip," the treatment of the speaker's body by these superficially concerned women reverberates with implications about the person identified as "you." And so it goes. "Out came the seam, and was pinned together in another place."

Furthermore, the bodies themselves produce the cultural contexts in which they become legible, rather than asserting their own independent legitimacy.[8] The speaker has lost weight because she is under emotional stress, of which her thinness is the sign. She also invokes the cultural preference for thin women when she responds to the fitter's concern by saying *"Tant mieux"* (so much the better). The working-class woman, dressed in "linty black," performs her role by the clothes she wears, beneath which she is not separable from her social status but simply another version of it, signified by her sweat.

Interestingly, the speaker herself may be seen to echo the hard-working fitter who has a "familiar and unknown face," familiar as the speaker's own face in the mirror, unknown as the guarded eyes from which the drooped eyes flee. The fact that all three women are brought together here in the circle of an economic relationship, and that somehow this relationship that groups them around an alienated body is meant to tell us something about the love relationship only gestured at but never described, implies Millay's instinctive comprehension of commercial culture's power to saturate every relationship, even that of a woman to her lover or of a woman to her own body.

In an earlier era, it was possible to speak of clothing as making an appearance merely. Characters in Hawthorne, Melville, Carlyle, and the early Henry James *do* so speak.[9] But under the clothes of Edna St. Vincent Millay are simply more clothes, signs covering and covered by other signs.

So Edna Millay wears a plaid dress. This plaid—as she describes it in the poem—represents a form of violence, self-created, perhaps, but color-coded by its inscription in culture, the reading of her behavior in a social context. Listening to the first stanza once again, we can hear the voice of middle-aged dissatisfaction:

> Strong sun, that bleach
> The curtains of my room, can you not render
> Colourless this dress I wear?—
> This violent plaid
> Of purple angers and red shames; the yellow stripe
> Of thin but valid treacheries; the flashy green of kind deeds
>     done
> Through indolence, high judgments given in haste;
> The recurring checker of the serious breach of taste?

But why do I say that this plaid dress is color-coded by intertextual reference? In the first place, the colors themselves are conventional: purple for anger, yellow for cowardice and betrayal. Then there is the denotative level of Millay's terms—shame that involves public embarrassment, shortly followed by that wonderful line: "The recurring checker of the serious breach of taste." Both shame and taste insist upon the social constitution of meanings. Nothing is shameful or tasteful without a community to judge it so.

In the pattern of plaid, with its repeating rectangles, we might even see a visual echo of the mirror image. The checker is an echoing frame, as well as an oblique reference to the checkerboard, perhaps. Furthermore, as the poem continues, we once again encounter a problem with our usual expectations regarding clothing, for the poem concludes:

> No more uncoloured than unmade,
> I fear, can be this garment that I may not doff;
> Confession does not strip it off,
> To send me homeward eased and bare;
>
> All through the formal, unoffending evening, under the clean
> Bright hair,
> Lining the subtle gown . . . it is not seen,
> But it is there.                                    (Millay's ellipses)

Just as in "The Fitting," in which drooped eyes meet guarded eyes in a glass where both are representations and neither is determinant, here the covering dress and the plaid dress form an unbroken circuit of interconnection and fleeting regard. There is no secret body beneath the layers of signification. At first, one might conclude that the phrase "it is not seen" means that there is an appearance-reality distinction at work here. If we do not see the plaid dress, perhaps the poet is nonetheless claiming that it represents the truth about the self, a truth that persists even when covered over. But further reflection reveals that the dress itself is the result not of an inner realization but of other moments of self-exposure. This social occasion ("the formal, unoffending evening") is simply one of a series of public appearances, interchangeable with others where "high judgments [were] given in haste" or where the speaker exhibited her penchant for "thin but valid treacheries" and "the serious breach of taste."

There is what we might call a *commutative principle* at work here. One occasion replaces without obliterating the other, just as the word "subtle" modifying "gown" could as easily (and perhaps more reasonably) modify "lining"—since *subtle* not only means fine or delicate but also carries the implication of secrecy, of something going on under the surface.

Yet, as I have said before, there is no secret body here, no hope of "getting down to basics," as one might say. The plaid dress worn on the inside during the formal, unoffending evening seems to be worn on the outside in the first part of the poem and can occupy either position equally well, it seems. The important point is that "Confession does not strip it off, / To send me homeward eased and bare." Why not, one might ask, if what is at stake here are only the venial sins mentioned above? Perhaps there is no hope of absolving oneself of the narrative of one's experience because there is no master trope to counter the force of endless replication. One version of the body calls up another, but none may be genuinely claimed as one's own. I think the conclusion we must draw from the reference to the issue of confession is that in the world of spectacle the Real as a substance has evaporated.

But this is not the same thing as saying that nothing is hidden. As Guy Debord writes, "Secrecy dominates this world [of the spectacle], and first and foremost as the secrecy of domination" (*Comments* 60). What is obscure are the power relations that have eviscerated ideas of self, love, God, or the state. And here is where a recognition of the vulnerability of the signifier, the Female Body, emerges at the intersection of culture and gender. Here is where twentieth-century politics (in which the buck stops nowhere) and twentieth-century economics (where everything is exchange value) and popular culture (with its emphasis on replaceability) come to greet a woman, who thinks they are admiring her body, but who in the end learns that in their eyes she is little more than a prostitute, briefly alluring but ultimately dispensable.

This is what is implied by considering Edna St. Vincent Millay as a postmodern instance. The woman we discover is not exactly a heroine, but her story is instructive and it may be summarized in a few words. Millay was a skillful poet and perhaps most skillful in her capacity to capture in memorable language physical experience, *not* sex—as was previously thought—but muscular tension and movement. Like many in our culture, especially women, she had no stable sense of her own identity. When young and attractive and flirtatious and talented, she was encouraged to trade on her charms, which she did with great success for a while. But as she grew older and kept trying to retail the same product, she found it no longer sold as well as it once had. Then people said that she had lost "it" or that she had never really had "it" in the first place. Shoddy goods.

What interests me in Millay's work is not so much that she understood the commodification of either the female body or its relations in consumer society, although there is evidence that she had ideas about such matters, most notably in *Conversation at Midnight*. What interests me is that Millay's work bears the unmistakable imprint of the stresses and fault lines of our superficially seductive, scopophilic culture. Millay herself was no postmodernist and even believed in such seemingly "old-fashioned" abstractions as Beauty. But her poetry, which has been criticized for its theatrical effects, is deeply interesting when its "theatricality" is understood as a sign of the society of the spectacle.

As a cultural figure, she had a lot to say to the women of her time about living courageously and not letting others inhibit one's pleasure. In the early days, she championed the rights of women to enjoy their bodies as they so desired. But her poems say more than she said about the lack of control one has over the semiotics of the female flesh, the way in which individual courage must in the end confront cultural de-realization. In the context of postmodern critique, her poems come alive again with a range of subtle and disturbing messages we would do well to attend to. She knew a lot, but in the long run, they know more than she knew.

## *Notes*

1. The classic essay on this subject is Laura Mulvey's "Visual Text and Narrative Cinema" (1975), which has now been questioned and revised by many subsequent considerations.

2. See my chapter on Millay entitled "Women on the Market: Edna St. Vincent Millay's Body Language" in *Masks Outrageous and Austere*, 135–64.

3. In 1950, after her husband's death from cancer, Millay wrote a frustrated letter to a friend who was collecting money for cancer research. In it she reveals her own astute observations about the way advertising can use the media to position its clients in the public's mind. (See *Letters*, 1952, 367.) Alfred Kreymborg mentions the extraordinary amount of publicity that preceded the opening of *The King's Henchman*: "The event was tremendously press-agented in advance" (445). Significantly, one of the main characters in *Conversation at Midnight* (1937) is a young man in the advertising business. Though cynical about his own occupation, he is also very shrewd and by no means the least sympathetic character in the bunch. In light of Baudrillard's comments above, it is interesting that he is the one who says, "Let me enlarge to you upon the comforts of modern transcontinental flight" (14). He knows the insubstantiality of life on the ground and has located the sublime where Baudrillard locates it, in connections made by air.

4. In " 'Material Girl,' " Susan Bordo argues that Madonna has become the toy of an objectifying media gaze despite her insistence that her creative work (as she told *Vanity Fair*) is ironic, ambiguous, and meant "to entertain myself" (that is, a product that she believes eludes objectification).

5. For an excellent discussion of Millay's work with the propaganda machine, see Schweik, *A Gulf So Deeply Cut*.

6. One hardly need mention the obvious phallic overtones of this tower, suggesting an unconscious devaluation of the female body even as the speaker is claiming it as her own.

7. Here I am using the term *Real* in the sense in which Jacques Lacan uses it, to signify an absolute (and ungraspable) reality outside of the

symbolic. When I refer to objects of perception, I do not capitalize the word *real*.

8. One could, of course, argue that all language must be understood intertextually, that there is no such thing as a signifier asserting its independent legitimacy. However, it becomes clear in the course of this poem that Millay's form of condensation (as in the remark "*Tant mieux*" discussed below) insists upon a particular intensification of intertextual reference that subsequently comes to deracinate all her terms. It may be that, in order for individuals to become agents, they must proceed *as though* their actions are for the moment outside of all language games.

9. I think particularly of Robin in "Young Goodman Brown" (Hawthorne), of Ishmael in *Moby Dick* and *Redburn* (Melville), of *Sartor Resartus* (Carlyle), and of Isabel Archer in *The Portrait of a Lady* (James), who argues: "Nothing that belongs to me is any measure of me; everything's on the contrary a limit, a barrier, and a perfectly arbitrary one. Certainly the clothes which, as you say, I choose to wear, don't express me; and heaven forbid they should!" (216). Isabel may be naive in this regard but she does have an inner self whose power is felt by everyone. She is an example of what I mean above when I say that agency requires the fiction of nonfictive status.

# 7 Love's "Little Day"

## Time and the Sexual Body in Millay's Sonnets
### Stacy Carson Hubbard

Much recent criticism of Millay evaluates her poetry in terms of its integrity, sincerity, and consistency or its capacity to liberate the woman poet from the constraints of contemporary gender roles or traditional literary forms. Too often, Millay is seen as either a victim of modern culture, especially its exploitation of female sexuality (Walker), or a victim of her own unstable emotions (Stanbrough). For Elizabeth Perlmutter, Millay's poetics defies the lyric's requirement for wholeness and sincerity; the theatricality of her lyric language is "vulgar" (170), a form of cheap and deceptive dressing, like that of a prostitute: the poems are tricked out "in costumes of net and lace, and slightly soiled satin, with thick seams and zippers for quick changes, broad gestures, and hints of knee and breast" (166). A similarly derogatory language of veiling, disguise, and gesture, set in opposition to such terms as "stable identity" and "consistent image of self" (Walker, *Masks Outrageous and Austere* 143–45) informs Cheryl Walker's and Jane Stanbrough's treatments of Millay. Stanbrough's self-described project is to tear the veil from Millay's poetic performances, the false images of her "liberation and self-assurance" (183), in order to get at "the truth of Millay's inner sense of herself" (191), which is the truth of her vulnerability and victimization. Similarly, Walker laments Millay's participation in the commodification of the female body, its "controlled self-exposure," an exploitation that ultimately "betrayed" Millay, and asks, "How should we interpret these contradictions in terms of Millay's individual experience and psyche?" (*Masks Outrageous and Austere* 139).

My intention in what follows is to redirect critical attention away from Millay's individual experience and "inner" (true, honest, undisguised) self toward the scene of literary history and its role in the rhetorical and cultural construction of sex and gender. I want to suggest that there may be more self-consciousness—and, specifically, more historical consciousness—in Millay's "gestur[-ing]" (Perlmutter 167) than has been acknowledged in recent discussions of her poetry's sexual politics. It is neither primarily twentieth-century culture nor temperamental instability that determines the range of gestures, postures, and utterances in Millay's poems; rather, it is language generally and the discourse of love poetry in particular that do not so much *veil* Millay's identity as a woman as make possible its performance, in the process revealing the instabilities of both gender and poetic authority. To measure Millay's poetic achievement in terms of its sincerity or its resistance to role playing is to seriously mistake both the nature of poetic language and the parodic and performative nature of gender.

According to Judith Butler, the notion of an inner, true self and a stable identity preserved from the falseness of display or gesture is itself a product of public discourse, one meant to protect against the knowledge of both self and gender as fictional (and fluxional) constructs. "The displacement of a political and discursive origin of gender identity onto a psychological 'core' precludes an analysis of the political constitution of the gendered subject . . ." (136). However,

if the ground of gender identity is the stylized repetition of acts through time and not a seemingly seamless identity, then the spatial metaphor of 'ground' will be displaced and revealed as a stylized configuration, indeed, *a gendered corporealization of time*. (141; emphasis added)

Such a redefinition of gendered identity suggests that the critical obsession with Millay's sincerity, maturity, and consistency (or, rather, her lack of these qualities) may obscure the extent to which the various roles she mimics and manipulates are the rhetorical products of a specific discourse (lyric poetry, and more specifically in what follows, the tradition of the *carpe diem* sonnet). This discourse is not merely a vehicle available for the expression of gendered interiority and sincere speech: it is, as Joel Fineman has so persuasively argued, the major literary venue for the production of these categories.

According to Butler, drag offers the best paradigm for the construction of the gendered subject, because drag serves to "displace the entire enactment of gender significations from the discourse of truth and falsity" (137). What if we were to reevaluate the charge that Millay "slavishly" submits to literary and gender conventions (Clark, *Sentimental Modernism* 67–68) in light of Butler's definition of gender as an imitative and parodic practice, one that must be performed over and over again, as a "stylized repetition of acts" (140)? Rather than lamenting Millay's obedience to conservative literary forms, we might consider the extent to which her arsenal of poeticisms, courtly gestures, and predictable plots may, like drag, work to undermine the very notion of an original—self, sex, or poem. The mannered literariness of Millay's poems—what has lead Karl Shapiro to lament, in a wonderfully theatrical scene of unmanning, that they "are such a parody of the great love poets that one is dissolved in tears" (qtd. in Clark, *Sentimental Modernism* 77)—opens up the possibility of rethinking poetic gender as an imitative practice and parody as one available response of the woman poet to a tradition predicated upon her silence. Millay's playful adoption of both masculine and feminine roles in the sonnet suggests just such an unstable notion of gendered subjectivity and signals her poetry's concern with the ways figurations of gendered and sexed bodies attach themselves to poetic forms, tropes, and narrative structures. If, as Suzanne Clark argues, sentimental literature, with Edna St. Vincent Millay as its most visible modern practitioner, has been made to fill the role of the abject in relation to modernism—that which it is compelled to expel by way of constituting its own identity (*Sentimental Modernism* 1–41)—then it may be worthwhile to inquire into the history by which women have come to figure such abjection and such endpoints in narratives of decay. Edna Millay, as the embodiment of sentimental abjection and empty posturing, the last gasp of exhausted literary convention, can stand for the death of Poetry. But how woman came to signify death *in* poetry and how her silencing has made possible both the constitution of male poetic subjectivity and the neat closure of poetic plots is a subject that Millay takes up repeatedly in her own poems, especially those in which she rewrites the male *carpe diem* tradition by insistently dislodging woman from her role as abject figure for the end of something.

The *carpe diem* tradition makes of the female body's vulnerability to decay a symbol of human mortality. The woman's body in poems such as Daniel's sonnets to Delia, Herrick's "To the Virgins, to Make Much of Time," or Waller's "Go, lovely rose!" is thus both an object of desire and an enemy to be conquered in a symbolic triumph over death; in Marvell's "To His Coy Mistress," the woman's body is actually transformed into an object of revulsion in its vividly imagined postmortem state. In these *carpe diem* seductions (and, more particularly, in those poems that employ the rhetoric of the *blazon*, as does Marvell's) the female flesh carries a double charge: desired in its intact and virginal state, it is haunted by its immanent disintegration, an undoing that is, strangely enough, to be initiated by the lover's entry into that "fine and private place," the woman's sexual body. The vision of her body dispersed by aging and death, its beauty fled, is held up to the female listener in hopes of persuading her to some lesser dispersal or loss, the opening of her body to the eloquent lover. As Marvell's invasive worms make clear, it is not only the barrenness and waste of virginity that prefigure death, but the surrender of the body to sexual love that also anticipates Death's possession.

That the lover in the *carpe diem* poem speaks in league with death, performing death's work of disintegration and possession, is an alliance not lost on Millay, who was throughout her life an avid student of classical and Renaissance poetry. Moreover, Millay's poems reveal an awareness of the dependence of the *carpe diem* poem's discursive logic on the woman's coyness, its inability to accomplish its triumph over woman or Time without her posited reluctance. Indeed, the extended verbal display of the speakers in these poems is made possible by the very deferral of sexual consummation that they so vigorously attempt to overcome. As Patricia Parker argues in her discussion of the classical and Renaissance traditions of rhetorical *dilatio*, the lover's discourse finds its own opportunities to dilate and delay in the obstructionist tactics of virgins, through a logic whereby the woman's refusal to "dilate" in a bodily sense both threatens to undermine "the master . . . project of the completion of the text," and surreptitiously figures the vagrant desires of romance itself (8–35).

The speakers of Millay's sonnets, many of whom draw upon the *carpe diem* motif, could never be accused of such sexual coyness: they are outspoken in their defiance of both Death and lovers whose possessiveness resembles Death's embrace. Itemizing the woman's bodily charms as perishable commodities, the *blazon* identifies the poet-lover both with the potential buyer and with the merchant who displays the woman's wares (Parker 126–32; Walker 135–45). Millay's women, on the other hand, aim to do their own spending. They refuse the association of sexual power with youth and beauty, portraying the body's ruin as its badge of sexual authority and the sign that it has been well used: Millay's speaker is the prize that robs itself, proclaiming to Death and its agents that with the "force I spend / . . . [I'll] leave thee hungry even in the end" ("Thou famished grave, I will not fill thee yet"). It is she who would "spend" her "force," burning her own candle at both ends, eating up life and love before they manage to eat her.

This flagrant, and often funny, rejection of feminine coyness in Millay's sonnets reflects more than a mere acquiescent response to the invitations of earlier poet-lovers (a giving of voice to the woman merely so that she can supply the required "yes") and more, too, than a simple reversal of the love sonnet's traditionally gendered roles. Rather, the pervasive promiscuity of Millay's speakers accomplishes two things. First, it provides a necessary escape from the *carpe diem*'s discursive logic, in which the female auditor's virginity and her associations with the grave virtually effect her silence and are figured by it; and, second, it accomplishes the temporal relocation of the woman in the poem, in an "after" far removed from the "before" of the addressed virgin. Millay's love-weary women exist beyond the wholeness that virginity bodies forth and that a poem such as

"To His Coy Mistress" threatens to undo. Although the traditional *carpe diem* urges upon the virgin a change of state, it is nonetheless the virginal body that it catalogs, precisely because it is the prolongation of the virgin's state that provides the poem's own principle of generation. Where the virginal addressee is a woman with a future bearing down upon her in the form of a lover with Time at his back, Millay's speaker is a woman with a past that has already taught her the ephemerality of all things.

Millay's women are not immune to the physical ravages of time; however, in a manner reminiscent of Shakespeare's mock-old man, they manage to draw authority from the experience that ripening age represents, reaping in memory what their senses have sown:

> Those hours when happy hours were my estate,
> Entailed, as proper, for the next in line,
> Yet mine the harvest, and the title mine.

Significantly, Millay's women do not cease to speak on behalf of the body, *as lovers*, even after their sexual "pride" has, to borrow Daniel's figure, "declined":

> . . . all of my late
> Enchantments, still, in brilliant colours, shine,
> But striped with black, the tulip, lawn and vine,
> Like gardens looked at through an iron gate.
> Yet not as one who never sojourned there
> I view the lovely segments of a past
> I lived with all my senses. . . .

Here Millay speaks from the other side of the "iron gate," which, in Marvell, marks the boundary between the woman's virgin desirability and her appropriated sexuality as well as that between life and death. In looking back through the bars of this gate, Millay signals her rejection of Marvell's terminal figures, his association of the hymen with the gateway into death. Surveying the "segments" of a sensual past rather than the unbroken wholeness of an earlier virgin state, Millay's woman speaks from beyond the ending of the earlier poem, making of the body's losses a narrative gain.

Traditionally, the bodily self-enclosure of the virgin necessitates her silence—her lips are sealed because she has no story to tell.

Millay's speakers, however, look back over a scattering of the sexual self among nameless and half-forgotten lovers and find in this lack of self-containment what, following D. A. Miller, we might call "narratable" experience. In place of the *memento mori*'s single-minded gaze forward toward death, these poems substitute half-rueful, ironical, sometimes sentimental, backward glances at the multiple deaths of love. As in the sonnet that begins, "When did I ever deny, though this was fleeting, / That this was love?," love itself is often made to carry the burden of mutability that had formerly belonged to female flesh. Millay's sonnets speak for the possibility of life after virginity; they imagine an endlessly renewable sexuality, a self-distribution without self-loss (indeed, one might say that giving and relinquishing are the very processes that constitute the feminine subject in Millay's sonnets, as they do in so much of the women's sentimental tradition). By converting female sexual experience from its status as a onetime (hence deferred and organizing) closural event[1] to a repeatable one, hence an opportunity for vacillation, indecision, and that general verbal and emotional irritability productive of narrative, Millay seizes for the woman the power of "dilation" in *both* its sexual and its verbal forms. Hence, "long-preserved virginity" gives ways to a well-used (and well-narrated) sexuality.

It is true, as some feminist readers complain, that the language of sexual conquest and possession remain central to these poems, but with the difference that the woman speaker often claims for herself the roles of *both* winner and loser, as in "I Being Born a Woman and Distressed," where she plays all the available roles in the sexual contest simultaneously: she is at once "zestful" and "frenzied" seductress and "staggering" victim, silent beloved and scornful mistress, "distressed," "urged," "undone," and "possessed," yet fully capable of a stylish exit. Since she submits to no one but herself ("the poor treason / Of my stout blood against my staggering brain"), she wins either way, making a game of such "undoing" by emphasizing its reversibility and repetition—"*once again* undone, possessed" (emphasis added). The poem's concluding refusal of conversation ("I find this frenzy insufficient reason / For conversation when we meet again") confirms what the internalization of the sonnet's erotic drama already suggests, that this is not an I/ thou encounter, but the woman's way of talking to herself. In its translation of the amorous tussle between man and woman into a battle of blood against brain, the poem illustrates Millay's strategy of displacing male/female poetic relations to the interiority of the woman speaker. Her response to the difficulties of the woman poet's self-positioning in the sonnet is to take up neither the male nor the female role, but to internalize the sexual drama, all but erasing the role of the eroticized and addressed Other. Such strategies have been labeled solipsistic; however, they may better be understood as a conflicted response to the difficulties of creating a feminine speaker in the amatory poem. The internalized erotic contest figures the woman poet's internalization of poetic tradition, her struggle with the love sonnet's seductive yet (for women poets) impossible plot: she both yields to poetic convention and walks away from it. The struggle within this poem between the inescapably masculine role of the speaker-seducer and the feminine role of sexual object, she who surrenders or *gives* herself bodily, supports Suzanne Clark's claim that Millay verbally cross-dresses, discovering in her "submission" to form "rebellious duplicities, the pleasure of the masquerade" (*Sentimental Modernism* 90).[2]

As performance or act, the woman's sex no longer invites analogies to things secret and sealed, preserved or else ruined. It is the double bind created by the overvaluation of woman's chastity—the preciousness of her sexual prize, to be given just once—that Millay snaps open in the following poem, sonnet XI, from *Fatal Interview*:

> Not in a silver casket cool with pearls
> Or rich with red corundum or with blue,
> Locked, and the key withheld, as other girls
> Have given their loves, I give my love to you.

The conventional association of the woman's privates with a casket, both jewel box and coffin, hence that "private place" that is the grave, is discarded in favor of "love in the open hand," "ungemmed, unhidden," like "apples in [a] skirt" (XI). These sexual treasures are displayed by the very skirt that was designed to hide them. By removing sexuality from the hidden interiority of the knotted ring with its secret spring ("Not in a lover's-knot, not in a ring," "where a secret spring / Kennels a drop of mischief") to the shameless exteriority of the child's open-handed offering, the poem attempts the defetishization of the woman's sex and claims for it an inessential status (not "I am all yours," but "*these* are all for you" [emphasis added]). Whereas above we saw Millay internalizing an intersubjective drama, here she externalizes female sexuality, so often figured as woman's special form of interiority. This speaker's self-display eschews the precious parceling (what we might call the verbal divide-and-conquer) of the Marvellian lover, in favor of a version of feminine sexuality as masquerade, a show or showing in which the woman gives herself, without ever quite giving herself away. Though such display does not entirely escape the logic or imagery of the *blazon*'s objectifications, it nonetheless unsettles these by placing them in ambiguous relation to a feminine voice, thus disturbing the imagined unity of body *and* voice.

As has been noted by more than one recent commentator, Marvell's dissection of his coy mistress is, for all its witty play, "punitive and morbid" as well (Barker 92; Belsey 107–9). It reveals a deep distaste for what is fleshly and feminine even as it requests access to it. The poem's obsessive feminizing of mutability begins to look like a different kind of coyness, a containment of the threat that the female body and the possibility of a less than mute and passive female sexuality may pose. Francis Barker has proposed an anti-reading of Marvell's poem, positing a text that underlies and challenges the male utterance by figuring as an "underside" "the woman's silent resistance, [her] refusal to enter into dialogue with the male voice . . . " (92). This imagined feminine resistance is "silent because it must yet find its own proper discourse . . . : it is the silence of Dora, who walked out" (93). Those of Millay's speakers who locate themselves, not outside where the male seducer begs entry, but inside the house of love and ready to "walk out," might seem to fulfill Barker's prediction of a not-yet-articulated feminine resistance to the *carpe diem*'s "sexual fixing." Like more traditional poet-lovers, Millay gains power by positioning herself in the in-between, where she can enforce transition and dictate change, but her chosen moment is more often the "after" than the "before."[3] The mobilization of feminine voice and feminine desire in the service of the love plot depends on the woman's refusal to be fixed by that same plot, her deferral of entry into the nonnarratable realm of fulfilled desire.

In their flaunting of feminine sexual energy and their frequent admonishments to reluctant or overly sentimental lovers, Millay's sonnets suggest that perhaps it is the death-obsessed male lover who is genuinely coy in the face of willing, even willful, female sexuality. In "Since I cannot persuade you from this mood," the woman wields her "yes" like a threat, as she vies with the dead for her lover's attention, trying to "shift [his] concern to living bones instead" (VI). However, in "Yet in an hour to come" (VIII), the speaker, her powers conflated with those of Death, competes with Life, personified as the second woman in a love triangle, for possession of the male lover. The reluctant lover, addressed as "disdainful dust," is offered a choice between love in life, "here / On the green grass, with sighing and delight," or love in death, "under it [the grass], all in good time, my dear," between the speaker's present tenderness and the violence that she will be free to unleash upon him once Death strips him of his right of refusal:

> And ruder and more violent, be assured,
> Than the desirous body's heat and sweat
> That shameful kiss by more than night obscured
> Wherewith at length the scornfullest mouth is met.

Here, truly, the poet speaks as Death's accomplice and threatens her addressee much as Marvell threatens his. But, unlike Marvell, Millay does not offer the lover a choice between the speaker and death's worms. The choice she offers is, strangely, between a consummation of the living—in which her force is held somewhat in check by his own—and a consummation of the dead—in which his strength will be sorely diminished by death, whereas hers will have increased to the point that she can wield Death's own power. Though life may momentarily hold the coy lover with her charms (and perhaps protect him from the speaker's dark powers), this attachment is characterized as nothing more than a temporary defection from his more enduring bond to Death: "Life has no friend; her converts late or soon / Slide back to feed the dragon with the moon." By replacing Marvell's worms with the hyperbolically phallic dragon, Millay calls attention to the element of masquerade present in all such apotropaic sexual posturing (the phallus properly belonging, as Jacques Lacan says, to nobody) and to the comic absurdity of such claims to orchestrate death's destructions in the service of one body's pounding blood.

Yet stranger even than Millay's retention of this aggressive phallic language in conjunction with a feminine speaker is her revision of the temporal distinctions that lend urgency and a certain dark logic to the choice proffered by Marvell's speaker. Whereas in "To His Coy Mistress" we are told that "The grave's a fine and private place, / But none, I think, do there embrace" (lines 31–32), in "Yet in an hour to come" the dead *do* embrace in the grave; the speaker's attentions are not to be eluded even there. The imperiousness of the speaker's tone throughout the poem emphasizes her power to command the situation and to make herself into the very embodiment of death, hence a creature unbounded by life's terminus. Her language asserts that she knows the future and that she is in a position to issue pronouncements and commands: "You shall be bowed," "This shall be," "all in good time," "be assured." The poem seems less invested in persuading its addressee to yield now than in asserting the speaker's power to prevail—precisely through the rhetorical trick of her self-personification—one way or another. The poem's tactic is not to speed up time (as in "To His Coy Mistress") but rather to elongate the time for love such that it extends beyond death. The speaker imagines herself as impervious to the sort of disarming (something short of deanimating) that awaits the object of her solicitations. Her identification of herself with Death (unlike Marvell's figuration of Death as a rival male suitor) invents for the speaker an amorous career without end. While death marks the point of passage from the realm of the addressee's consent to the place of his forced submission to the speaker as Death, it represents a mere conversion or crossable boundary rather than an absolute end to sexual opportunities. The poem's figures have the effect, therefore, of reinventing time; they accomplish the imaginary liberation of the woman from the fetters of mortality. Millay's poem continues to exploit the apotropaic effect of the female body that we have seen in the classic *blazon*, but it alters the significance of that body by giving it a voice with which to announce its own threats and desires.

This poem, then, is more concerned with the speaker's desire to reposition herself within the terms of a particular literary discourse than it is with her desire for a sexual Other. The indifference to the particular attributes of erotic objects that characterizes Millay's sonnets, and their unwillingness to either entirely abandon or entirely submit to the rhetorical conventions of the sonnet tradition, suggest that the Other in Millay's love poems is, more often than not, literary history itself and the individual poets who, like Shakespeare and Marvell, stand in metonymically for that history.

Millay's most sustained engagement of the Renaissance *carpe diem* tradition appears in her many sonnets that allude to Shakespeare's sonnet 73 (with its images of leafless branches, dying embers, and setting sun) and that together may be read as an extended response to that sonnet's appeal, its injunction to "love that well which thou must leave ere long." Sonnet 73 differs in one important respect from the male *carpe diem* poems discussed above for in it, the speaker catalogs his own, rather than a woman's, ruination by Time. It is he in whom the addressee is said to perceive a dying season, a dying day, and a dying fire. Yet this inventory of mutable parts functions similarly to that of the *blazon*: it serves to "fix" its addressee within a mortal logic:

> In me thou see'st the twilight of such day
> As after sunset fadeth in the west;
>
> . . . . . . . . . . . . . .
> In me thou see'st the glowing of such fire,
> That on the ashes of his youth doth lie
>
> . . . . . . . . . . . . . . .
> This thou perceiv'st, which makes thy love more strong,
> To love that well which thou must leave ere long.

To witness the speaker's decline is not to feel one's esteem turn to scorn, but rather to love the speaker more dearly for the signs of his enslavement to death, and as the poem's final turning of its self-portrait mirror-like toward the auditor makes explicit, it is to see one's own death bodied forth (not "I," but "*thou* must leave ere long" [emphasis added]). In Marvell's poem, the woman's imagined disintegration works like a death's-head to frighten her into compliance; in Shakespeare's sonnet, the specter of the speaker's deathliness works similarly to enjoin its auditor to greater devotion.

In her three sonnets that most directly engage sonnet 73, Millay toys with the notion of necessity that Shakespeare's sonnet assumes and with the ambiguity of the "leaving" that it predicts for the addressee. This leaving, though commonly read as indicating the death of the speaker and/or addressee, might just as well suggest the addressee's growing indifference and willful departure. In Millay's poems, mortality still casts its shadow, but the threat of boredom—the fragility of modern love—proves a more immanent agent of destruction. In the following sonnet from *Second April*, "Only until this cigarette is ended," Millay redirects attention from the death of the body to the death of affection; the dying embers of Shakespeare's sonnet seem to find their modern equivalent in the ashes that fall from the woman sonneteer's cigarette, marking the limit of her memory:

> Only until this cigarette is ended,
> A little moment at the end of all,
> While on the floor the quiet ashes fall,
>
> . . . . . . . . . . . . . . . . . .
> I will permit my memory to recall
> The vision of you, by all my dreams attended.
> And then adieu,—farewell!—the dream is done.
> Yours is a face of which I can forget
> The colour and the features, every one,
> The words not ever, and the smiles not yet;
> But in your day this moment is the sun
> Upon a hill, after the sun has set.

Her response to his setting like the sun is a brisk "adieu,—farewell!—the dream is done," and what cataloging of his features the poem allows is, ostensibly, all in the service of forgetting. It is not time that will erase these features, but the speaker, who will allow them only a moment in her memory. In spite of its flirtation with bathos, there is humor in the poem's trivializing of the fire of life in the image of the cigarette and an element of self-satisfaction in its willing acceptance of loss. There will be other loves, as there are sure to be more cigarettes.

In "What lips my lips have kissed, and where, and why," the speaker casts herself as a "lonely tree," in language that directly echoes Shakespeare's "Bare ruined choirs, where late the sweet birds sang":

> What lips my lips have kissed, and where, and why
> I have forgotten, and what arms have lain
> Under my head till morning . . .
> . . . . . . . . . . . . . . . . . .
> And in my heart there stirs a quiet pain
> For unremembered lads that not again
> Will turn to me at midnight with a cry.
> Thus in the winter stands the lonely tree,
> Nor knows what birds have vanished one by one,
> Yet knows its boughs more silent than before.

The aging speaker as songless tree is an abject figure, one that we might be tempted to read as a prototype of abandoned womanhood, pathetic and powerless, if it were not for the powerful alliance that such abjectness establishes between Millay's speaker and Shakespeare's. The speaker of Shakespeare's sonnet makes a spectacle of his abjection by way of persuasion; so, too, does Millay's, but with the further motive of authorizing herself through poetic echo. To read such self-abjection without a view to literary history would be to mistake it for mere self-pity, a sentimental attachment to the figure of woman as victim,[4] rather than the bold poetic affiliation that Millay surely intends it to be. Male desire in the courtly love sonnet was always a masquerade of feminine weakness and sentimentality; wan, beseeching, and consumed by desire, the male lover speaks with the authority of suffering and, perhaps more importantly, with the authority of convention. When Millay masquerades as a male poet masquerading as a lovesick woman, our sense of where sincerity meets gesture and how authority aligns itself with gender is confused. She is either too sincere or not sincere enough, excruciatingly vulnerable in her self-exposure or cynically manipulative of rhetorical conventions and pathetic "postures." The result is, as Dorothy Mermin argues in her discussion of Barrett Browning's love sonnets, embarrassment and unease:

The embarrassment arises from the clashing of apparently incompatible roles; we are made uncomfortable by the appearance of a woman where we expect a man, by the fact that as subject of desire she denigrates her attractiveness as desire's object, and by the manifold incongruities between amatory convention and . . . [modern] courtship. (141)

In Millay's version of the denuded tree, in contrast to Shakespeare's, it is not the speaker's youth and beauty that are said to have fled like birds or leaves—it is "unremembered lads," lovers so numerous that their names and faces cannot be recalled but who remain in the form of something like tactile traces, as links in the chain of experience constituting the body's history, and in their individual forgetability, making possible its continuation. Her body is not the locus of any permanence that might mitigate its debt to time—it cannot be permanently possessed, nor does it promise to reproduce itself as a stay against mortality. Millay's sexualized body produces nothing but ephemerae. This body spends its powers in hopes of having them, too, and the force of this spending is a perpetual and willful forgetting that makes possible the repetition of love's story:

> I shall forget you presently, my dear,
> So make the most of this, your little day,
> Your little month, your little half a year,
> Ere I forget, or die, or move away.

Shakespeare's famous anticlimactic sequence—"yellow leaves, or none, or few"—finds its echo in the willful disintegration of feeling in Millay's equally anticlimactic line—"Ere I forget, or die, or move away." The inexorableness of nature's process so wishfully reversed in Shakespeare's line meets its flinty equal in the forgetfulness and restlessness of women in Millay's.

The judgment of Millay's sonnets as logically and verbally thin—their emotions temporary, their gestures briefly held—is not entirely unearned. Many of these poems do have a throwaway quality. Millay often chooses not to exploit the sonnet's potential for condensation, punning, chiasmus, paradox, and the other self-enclosing devices that give the sonnet its characteristically well-wrought—one might even say monumental—feeling. Many of Millay's sonnets seem, contrarily, to resist the form's closure, exhibiting instead a narrative pull that invites one to read these poems as fleeting gestures, briefly held poses in a sequence of self-inventive—and necessarily temporary—posturings. Millay's sonnets read less like jeweled caskets than like lines tossed over the shoulder in passing, throwaway poems for throwaway loves. The woman's promiscuity—her self-dispersal—implies a rejection of monumentalizing, immortalizing love (and its poems) as well as a refusal of that "fixing" inherent in the *carpe diem*'s fearful invocation of the movements of Time. Millay's sonnet-lover attempts in the opening of her hand an open mouth and an open door as well. By working to unfix feminine sexuality from death, she attempts to convert it from its status as the *carpe diem*'s object and terminus, into the very principle of narratability itself, that upon which the woman poet may "dilate" without end. In her willingness to embrace small deaths—forgettings, farewells, and surrenders of reason to passion—and her wry and worldly acceptance of the body's lack of discrimination and memory's short lease, the speaker of Millay's sonnets attempts to outlive the seductive voices of those Renaissance lovers whose invitations were always to silence.

The critical attempt to legislate what counts as legitimate identity and emotion in Millay's poems is related to the regulation of gender that these poems so determinedly evade. Millay's claims to rhetorical and emotional power will appear as posturing in a cultural context that denies such power to women; conversely, her expressions of vulnerability will be read as sentimental within a literary tradition that founds itself on authoritative self-assertion. Millay disturbs our critical categories by rendering permeable the boundaries between authority and abjection, modern literature and dead forms, the poet as woman and the poet as man. She gestures to us from the afterlife of that rhetorical tradition whose death she declines to signify.

## Notes

I owe special thanks to Irene Fairley, Susan Gilmore, Jo Ellen Green Kaiser, and Deidre Lynch for their help in developing and improving this essay.

1. "If the Freudian Oedipal myth can be taken as a version of the cultural sense of value and purpose—with the woman as object of desire—the same story will appear repeated everywhere. *The open narrative is closed by the figure of a woman*" (Clark, *Sentimental Modernism* 90; emphasis added).

2. See also Fried, "Andromeda," on the complex relation of "mastery" to "being mastered" in Millay's use of traditional poetic forms.

3. See also Clark: "[Millay] maintains herself on the borders of literature, in the position of the extra one, the child, the girl, at the limits of inside/outside where she is that which exceeds the experience, that which is more than the (circular and repetitive) plot" (*Sentimental Modernism* 83).

4. See, for example, Stanbrough: "Millay's victims are . . . all embodiments of Millay, the anguished, writhing, defenseless, and finally defeated victim" ("Language of Vulnerability" 194).

# 8   *A Moment's Monument*
## *Millay's Sonnet and Modern Time*
### Robert Johnson

Surveying the emergence of lyrical poetry in Renaissance English literature, John Williams has proposed (especially in his preface) that an essential tension exists between the "Native" tradition of common speech evoked to name basic human concerns and the attractive power of the "Petrarchan style," of which the sonnet is probably a central manifestation. This latter influence prods verse to balance the needs of precise rhetoric against the truth of feelings, engendering a kind of difficult poise demanded in English lyrical poetry ever since. The sonnet, as a practical result, has become a testing ground for each age of art to refine its own vision of life, a crucible in which poets simmer feeling with linguistic limitation, tradition with the best new thinking.

In just this fashion, the sonnets of Edna St. Vincent Millay reflect the artistic problems of her age. Specifically, they often balance the urgency of human emotional responses and the concomitant need to name what one feels against the limitations of attempting to describe the felt moment. Experience becomes a kind of *topos*, a precarious foothold maintained within the ceaseless flow of change and time, against the sure loss of sensory awareness, the inevitable death of imaginatively evoked correspondences and all the names that language can throw at the world. In Millay's sonnets, art becomes a speaking to and against the power of time to limit, to deny, yet also to nurture human understanding—in language—of experience. The search for understanding feels to be a wrestling with time itself.

Responsibility for the presence of this sensitivity to change and time has been attributed variously by critics. Standard reactions suggest that Millay's readings in Renaissance literatures and the metaphysical ironies of writers such as Donne marked her verse with a profound respect for mutability.[1] As literary historians have demonstrated, Millay has so often been linked with traditions older than those of the early twentieth century that she is frequently denied by her critical contemporaries an acknowledged role in the artistic climate of her own era. Suzanne Clark writes that Millay's work was originally read as altogether too "sentimental" to be considered rightfully modern. "Modernist poetics," Clark notes, assume "an estrangement between the poem and the reader," while Millay flaunted her passions and invited "commonality" (*Sentimental Modernism* 71, 69). The very subjects in which Millay reveled—emotions, understanding, relationship—Clark shows, "were disenfranchised by the practices of modernism" ("Unwarranted Discourse" 141). Millay confronted prejudices favoring the distanced and the cerebral with a language of experience and of the heart.

Indeed, even some recent studies have maintained that Millay is best read as a sort of anomaly, a writer not comfortably fit to her intellectual environment. Summarizing the twentieth-century sonnet tradition, Janis Stout places Millay as a poet "of great technical ability," who nonetheless at times "so smothers her work in stale poeticisms and sentiment that it seems tritely sentimental and outmoded" (30). Judith Farr admires Millay's work, but notes that, like Elinor Wylie, Millay spoke in a "consciously inherited manner" and that many of her lines could "pass" for being Elizabethan (288–89). Cheryl Walker, too, admits the richness of Millay's accomplishment but judges her, finally, not "subversive" enough truly to be modern *and* feminist, especially in her view of women's roles and women's bodies. Millay "never worked out a large conception of women's place in American culture," Walker sums up (*Masks Outrageous and Austere* 164). Evaluating the portrait of women's identity as reflected in language and writing of the age, Jan Montefiore must conclude of Millay that the "experiments of Modernism passed her by" (115).

Yet I believe Millay's sonnets can be shown to demonstrate clearly modernist attitudes, at least about time. No doubt her poetry reflects Renaissance influence—the era gave Millay her tool, the tightly wrought little sonnet machine. And, as Farr reminds readers, to "write in the style of a particular period is temporarily to assume its convictions" (305). One cannot pen sonnets without, in so doing, gathering the world up into Renaissance logics. "Poetic forms," writes Debra Fried, "are not natural but ideological" ("Andromeda" 17). That is, sonnets, as C. L. Barber argues of Shakespeare's attempts, offer a remarkably intense case of just such influence: they ask for "a special sort of attention because in them poetry is, in a special way, an action," yoking the needs of writer, form, and subject ("Essay" 303). In sonnets, readers perceive the writer's voice exercised against the rigors of a demanding, deliberately limiting—all the while lyrical—and specifically Renaissance genre. The very limitations that the form places on the reader require the reader to think the way the sonnet thinks.

However, Millay's is also clearly an art of her own era, and in more ways than by challenging the moral biases of the popular culture into which the poet was born. Again, an essentially modernist quality of Millay's sonnets can be discovered in their portrayal of the emotional experience of time. Moreover, in demonstrating this modern perception of time, Millay confirms the role of the sonnet as a place where poets journey to test the old against the new. This modern temper might best be appreciated after first reviewing a few general contrasts between Renaissance and modernist attitudes regarding time.

## Living in Time, in Sonnets

For the Elizabethan mind to which Millay was exposed in her reading of early English sonnets, historians surmise, time is quantitative, a "precious commodity" (Quinones 11). Born of the explosive growth in international political and commercial activities during the period, this Renaissance thought regarding time's powers not only respects the ability of time to change everything humans know—witness, say, Spenser's or Shakespeare's sonnets and their embracing the worth of trustworthy emotions—but also the importance of investing time well. In a classic essay, C. L. Barber notes the tension in *Henry IV* between meeting the responsibilities of everyday time and the ritualized revel and waste of the time spent on holiday ("From Ritual to Comedy"). Georges Poulet explains that in the Renaissance, time is part of a world best understood as a "gigantic network of interchanges" (9), one more substance over whose husbandry humans bear responsibility. Renaissance time, Ricardo Quinones suggests, is ever a product to be nurtured and budgeted and spent well (16). Defined in general terms, Renaissance time exists *outside* the human mind, as a process working toward its own ends, as something of which humans must be wary, and with which they must reckon. Time has the power to alter and shape everything humans experience and need. Since it bears a personality of its own, time can be friend—or enemy.

Most assuredly, a respect for changeful time imbues Millay's sonnets. As Patricia Klemans has written in her study of the work and of its intellectual heritage, time is often portrayed in the sonnets through nature images, suggesting the endless cycle of gain and loss manifested by the seasons (Klemans 15). Like leaves falling from trees, all beauty will pass, Millay writes in her poem "And you as well must die, belovèd dust." "Unscrupulous Time," she notes, will ever be waiting to tear lovers from their embrace, she notes in her sonnet "Oh, my belovèd, have you thought of this." Truly, the cycles of nature appear in her sonnets as a great leveler, reducing all experience, all hope and dream, to dust:

> I see so clearly now my similar years
> Repeat each other, shod in rusty black,
> Like one hack following another hack
> In meaningless procession. . . .

And in another sonnet, she writes: "Read history: so learn your place in Time; / And go to sleep: all this was done before." Millay even represents in her sonnets the properly Renaissance debate over whether one can expect time's destructiveness to assure that a thwarted lover's heartache will pass, arguing at one point that even as time brings maturity to the body, "Time, doing this to me, may alter too / My sorrow, into something I can bear" ("Sonnet").

Yet she can lament: "Time does not bring relief; you all lied / Who told me time would ease me of my pain!" Consequently, the critical stand that Millay's sonnets show affinities with the spirit of Renaissance models of time appears substantial. Yet, there is more here than the recognition of loss and natural process. There is a decidedly modernist tone.

Modernist notions of time, if one accepts the modern period as coming to fruition in the late nineteenth and early twentieth century, generally shift their analyses from perceptions of loss and change to studies of time as a personal experience, as a *duration*. Time becomes a point of view, a species of imaginative memory. Theorizing from the heart of modernist thinking and during the decade when Millay's reputation was founded, Henri Bergson proposes that when humans are consciously aware of time, they project upon their shifting, accumulating sensory experience the simultaneous burden of a remembered past and an anticipated future. Time is not a thing, a substance, but a flow of data knit into reasonable patterns, in order that humans might create a spurious but necessary sense of a "now-point" where they can imagine themselves, instant by instant, to exist. Against this juggling, humans find it useful to balance mechanical measurements of some movement through space—say, the turning of hands upon a clock face, the swing of a pendant, the pulsing of an electronic charge. Figuratively, such measurement is then called *time*. Yet, real time, modernism insists, one way or other, is not its mechanical complement but the very consciousness of passage along that hazy continuum out of the past into the anticipated future, every bit of data accumulated in the steadily growing memory interacting with the bombardment of new sensory information received along the way. Real human time, Bergson judges, can only be measured in "counting simultaneities" (218–27, 230).[2]

To borrow the language of modernist linguistics, one moment in time is the intersection of the human ability to name experience with a fleeting configuration of sensory data simultaneously received from the physical world. As sensory data are constantly being received from the world, each intersection in real time is lost the instant it receives a name, for by then, the speaker exists at a new intersection. Therefore, one critic notes, modern time is "value neutral" and, like primitive notions of life as repeating cycles, does not necessarily support progress (Meyerhoff 103). The popularity of techniques like stream-of-consciousness makes clear that the stage on which modern time is evaluated is not to be found in commercial houses and banks, or in castles swirling with political deals, or on clock faces—or even in the passage of beauty, love, friendship, art— but among the imaginative constructs of mind (Meyerhoff 38–39).

In sum, humans project their accumulated names for experience against the shifting images they receive from the world, creating moments that they know are not physically actual, that they know are only concepts, and yet realizing, all the way, this is the best they can do. Unlike the Elizabethan, who focuses on experiencing substantive loss through time, the modernist grapples with the realization that all understanding is a game willingly and knowingly played. The modernist flows through time like those passengers on Mr. Eliot's train in the London underground, moments flickering by the window, new stations always approaching, others always receding into memory.[3] Each moment lives as a facet in some imaginative continuum, like all those folds and panels in Duchamp's nude walking downstairs or the flurry of legs whirling beneath futurist dachshunds puttering along the sidewalks of Paris.[4] For the modernist mind, time often seems reformed as a relationship between the imagination's musings, its relentless search for stability and meaning, and the equally relentless inundation of the senses with data. Humans must labor even to manufacture a *now* to sit in long enough to store up treasures they can lose!

Working from this definition, one can recognize the distinctively modernist tone of time's engagement as it is portrayed in Millay's sonnets. The narrators in these poems—all the while conjuring Renaissance convention—also create the very type of relationship to the moment that is associated with modernist art. They consciously grasp moments out of the flow of experience and then, with words, consciously construct a still point from which to view the course of life's happenings. They claim time by naming the moments they exist in. In one striking example, an early sonnet suggests of a lover:

> Only until this cigarette is ended,
> A little moment at the end of all,
> While on the floor the quiet ashes fall,
> And in the firelight to a lance extended,
> Bizarrely with the jazzing music blended,
> The broken shadow dances on the wall,
> I will permit my memory to recall
> The vision of you, by all my dreams attended.

What an apt image this glowing cigarette's tip provides for the modernist notion of the moment: one willingly isolated, fleeting bundle of sensory data, captured against its physical background, while the mind knowingly toys with a vision soon to fade, the boundaries of that moment imaged by the burst and waning of the burning cigarette's light. Following will come another moment, but by then, this initial burst of light will be the past. This is, of course, just the kind of fluid experience of time described by Bergson in 1922, a year after Millay's sonnet was published.

Millay embraces, too, the modernist recognition that only people know time as instants. For example, one sonnet holds, against the background of a "mute clock, maintaining ever the same / Dead moment, blank and vacant of itself," that a significant lesson to be learned from the dead is that "things in death [are] neither clocks nor people, / but only dead" ("There was upon the sill a pencil mark"). Moments and articulated time, that is, can only exist in a living consciousness. A parallel reminder of how incremental time is a human notion is offered in another sonnet when the speaker laments that while love exists in moments soon lost, a disappointed lover, returning to the sea shore, will discover that the "sullen rocks and skies [are] / Unchanged from what they were" when she was young ("I shall go back again to the bleak shore"). Nature's cycles and the cycles of human understanding, to use Bergsonian terms, are simultaneous but separate. We may lament that our moments are "under-said and over-sung" but nature merely *is*.

Indeed, Millay's sonnets' entire portrayal of love seems relentlessly modernist in its tone toward time seen as a willing manipulation of moments snatched from the flow of inescapable emotional changes. Instants are here celebrated in art as a way of preserving them from being lost in the relentless flux of memory. Note the typical warning of one sonnet:

> I shall forget you presently, my dear,
> So make the most of this, your little day,
> Your little month, your little half a year,
> Ere I forget, or die, or move away,
> And we are done forever. . . .

Surely, such lines do invert the roles traditionally attributed to women and men in love poetry—as feminist critics have rightly noted[5]—and they do reflect age-old warnings to seize the day, but they are also directly conscious that time *is* a flow of instants, endured, knit by deliberate imaginative will.

Perhaps, though, a most direct indication of Millay's mixing of traditional and modernist notions of time can be found in her celebrated 1931 collection, *Fatal Interview*. Containing fifty-two sonnets, the actions in which are spread through the four seasons, the group seems, in format, clearly meant to represent one complete (fifty-two week) cycle of the year. This cyclical, year-long structure can be likened to that of Renaissance works like Spenser's *Shepheardes Calendar*, classical prototypes, or as one critic notes, even the biblical injunction that there is fullness and a season for everything. An additional structuring device can be seen in Millay's opening and closing the group with references to the myth of Selene and Endymion, establishing for the cycle what has been called a strong "pagan base" as well and a model for frustrated love (Klemans 15, 13). Yet, readers soon note, the individual sonnets within the enveloping larger patterns of *Fatal Interview* are also connected by content. They demonstrate the emotional life of a woman speaker as she lives out the captured year, each sonnet representing some one moment of insight into a growing, then faltering, apparently extramarital, love affair.[6]

Within this combination of framing device and content, Millay evokes the modernist notion of the experience of time. Even as each sonnet offers a moment in the narrator's emotional life, a good number of them capture the struggle of that narrator to balance the demands of anticipation, memories of and references to the past, and her desire to have her love stabilized and graspable in the now—a now for which the individual sonnet stands as objective correlative. As an instance, sonnet VI finds the woman chiding her lover for his fascination with literary women of the past, whom she calls "buried girls." Looking forward in time, she then warns that he should prepare himself to call upon these same girls when he is old—"When you lie wasted and your blood runs thin"—while she would, by contrast, live in the moment and honor the "rude sea / Of passion pounding all day long" in her own veins. This is, in rather precise terms, the very model of the modernist notion of duration: imagined futures and recalled past balanced around the constant yearning to feel palpably alive, in between, in the now. All of this struggle is played out against the constant slipping away of each moment into the past and the rush of life itself toward a sure grave—what the Selene voice refers to as humankind's constant "hastening headlong to" its "dusty end" (I).

With almost existentialist fervor, these sonnets ever remind the reader that the single defining event in life is death. The lover is warned that years will "cover up our eyes" (XXXI), that time will make "veins" into "frosty channels" (XXVIII), that dawn is ever waiting to take her lover away (XXVII), that time brings its "gross decree" of loss to every meeting (XIV), that the love of two offers a defense against the "yelping" future years certain to attack one who is alone (XXXIX). Such warnings to command the moment root themselves deeply in ancient literatures. But, here, within the context of this turning cycle of observations lies, too, the modern model of the mind's play with each passing instant of consciousness. Each sonnet erects with words a balancing point for some brief attempt to grasp the meaning of an instant impinged upon by the demands of memory and the hope or dread associated with the future. Victorian thinking holds that the sonnet can stand as the moment's "monument."[7] Millay's sonnets stand as monuments to the very attempt of the mind to erect a stable insight of words, while experience seems ever to be slipping away. That is why doubt is such an enemy in this cycle—it corrupts the confidence that each moment can be erected and held fast. The Selene myth also adds credence since the framing first and last sonnets demonstrate that only mortals *can* feel love as it is being experienced by this narrator. Death must exist, as must language and the swift flow of endured time, for the love of which she speaks to acquire value. This love, this tortured but true affection, only has worth when measured against a flow of experiences, captured in language, verging toward certain loss. This love is as much a connection with the moment as with any other heart; it is an imaginative act within the fleeting moment that forges its identity.

Additionally, this fragile, human moment, sonnet X reminds, is a "stern" master. Even in the summer of adoration, allows sonnet XXXV, the mind at play possesses "winter" visions and reasons to doubt love's heartiness. Emotions themselves determine human experience of the moment. Doubt, time's accomplice (XXXIV), is at the ready to teach the blaspheming, painful truth that love cannot be trusted, even as the speaker protests her loyalty, hoping that with belief a hiatus in the steady process of loss might be erected and maintained. The moment of the lovers' first kiss holds seeds of their destruction, the "season-wise" narrator confesses. She can only hope for a "fairer summer and a later fall" than usually anticipated, but she cannot "defy the frost" (XLVI). The moment, too, can seem a "mournful" prison room against whose suffocating reality the lover's pulse beats mark the passing time's duration (XVIII). In each case, a central point being made is that time *is*, in fact, an experience the character of which is determined by the imaginative juggling act Bergson described: past and future connected through the imaginatively grasped now.

Notably, of the fifty-two sonnets in the group, only some half-dozen speak solely of the present; only seven, purely of the past or future. Over half (twenty-nine), though, connect the now with memories or anticipated future events. Eight refer to past, present, and future, linked. The present is, thus, portrayed here as a point of balance soon lost to changes in love, in experience, in time.[8]

## The Case for Millay

One returns to the original task: placing Millay's sonnets. As John Williams has suggested, in Millay's work the sonnet continues as a testing ground, adapting tradition to the clear and common voice of the new—in this case, championing an emotionally rendered and *felt* now. The fact that Millay captures as well as she does this theoretical rethinking of how humans actually live in time, without herself posing as a theorist, founds Millay's power. Like a palimpsest, her sonnets bear the etchings of the spirit of her intellectual milieu; as a group, they expose a latent print of the theoretical biases of her generation.

Consequently, I believe, Millay's accomplishment in these sonnets answers some questions that have been raised about her role in modern literature. In spite of critical tussles, it seems to me that the very nature of Millay's grasp of the now, of how the moment is assembled in and by consciousness, roots her *directly* in her age. The key element in this portrayal, ironically, is her relentless chronicling of human emotions. The same "sentimentality" that irks commentators who hunger to find in proper modernist poetry a cool distancing of poetic voice from physical realities—most certainly from those of the body—allows Millay to evoke the modernist feel of how time is known: by human consciousness; in sensual, needy, dying bodies. Millay brings theoretical time back to fleshy earth. In so doing, she, in effect, heals sterile theory. Millay narrates a passionate woman's actually having lived in the flow.

Thus, while debate over Millay's position among recognized modern feminist writers continues, regarding her speaking of time, at least, a case can be made for the legitimacy of her credentials. In her own way, Millay has matched what Cheryl Walker describes as the poet H.D.'s modernist revolt against the confines of masculine-centered, linear concepts of history (Walker, *Masks Outrageous and Austere* 109). Millay is perhaps the most dangerous kind of feminist subversive: the deep-cover agent, willingly accepted by the general public (her kitchen was featured in *Ladies' Home Journal* [Clark, "Unwarranted Discourse" 139]), all the while undermining its foundations—in this case the belief that time can be encountered outside the life of the emotions. French critic Julia Kristeva theorizes that, traditionally speaking, women's time might best be conceived of as lying between the extreme experiences of cycle (e.g., gestation) and eternity, the sense of being lost in one infinite, mythical moment

("Women's Time" 191). Millay's sonnets reconcile polarities, though, by showing time felt and lived in bursting moments, each a small eternity of its own. As a result, Millay is, perhaps, as Debra Fried has argued in larger terms, closer to T. S. Eliot, Ezra Pound, and other more traditionally accepted modernists "than we might initially suppose" ("Millay" 294). Millay evokes the modernist model for time and demands, all the while, like many feminists, that art honor connection, community, and relationship.

Cheryl Walker notes Millay is a poet "formed by her culture" (*Masks Outrageous and Austere* 164). Retreating from restrictions placed on women's lives and emotions in that culture, Millay, if only by default, assumes a feminist-modernist position for her era. While Millay may not speak as deeply as do more self-consciously feminist writers to the political issues of women's lives, Millay nonetheless links modernist and feminist camps in her sonnets by speaking emotionally about time. Again noting Walker's perceptive analyses, one must admit that later feminists have found limitations in Millay's documenting the life of the body. But, to paraphrase Suzanne Clark, I think one's judgment of Millay's feminism must be carefully made. One's conclusion will depend "on how we read her" (*Sentimental Modernism* 96)—from inside or outside her time, pun intended.

Finally, Millay's sonnets demand continuing attention for their reminding readers of the power of lyric—even within the fold of modernist vision. If a major element of poetry in Millay's age was a growing distrust of emotional language and an abandonment of traditional literary figures for attempts at pure image, Millay's work offers a bold reality check.[9] By embracing sonnets while remaining inescapably emotional, Millay revalues the lyrical as mood, all the while echoing the modernist notion of living in time's relentless current. The sonnets document how necessary it is to honor feeling within that model for experience. As Barbara Hardy writes, the lyric, historically and practically, does not aim to "provide an explanation, judgment or narrative. . . ." Lyric "creates and discovers feeling" (1). Composing lyrical, *modernist* sonnets, Edna St. Vincent Millay reminds students of the modern in art that even the "academic priesthood" (Clark, "Unwarranted Discourse" 141) must learn to live in bodies or lose their lives.

## Notes

My thanks to Barbara Black, Skidmore College, for her suggestion for a revised title; to Diane Freedman and K. McCormick Price, who made suggestions for my revising the essay.

1. For a discussion, see Jones, "Amatory Sonnet Sequences."

2. I have chosen to quote Bergson from the Sherover anthology because the collection offers such an excellent history of attitudes toward the experience of time, one I thought potentially useful to readers of this essay.

3. See, especially, section III of *Burnt Norton*.

4. See Duchamp's "Nude Descending a Staircase No. 2" and Giacomo Balla's "Dynamism of a Dog on a Leash," for example. Both paintings are from 1912. For a good brief commentary, see Hughes, *The Shock of the New*, chapter 1.

5. Klemans, " 'Being Born a Woman,' " provides an overview.

6. See Brittin, *Millay*; Jones, "Amatory Sonnet Sequences"; Klemans, " 'Being Born a Woman' "; and Montefiore, *Feminism and Poetry*, for helpful discussions of the group's structure.

7. See Rossetti's introduction to his *House of Life* series.

8. By contrast, reading through sonnets collected from Sidney, Spenser, Shakespeare, and Petrarch—the last, admittedly, in translation—in common university anthologies, I find that over half perch comfortably in some one grammatically steady place in time. The verses may lament loss or fear coming events but do not generally appear to be about the business of having to cobble together a believable moment from which to speak, before proceeding with their explications of thought. If this is the tradition from which Millay's sonnets, at root, spring, she has most certainly altered the tone of that tradition in her practice.

9. See Cox and Dyson's introduction to *Modern Poetry* for a concise history of the shifting moods within modern criticism of poetry. Their study provides an excellent guide to the essential trends in modernist poetics.

# 9 Vampirism and Translation
## Millay, Baudelaire, and the Erotics of Poetic Transfusion
### Marilyn May Lombardi

A covert vampirism underlies Edna St. Vincent Millay's response to the task of translation. Collaborating with George Dillon on his 1936 edition of Charles Baudelaire's *Flowers of Evil*, Millay writes a preface in which she insists that the process of translation is "as complicated as blood-transfusion" (xi). Developing her *topos* for translation—the imbibing of another poet's bodily fluids—Millay comments on Baudelaire's own evocations of the artist as parasite, sadist, and necrophiliac. Adapting Baudelaire's erotic tropes to describe her own enterprise as a consumer and transmuter of texts, Millay stages a psychosexual encounter with the most influential poet of modernity. This translator's preface speaks to Millay's position as a woman poet in the modernist era—an artist forced into endless efforts of absorption and transcription each time she approaches the inherited poetic corpus.

Calling the Baudelairean lyric a "cemetery flower," Millay promises to handle each poem as though it were something organic and subject to corruption (xxxiii). For Millay, the peculiarly French rhyme schemes, meters, and stresses that surround a Baudelaire work serve as a sonorous and sensuous envelope. Translation must inevitably inflict a "wound" on this fragile tissue of sense and sound. According to her graphic description of the translation process, the poem's original vitality is first drained away ("stripped bare to its bone"), and then the emptied vessel is infused with the foreign blood, or psychic force, of the translator who must "be able to fill the veins of the poem . . . with his [*sic*] own blood, and make the poem breathe again" (xiii). Millay demands that the translator preserve as faithfully as possible the body of the original verse, the outer sheath, the physical character of the poem on the page, even as s/he animates it with his own spirit. To do otherwise is to "betray the poem" with "brutal prose renderings" (vii, xii). Nevertheless, she acknowledges that even the most literal attempt to replicate French metrical verse in English will result in a free "adaptation" rather than a transcription (xxv). In the end, the original lyricism may be revived in body, but its spirit is no longer entirely its own. The French verse, "shipwrecked into English, and fitted out with borrowed clothes" (xxxiv), possessed by an alien will, rises again like the living dead.

Millay insists that literary transfusions of this kind are complicated because the donor's blood type (his language and sensibility) cannot be relied upon to match or sympathize with that of the recipient. Inspired no doubt by Baudelaire's own erotic imagination, Millay's preface stresses the delicacy of the operation, arguing that all too often translation may be likened to a sexual assault, a sadistic coupling of two incompatible personalities. Even under the best of circumstances, the two warring languages are "at each other's throats for weeks" (xxiv). Only "at rare intervals" do they reach a truce, and grow "suddenly mild and tractable" (xxiv). Typically, they remain at odds with one another, until the original work of art surrenders, the victim ultimately of a "pious rape" ("I will put Chaos into fourteen lines").

Millay's physicalized notion of translation may be seen as both the product of her immersion in Baudelaire's blood-soaked verse and a subtle response to literary modernism with its emphasis on the poet's role as a translator recuperating and resuturing a fragmented body of knowledge. Pound, we recall, used the figure of the translator as an analogue for his own enterprise as the reinvigorator of a moribund cultural past. *Canto I*, for instance, begins by associating the modern poet with Odysseus who poured sacrificial blood into the ground so that the lifeless shadow of the soothsayer Tiresias might drink and be revived to speak once more.[1] In *I Gather the Limbs of Osiris*, Pound sees his task as a gathering together of ancient texts, which, like the scattered limbs of the desecrated Egyptian god, must be infused with fresh virtu or life-force so that, in the words of James Logenbach, they may reappear in the present, "*blooded* by the imaginative vision of the poet" (116; emphasis added).

A fear of masculine incapacity hovers over Pound's adaptation of the Osiris myth. Linking his mission with that of Isis, who gathers the limbs of her dead husband, Pound obviates the need for women altogether by asserting his own artistic androgyny. In offering his own blood, or virtu, as a form of sacrificial libation, he proclaims himself to be a universal donor, one whose life-force speaks for all ages, transcending place, time, and gender. Yet, in practice, Pound is never a neutral conduit for history. Appropriating the past for his own purposes, he conceals the evidence of error and subjectivity that inevitably marks the process of translation. For Pound, the poet-translator's mission is to suffuse the debilitated culture with his own "potency," lending a new virility to a past demasculinized by the forces of prelogic and primitivism. In this way, the modernist poet defends his culture against the powers of chance and chaos unleashed by a host of female Furies, those age-old emblems of irrationality and desire.

When Millay set out to gather and revivify the lyrics of Baudelaire, she confronted Pound's modernist myth of translation in a strangely literal sense: Baudelaire's original title for *Les Fleurs du Mal* was, after all, *Les Limbs*. But Millay proved to be an idiosyncratic Isis, for she and her collaborator underscore their selectivity. Having gathered together only those poetic "limbs" for which they felt an affinity, Millay and Dillon end up translating only a fraction of Baudelaire's lyrics, leaving great rifts in the corpus. Thus, the panoramic and encyclopedic ambition of the modernist translator is not apparent in their production—and neither is Pound's celebration of the translator as martyr offering his lifeblood to recoup the past, a notion Millay apparently found untenable. As her sonnet "Not with libations, but with shouts and laughter" suggests, pouring one's blood upon the altar of vanished time cannot resurrect dead love and buried vitality.[2]

Contradicting the modernist ethos of translation, Millay points out in her preface to *The Flowers of Evil* that the translator almost always victimizes what she once sought to revitalize. Rather than conceal the potential intrusiveness of her task, Millay leaves the lingering impression that she could all too easily betray Baudelaire's original intent. In this way, she paints herself as something of a "femme damnée," the treacherous female succuba that haunted Baudelaire's *fin-de-siècle* culture. Her notion of the translator as ravisher evokes such Baudelairean fantasies as "Femmes Damnées Delphine et Hipployte," one of many works in which the poet pictures the meeting of two alien sensibilities as a predatory dance climaxing in a fanged kiss.

Given her violent vision of translation, it is not surprising that Millay appears troubled in her preface by the whole question of "sympathy" and the extent to which she can empathize, as a poet, a translator, and a woman, with Baudelaire's poetics. If their sensibilities prove incompatible, then there would be nothing to prevent a brutal violation of Baudelaire's prone and malleable text. Certainly, Millay knew (and knew how to exploit) the indignities of laying oneself and one's work open to unsympathetic attacks. In one well-known review by John Crowe Ransom, "Miss Millay" was accused of possessing a "womanly" mind that, being "less pliant, safer" than a man's, rarely stretches itself but instead "remains fixed in her famous attitudes" forever ("The Poet as Woman" 784). No doubt the review reveals (like a stake through the heart) just how blandly a woman writer could be "fixed" and pinioned by the cultural orthodoxies of her day—particularly when her poetry ventured so often into the scorned terrain of the personal and affectional.[3]

Millay must have been acutely sensitive to the power she might wield over a dead and translatable poet, since she was not averse herself to marketing her own vulnerability, or penetrability. She often portrayed both herself and her art as painfully dependent on the kindness of strangers—strangers who frequently appeared to her in vampiric guise. In fact, Millay invited her reading public to imbibe and devour her or, in Cheryl Walker's words, "to get the juice out of her poetry, to consume it (and her) in order to keep her spirit in circulation" (*Masks Outrageous and Austere* 143).[4] Millay embraced this brutal economy, promoting herself as an exquisitely anemic woman whose body, already bled by Life, would in the end leave Death with a meager diet. Everyone was called upon to witness, and even to participate in, Millay's beautiful wasting away:

> Grief of grief has *drained me clean*;
> Still it seems a pity
> No one saw,—it must have been
> Very pretty.
>
> ("Three Songs of Shattering"; emphasis added)

For those who had been following Millay's bohemian project since the appearance of *Renascence and Other Poems* in 1917, it became clear that the poetics of "burning one's candle at both ends" was inspired, at least in part, by the appetitive aesthetics of the French decadents. But Millay could not envision herself as the triumphant devourer of life, and her poetic self-studies inevitably convey an image of the artist as masochist rather than sadist. When vampiric *topoi* emerge in Millay's verse, her poetic persona is usually seen as either the blood-drained vessel or the victim compelled to drink life's sorrows to the lees. This stands in stark contrast to Baudelaire's vision of the male artist as predator or psychic parasite immobilizing and draining strength from the female objects of his attention. As a woman, Millay could not comfortably adopt a Baudelairean approach towards her subject matter, particularly when her own womanhood became the primary object of her poetic attention. If a woman writer were to fall in line with such an aesthetic, she would be forced to violate her own person.

In her preface to *The Flowers of Evil*, Millay is ever conscious of Baudelaire's blood-sucking tendencies and the connections he draws between sexual and artistic predation: "The efficacy of blood, of the sight of bleeding wounds, as a stimulus to sexual ardour, is often indicated and sometimes broadly developed in the poetry of Baudelaire" (xxviii). Her point is demonstrated by poems like "Metamorphosis of the Vampire," in which a vital, assertive woman is transformed into a desiccated pile of bones. At first, the poem's title character, a female succuba, appears as a substantial threat to her male lover's potency. But we soon find that the artist has offered this glimpse of the phallic woman only to indicate just how much vitality he will drain from her once he is able to draw the lifeblood of his art from her prone and enervated body. In the morning's light, this erstwhile lamia has shrunk to a loathsome skeleton, sucked dry. A similar shock awaits the reader in "A celle qui est trop gaie" ("A Girl Too Gay"), one of the poems that Millay draws our attention to in her preface as illustrations of Baudelaire's "cult of the wound." In this, Baudelaire's most explicit poem of sadistic sexuality, he dreams of carving "a deep seductive wound" upon the "perfect form" of his mistress (lines 31–32) and "through those bright novel lips, through this / Gaudy and virgin orifice" (lines 34–36) infuse her with his venom. This poisonous insemination will kill her, allowing him to expend his passion in necrophilia. In "Une Martyre" ("Murdered Woman"), when Baudelaire fantasizes about consummating his lust on a woman's "inert, obedient body" (line 47), he expresses a fear of his own destabilizing passion for the woman, his own emotionalism and penetrability. Using his art to skewer and capture this wayward woman, he reasserts the penetrating powers of his mind.

The image of the male artist as psychic parasite feeding off the energies of the women around him had become so fixed in the collective consciousness by the end of the nineteenth century that the "true artist" was understood to be lethal. Baudelaire may have been introduced to the vampire as a metaphor for artistic consumption and consummation when he translated Edgar Allan Poe's fiction into French. D. H. Lawrence will later tease out the various layers of meaning that Poe attaches to "vamping": "The desirous consciousness, the SPIRIT, is a vampire, [for] to try to *know* any living being is to try to suck the life out of that being" (Lawrence 335). The consumptive woman of Poe's imagination is "the passive body who is explored and analyzed into death" by the probing mind of the male artist (336). Lawrence argues that the masculine longing to "know" or to consume inevitably saps energy from the beloved, but it is also safe to say that the beloved is finally pacified by her lover's insistence that she remain only a convenient "thing" to be known and digested. Leo Bersani locates at the heart of Baudelaire's poetics a similar need to pacify, or de-fang, the "thing that he loves":

> Ultimately, there is perhaps only one escape from the hell of insatiable desire; the forced and permanent immobilizing of the desiring woman, that is, murder. . . . To a certain extent, necrophilia is the Baudelairean erotic ideal; it is sex with an absolutely still partner who, at the extreme, may even be devoured. (69–70)

According to Bersani, the misogyny in Baudelaire stems from the poet's fear of his own desiring self—his fear, that is, of the woman within. After all, Baudelaire defined the male artist as a "sacred prostitute," open and receptive to wounding experience. Baudelaire resorts to murderous fantasies in a "panicky effort to reject the feminine side of his own sexual identity" (66).[5]

Even this brief rehearsal of Baudelaire's eroticized poetics is sufficient to raise a crucial question for our reading of Millay's translations: was it possible for Millay to "sympathize" unequivocally with the poetic ideals of her French master, based as they were on an image of the artist as rapist and psychic interloper? If we look backwards through even her earliest poetry, we find that Millay continually tested the limits of her sympathy. She would become famous, in fact, for a poem that wrestled with precisely this issue: To what extent must a woman writer cultivate empathy and selflessness at the expense of critical penetration and accede to the cultural injunctions of her age? In "Renascence," the poet's efforts to critically "probe" the Universe rebound against her as the weight of vast Infinity presses down on her, bending back her arm upon her breast. The image is strangely reminiscent of another found in Baudelaire's "Remords Posthume," a title Millay translates as "Remorse Too Late" (*Flowers of Evil* 26–27). Baudelaire's speaker reminds his untamed lover that one day she must feel the "oppressive stone" of the tomb "upon [her] frightened breast" (line 5) when death bends down and binds her feet, once "so roving, so unwise" (line 8). In both poems, Infinity or Death restrains a "girl too gay," too inviolable, too mobile for love to leave its mark. In Millay's translation of the Baudelaire lyric, the woman is imaginatively immobilized, her heart gnawed by remorse for having "no warm memories of true love to keep" (line 13). The unsympathetic or unyielding woman is punished in both "Renascence" and "Remorse Too Late" for having lived impervious to love, for having sunk her teeth in life without feeling its bite in return.

The heroine of "Renascence" is transgressive both because she refuses to sacrifice herself to love and because she uses her critical intelligence to expand the boundaries of her knowledge ("cleaving" the Universe to the Core and laying it open to her "probing sense" [line 49]). She dares to challenge the male monopoly on penetration. But the Universe and Infinity bar her ascension, and the world violently impresses its law on her body and soul. As a woman, she must expand not her critical but her affective faculties, since sentimentality is her "natural" medium. Paying for her audacious exploration of the Universe with an "infinite remorse of soul" (line 56), a phrase that echoes Baudelaire's "remorse too late," she must "suck / At the great wound, and could not pluck" her lips away till she had "drawn / All venom out . . ." (lines 51–54). Rather than carve her deep mark on the Universe, she must absorb its pain, and serve as the compassionate "rod" (line 81), the conductor, the conduit, the bearer of all human suffering. Only with a soul fed on the carrion comfort of remorse and with a heart swollen with empathy can a woman hope to keep the sky from caving in on her by and by.

In "Renascence," then, Millay's poetic persona becomes a strangely hobbled vampire, one that inflicts no wounding kiss on the world, but instead, ingests its poison like a medicinal leech, or selfless martyr. Millay's ravished persona undergoes a significant transformation, however, when she takes on the "heady and exhilarating task" (preface v) of translation. Millay's preface delights in pointing out the opportunities for aggression and dominance implicit in her new position as translator. And in her renditions of Baudelaire's verse, it is apparent that she withholds her complete sympathy from his poetic project. For one thing, she personalizes his faceless (even "headless") women, breathing new life into these bruised flowers. In this way, Millay the translator effectively reverses the dynamic of power so often reinforced in her own verse. While she imagines herself objectified, brutalized, and enervated within the boundaries of her own poetry, as a translator she finds herself capable of objectifying, even violating, the body of Baudelaire. Under Millay's gaze, Baudelaire's "limbs" are rendered as "mild and tractable" as those of a ravished woman. Exploiting her new position, Millay refashions herself as a Baudelairean lamia, "a beast of prey / Who seemed to have replenished her arteries" ("Metamorphosis of the Vampire," lines 22–23) at the expense of her host.

Millay's translations offer her the unique opportunity to "consummate her lust" on the "inert, obedient body" of Baudelaire's art. Her rendering of "Une Martyre," another example of the French poet's "cult of the wound," is a case in point. The poem focuses on the raped and headless corpse of a woman, a grotesque body that is nevertheless arranged provocatively, becoming the object of a succession of gazes. The woman's torso is posed on a settee whose white pillows lap up the blood from the severed head. The poem's subtitle tells us that this central image is inspired by a drawing of an unknown master who has mastered, to be sure, both the ravished woman and the art of titillation. Within the poem (itself a verse translation of a drawing), the reader's gaze is directed to a painting of a naked woman that hangs behind the murder victim; the pose of the painted nude exactly replicates that of the ravished corpse below. The poem is thus the last in a long line of commodifications, making the painterly tradition of the nude a vehicle for Baudelairean irony.

By presenting himself as a voyeur—a surrogate for the reader/viewer—the poet compels his audience to identify not only with the necrophiliac and the sadist. Like the speaker, the presumably male reader is meant to be aroused both sexually and aesthetically by the idea of a decapitated woman—a woman, that is, whose mind is no longer an obstacle to masculine satisfaction and whose pudendum, or "secrète splendeur" (line 23), is made permanently available. The first indication that Millay's translation of this poem will be one of her less self-effacing "adaptations" is given in the English title she has chosen for the work. Rather than retain Baudelaire's original "Une Martyre," with its implication of blood sacrifice in the name of some higher purpose, Millay desanctifies the violence by renaming the poem "Murdered Woman" (*Flowers of Evil* 205). In Millay's version, the "headless trunk . . . in loose abandon lies, / Its secret parts exposed, its treasures all outspread / As if to charm a lover's eyes" (lines 21–24). Millay stresses the woman's helpless subjection to "exposure," while Richard Howard's translation of the same lines, by contrast, underscores and even intensifies the callousness implicit in Baudelaire's lines. Rendering "la secrète splendeur" as "the splendid cynosure" (line 23), Howard further etherealizes Baudelaire's image, transforming a woman's wounded "parts" into an artist's guiding star.

Choosing to add her own phrases of commiseration ("ah, poor child," "mysterious unfortunate" [lines 44, 56]) to Baudelaire's colder dissections, Millay conveys the ambiguity of her position as a female artist estranged from the poem's male interlocutor. Millay's "poor child" is Howard's "lovely enigma" (line 55), while Baudelaire remains conspicuously silent on the subject. Ultimately, Millay's emphasis on the "exposure" of the corpse to the public gaze, both complicates and enhances the irony of the poem's parting prayer:

> Far from the mocking world, the peering crowd, oh far
> From inquest, coroner, magistrate,
> Sleep, sleep in peace; I leave you as you are,
> Mysterious unfortunate.
>
> (lines 53–56)

The exhibitional nature of the dead woman's afterlife guarantees, of course, that she will be subjected forever to the prying eyes of "the crowd." Millay, a victim of exposure (or overexposure) herself, could not help but view the beleaguered corpse with a private sense of outrage capable of affecting her translation. Sure enough, she interjects a wholly fabricated image into her rendering of the poem—an image with no equivalent in the original French that proposes a new motive for the crime of ravishment. Millay seems to suggest that the woman was murdered by her lover because he feared her lamia-like powers: even in death, her "whole form [was] / Lithe as a teased and fighting snake" (lines 39–40). While her torso lies vanquished in Howard's version of "A Martyr," the murdered succuba of Millay's imagination still writhes, struggling even now against the masculine gaze.

When Millay translates Baudelaire, she liberates the "teased and fighting snake" of female sensibility by bringing out into the open the emotionalism latent in the original poem. Suzanne Clark has shown how Millay reinjects the female into Baudelaire's depersonalized poetry, making it more accessible to a readership familiar with the sentimental tradition. As in her version of "The Owls," Millay consistently unveils the "lovely face" behind Baudelaire's "ombre" or passing shadow. Her own face emerges from behind the protective scrim of her role as translator, revealing a mobile and disruptive mind at odds with the French poet's aesthetic and erotic ideals. Time and again, the Baudelairean protagonist conceives of his task as the verbal equivalent to pacification: he asserts his will over recalcitrant material so that the poem emerges as a haven of quiet, meditative calm that has triumphed over restless, tortuous desire. If only the world would behave like a murdered woman, lying absolutely still, arousing none of the passionate agitations that drain the poet's strength. Craving the wise passivity of his petrified owls that "shun all action, all surprise" (line 10), Baudelaire recognizes in the "girl too gay" an enemy to his peace, an emblem of devouring Time and uncontrollable Nature.

It was Baudelaire's unobtainable dream to impose his will on Nature's inert form, wresting from the world an "artificial paradise." Ironically, after his death, Baudelaire's poetry lay defenseless under the gaze of a succession of translators, each viewing it as Baudelaire himself once viewed a woman's dense tresses: ". . . the dark gourd / Whereof I drink in long slow draughts the wine of dreams" ("The Fleece," lines 34–35). Millay found much in Baudelaire that spoke to her own private fantasies, and she came to his verse the way a Baudelairean lover might approach his mistress's body. For her, the French poet's "slow, rich, *mouth-filling* lines" (Millay, letter to Dillon 11; emphasis added), as she called them, became "the wine of dreams" from which she could draw her own sustenance.

Still, Millay was always conscious of the petrifying effect her gaze might have on Baudelaire's work. She complained that her own translations, set beside the efforts of George Dillon, "seemed so set, so *there*, so inert . . ." (Millay, letter to Dillon 11). The comment opens a window onto her feelings about the goals and purposes of art. She insisted that translation retain the "sonority and sensuousness," the flexibility and movement, of the original verse, and she rejected lines that struck her as too fixed or too "glib" (Millay, letter to Dillon 11). This same aversion to the immobilization or calcification of the "sweet," restless rhythms of a dead poet's verse must have influenced her in more ways than one when it came time to "fill the veins" of a Baudelaire poem with her own blood "and make the poem breathe again" (Preface, *Flowers of Evil* xiii). She could not help but notice how often Baudelaire violated or etherealized the physical reality of women's lives. The task of translation offered Millay a chance to exercise what she once called her "masterful and cruel imagination" (*Letters*, 1952, 22). Under her gaze, Baudelaire's poetry "lies, / Its secret parts exposed, its treasures all outspread / As if to charm a lover's eyes." Using her "womanly mind," "Miss" Millay lovingly drained and devoured the father of modernity.

## Notes

1. For a fine discussion of Pound as historian-translator, see Longenbach, *Modernist Poetics*, particularly chapter 5, "*Three Cantos* and the War Against Philology," 96–130.

2. See Fried, "Andromeda," for a discussion of Millay's "revisionary force as a woman poet" working with traditional forms in an age of free verse. Fried's reading of "Not with libations, but with shouts and laughter" focuses on the sonnet's central image of futile blood-libation.

3. For a lively account of Millay's "communal understanding" in an age that rejected the power and value of sentimentalism, see Clark, "*Jouissance* and the Sentimental Daughter: Edna St. Vincent Millay," chapter 3 of *Sentimental Modernism*, 66–96.

4. My focus on the covert vampirism in Millay's work supplements Walker's interest in "the drama of consumption" operating in the poet's "controlled exposure and packaging" of her own body for the marketplace. See "Woman on the Market: Edna St. Vincent Millay's Body Language," chapter 6 of *Masks Outrageous and Austere*, 135–96. See also Stanbrough, "Language of Vulnerability."

5. See Bersani, *Baudelaire and Freud*, especially chapter 7, "Desire and Death," 67–89, where he locates the parallels between Baudelaire's poetic and erotic ideals.

Part IV    *Millay's Drama
of Impersonation*

# 10 *"I Could Do a Woman Better Than That"*
## Masquerade in Millay's Potboilers
### Deborah Woodard

In May of 1924, midway through her honeymoon cruise, Edna St. Vincent Millay took time to scribble a quick blurb for a fellow writer, Nancy Boyd, whose satiric writings were being brought out by Harper's under the title of *Distressing Dialogues*:

Miss Boyd has asked me to write a preface to these dialogues, with which, having followed them eagerly as they appeared from time to time in the pages of *Vanity Fair*, I was already familiar. I am no friend of prefaces, but if there must be one to this book, it should come from me, who was its author's earliest admirer. I take pleasure in commending to the public these excellent small satires, from the pen of one in whose work I have a never-failing interest and delight. (vii)

Millay had good reason to be conversant with Miss Boyd's career. Nancy Boyd was her pseudonym, and she had labored so long over Boyd's witticisms that she could reel off many of the tales by heart. But if *Distressing Dialogues* paid tongue-in-cheek homage to her alter ego, it also signaled the close of Nancy's tenure. Millay's preface was, in fact, a sort of "Dear Nancy" letter; marriage and increasing poetic acclaim had ensured for Millay a climate of relative financial security, and so her money-grubbing alias was mothballed.

Nancy Boyd's exit signals the concomitant loss of much of the playful theatricality that characterized the first phase of Millay's career and abetted her immense popularity. Later on, both these theatrical affinities and her large reading public would render Millay suspect, providing the New Critics with fuel for her literary undoing. But perhaps their most telling indictment of her poetry was that it was not substantial; its theatrical indulgences rendered it an irremediably feminine product, devoid of "serious" engagement with ideas. In "The Poet as Woman," John Crowe Ransom defined Millay as the quintessential woman poet, declaring of the woman poet and of Millay at one and the same time:

Less pliant, safer as a biological organism, she remains fixed in her famous attitudes, and is indifferent to intellectuality. I mean, of course, comparatively indifferent; more so than a man. Miss Millay is rarely and barely very intellectual, and I think everybody knows it. (78)

Ransom's "everybody knows it" strikes a note of triumph. Millay's limitations are integrally linked to gender, to what one can in the first place "reasonably" expect from the poet as woman. Millay herself was certainly not oblivious to this charge. She adopted a "discreet" mode of self- defense, establishing—albeit idiosyncratically and intermittently—her own code of aesthetic ethics, which ironically seemed to second Ransom's judgment upon herself and "women." Thus, for example, when she collected her sauciest feminist verses in a chapbook entitled *A Few Figs from Thistles*, her idea was to winnow out her light verse, saving her "heavyweight" poetry for her second full-length collection, *Second April*. This strategy backfired rather badly, however, for *A Few Figs* proved an overnight sensation; it seemed the public could not get enough of Millay's "bad girl" persona.

Nancy Boyd was likewise invented to preserve canonical proprieties. But in retrospect, it seems clear that no alter ego, however cunningly employed, could have shielded Millay from charges of artistic trivialization. Such charges went along with the (gendered) territory. What makes Nancy Boyd worth reconsidering, I would suggest, is precisely her illegitimate status. Through Boyd, Millay could foreground the construction of woman and woman artist in ways that reflect back upon her own precarious positioning as "representative" woman poet. As we shall see, Nancy Boyd functioned both as an outlet for "improper" musings and as a foil against their getting too far out of hand.

Nancy Boyd was the brainchild of *Ainslee's* magazine editor, W. Adolph Roberts. A great fan of Millay—and reputedly one of her suitors—Roberts wanted to pay the young poet more than the publication of her verse alone made possible. Even potentially immortal lyrics (Millay's supporters believed she was producing nothing less) were poorly reimbursed compared to the potboiler romances that were *Ainslee's* mainstay. And so, Nancy Boyd, willing accomplice and alter ego and indefatigable scribbler of potboilers, made her entrance. From mid-1918 to 1921, *Ainslee's* readers continued to be regaled by Millay's poetry—alternately elegiac and daringly advanced in its views on the post–World War I "new" woman—but once they had digested this snippet of Miss Millay's "authentic" art, they could relax with Nancy's latest prose confection.

Nancy's initial efforts were, indeed, standard filler that faithfully reinscribed the codes of potboiler romances. Their plot runs something as follows: an ostensibly bold and Bohemian young woman falls in love with a sensitive, self-sacrificing, and likewise artistic young man who, discerning her essential fragility, is given to proposals of marriage and exclamations of "Oh, my poor child!" Boyd thus manages to start with the vaguely risque and conclude with the overwhelmingly sentimental.

"Mr. Dallas Larabee, Sinner" puts a more subversive spin on this saga, however.[1] It features another young innocent, Keane Sailor, whose name presumably denotes her yen for experience. In the course of one of her aunt's interminable teas, Keane meets the worldly wise Sophie de Witt who informs her that she is "an extremely handsome woman" (82). Once the role of woman is proposed to her, she quickly begins to pull together the accoutrements of the part. Before long, Keane—who yearns to do "one unconventional thing, and by it be delivered forever from the restraint of propriety" (85)—appears in the doorway of Mr. Dallas Larabee's apartment, dressed to the teeth in one of Sophie's gowns and trying very hard to look the femme fatale: "Before him stood a very beautiful woman, with smoldering red-brown eyes, a great deal of gold-colored hair piled high upon her head, and a slightly parted, perfect scarlet mouth, through which the breath came quickly" (84).

In contrast to the heroines of the earlier stories, whose femininity is presented as innate, it is clear that Keane Sailor's womanliness has been worked up for the occasion. In fact, Larabee, one of Sophie de Witt's erstwhile paramours, recognizes some of the props:

Dallas Larabee knew the gown, he was sure of that. . . . Curious that he should remember the gown so much more distinctly than the girl! Well, he had an increasingly bad memory for faces, that was the truth of it. (84)

But clothes do not (completely) make the woman, and when Keane denies being "a beautiful child" (86), the worldly "sinner" Mr. Larabee knows immediately that is just what she is. Having unmasked her as a "poor child," Dallas promptly falls in love with her. As incipient woman—looking the part at the same time as her actions deny it—she is irresistible. Yet by the time Larabee eventually proposes (" 'Take me,' he begged. 'I'm awfully eligible' " [89]), Boyd hints that, realizing its potential as a role, Keane has begun to exploit her own youthful naïveté. Her aunt has, after all, promised not to send her back to Wichita if she makes a brilliant marriage. Keane's final gesture, the little bright sweet smile to which Larabee has previously shown himself susceptible, seems manufactured, though few of *Ainslee's* readers were likely to view it in that light.

The parody of the "sweet young thing" implicit in "Mr. Dallas Larabee, Sinner" is stunningly overt in "The White Peacock," a story that we might view as an urtext for Boyd's "post-potboiler" productions. Of all the *Ainslee's* pieces, it presents by far the most radical depiction of womanhood/identity as construct and most devastatingly undermines romance plot givens. In "The White Peacock," moreover, style echoes content, becoming increasingly parodic. The heroine's name, for starters, is Antoinette Devilfish-Moonflower du Forêt. She is the daughter of a Chinese princess and a Frenchman—who was himself the offspring of a French millionaire and a geisha. Sent to America to attend a Quaker school by her now-deceased father who feared for her "so strange soul" (100) nourished on at least three religions and four cultures, she lives (as her suitor John Bailey discovers) surrounded by a formidable array of signifiers:

John Bailey's eyes traveled about the great room, taking in the paper *shoji* which screened off the door to his hostess's kitchenette and bath, the sandalwood chest, the little teakwood table with its inkstone, writing paper, and brush, the toilet case on the floor—a round mirror of polished brass, supported by a tiny easel with lacquered legs—the intricately carved cabinet, on which squatted a large Buddha with a Roman Catholic rosary hanging from his neck. (99)

The description pokes fun at the 1920s' penchant for Orientalisms— a vogue in which Millay participated—but it is also clearly a reflection of 'Toinette herself as a pastiche, a subject propped up by the bric-a-brac of various mythologies. She calls herself, in fact, a hybrid or "hash," thereby highlighting the arbitrariness of her "essential" nature and hinting at the paucity of existing categories of woman.

In the time-honored tradition of his *Ainslee's* predecessors, Bailey longs only to unveil the sweet young thing that lurks beneath his beloved's show of machisma. Aligning himself with her father, he beseeches 'Toinette to cut herself free from the flotsam and jetsam of her exotic heritage: "These candles and gods and crucifixes and litanies, and—and *spells*. . . . You wouldn't need them, dear. You wouldn't have to worship so much if you'd only let yourself love a little" (100). For 'Toinette, the issue is indeed one of idolatry versus love. As Bailey eventually discovers, his real rival is a tapestry of a white peacock she keeps concealed behind a screen in her bedroom:

Covering the wall was an immense Chinese embroidery: on a black ground shot with threads of gold, a white peacock, with a sensuous, languid body, and a cruel head, on which sat like a crown a fan-shaped jeweled aigrette, and from which winked and leered a slanting, ruby eye. (101–2)

Earlier, 'Toinette has told Bailey of a white peacock in the courtyard of her Chinese mother's palace in Canton that " 'I feared, and ran from, and loved, and followed. He died' " (100). A representation of that peacock, the tapestry is, like 'Toinette—and like her story— overwrought, pure artifice, maybe even a little absurd. In a sense, 'Toinette has transformed the peacock into a dissociated, narcissistic version of self, one that is both languid and sensuous ("feminine") and cruelly powerful or phallic. This mode of self-presentation allows her to play out her fantasies of abasement and dominance— to be simultaneously the daughter of a purveyor of female power (the princess) and the granddaughter of a representative of female erotic servitude (the geisha).

Although he spares himself such ruminations, the right-thinking, single-minded Bailey finds the peacock repulsive. He storms out of the apartment, and when he returns (drawn thither by the force of his passion), it is to find 'Toinette lying prostrate before the tapestry in the throes of orgasm:

> At first sight, she seemed to have fainted. But as he looked at her, a sudden shudder passed over her from head to foot, then another, and then for a moment her whole slender body vibrated delicately, like a string which gives forth tone. . . . Her eyes, over whose blackness there seemed to have been drawn a film of mist, stared up at him without recognition or interest. Her face was deathly white, her lips open. Only her nostrils appeared to be still alive. (102)

His fighting spirit roused by this spectacle of tapestry-induced auto-necrophilia, Bailey tears the tapestry peacock from the wall and burns it, consigning his odd rival to the flames. He then makes love to 'Toinette. She displays the "appropriate" emotions and all seems well. But when Bailey returns the next morning, he finds her shaking a statue of Saint Anthony, exhorting it to restore her peacock. 'Toinette brusquely informs Bailey that she can never love him: " 'Last night—poof! What was it? A man and a woman in each other's arms! Sweet, yes—perhaps you call ecstasy, but, la! not rare!' " (104). To underscore her point, 'Toinette uncovers the brass bowl she holds in her arms, revealing to her stunned lover the ashes of the white peacock. This apparently *is* rare.

Why has Bailey failed? Perhaps he himself is not sufficiently a hybrid or hash, or—equally damning—is oblivious to any status he may have as such. Telling him that she would love him wholly if he were *three* men, 'Toinette bids him adieu with the wish that " 'thee find for thyself soon a lovely lady with yellow hair, that is but one lady always, and does not change at all!' " (103). Such a lady would be the "authentic" heroine into whom Bailey thought he could remake 'Toinette. For 'Toinette, only the peacock (her mirror and the elusive "other" she adores) can sustain her proliferating selves.

Despite her manifest improbability, 'Toinette is the most memorable of Boyd's *Ainslee's* heroines. This creature who can leapfrog from mood to mood—and intertwine the elegiac with the droll—has a great advantage: belonging to nothing, she can appropriate everything. (She will, for example, reward Saint Anthony for the restoration of the peacock with incense stolen from the Buddha.) We might say she articulates the multiple possibilities available to the woman artist, whose literary heritage is, like 'Toinette's family tree, " '*quel mélange*' " (99). And yet, fluid identity seems a mixed blessing, for the cult of the white peacock underlies our heroine's élan. Fetishistic bondage is the price of her liberation, and consequently, 'Toinette comes across as a little dead-ended, trapped in the arias of a solipsistic grand opera.

'Toinette points to the dangers inherent in any performance that may be read from without as self-aggrandizing narcissism. Millay shared with 'Toinette a flair for the theatrical, and her work would eventually be tagged as both retrograde and grotesquely "excessive." Reviewing her *Collected Poems* in 1957, Karl Shapiro conjures up the suspect figure of the actress/seductress: "The poems have an intimacy which makes the reader recoil, even if he is susceptible to this flirtation. What is worse, it is the intimacy of the actress and (off-stage) the *femme fatale*" (13). In a more recent appraisal, Elizabeth Frank finds Millay's persona of the Girl to be a carefully contrived vehicle for self-pity and emotional indulgence, one that is "all so staged, so visible, so temporary . . . " (134).

For Millay, keeping gender and the body in plain view meant constant judgment as poet *and* woman: Ransom's poet-as-woman. Reveling as they do in the staged, the visible, and the temporary, 'Toinette's histrionics both raise the ante on these charges and point to a quandary. Millay's gesture in writing "The White Peacock" might be translated like this: call me the poet-as-woman, and I'll give you "woman" with a vengeance. However, in venting her spleen, she ran the risk of endangering her own candidacy for "major poet." Finally, Millay's own ambivalence toward "woman" must be factored in. She did not want Edna St. Vincent Millay confused with Nancy Boyd; she did not want to make a "hash" of her preferred identity. And yet, even relocation to the more modish and better-paying *Vanity Fair*—a move facilitated by another of Millay's beaus, Edmund Wilson—would not serve, as we shall see, to banish "woman" nor to muffle the irrepressible Miss Boyd.

Nancy Boyd's *Vanity Fair* satires, later reprinted in *Distressing Dialogues*, reiterate the problem of woman as self-constructed artifact. If Boyd deconstructed the bildungsroman of the sweet young thing in the *Ainslee's* stories, her *Vanity Fair* pieces survey the rubble of the romance plot, often abandoning even parodic narrative for a still more fragmentary mode of presentation. Many of the sketches take the form of playlets in which the deliberately overblown stage directions threaten to suffocate the dialogue proper. In "Powder, Rouge and Lip-stick," for example, we meet Robert Avery-Thompson, who is "subject to recurrent attacks of acute idealism" (111), and his wife, Gwendolyn, whom (as the stage directions indicate) he has just accused of using too much makeup:

Silence falls again like a shawl over a parrot cage. Mrs. Avery-Thompson, under the impression that her countenance has become distorted with passion, proceeds to make up all over again. Having squeezed some cold-cream from a tube out upon a many-coloured cloth, with one sweep of the hand, and rather in the manner of a painter scraping his palette-knife across a finished canvas, she destroys the whole effect. Then she begins. She carefully removes all traces of the cold-cream, and applies another kind of cream, which smells of camphor. This she manipulates softly about her chin and the corners of her eyes. Having as carefully removed all traces of this, she dabs her forehead, cheeks and chin with a linen cloth soaked in rose-water, and for the ensuing two minutes sits blandly at ease, doing nothing at all, allowing this to dry. (115)

Gwendolyn's self-construction is fairly obvious, and of course it reflects back upon *Vanity Fair* as a toney woman's magazine. Boyd is gently satirizing her host medium. But the humor becomes more trenchant when Gwendolyn finally promises her husband to abstain from face paint and, true to her word, presents quite another picture on the eve of their next engagement:

*He* [. . .]: Gwen, for Heaven's sake, what have you been doing to yourself?
*She* [*modestly, with awkward, purplish hands smoothing down her magnificent black and silver evening gown, above which rises a rather boyish neck, sunburned into a V, a fairly well-shaped but sallow face with a pale mouth, a pink and gleaming nose, and no eyebrows whatsoever, from which in turn recedes honestly a flat surface of straight and sand-colored hair*]: Nothing

at all, dear. That's just it. I'm my own sweet, simple, natural, girlish self. (120–21)

The Avery-Thompsons play their final scene "in the accepted manner" (121), but the freshly made-up Gwendolyn deals one final jab when she forces her husband to adopt the baby talk that he has routinely coerced from her:

*She:* Mind the paint! [*She whispers in his ear.*] Whose little girl am I now?
*He* [*ruefully, and in a low voice, snuggling his head upon her shoulder*]: Bobby'th. (122)

As we can see, these pieces approach the slapstick (they appeared in a section of the magazine entitled "Literary Hors D'Oeuvres"), but even as she jokes, Boyd implies that the transgressive pleasure of histrionic display masks a potential violence against the self. Two concepts are relevant to why this is so. First, Boyd's character, Gwendolyn, takes on the part of woman. In other words, she engages in that ambiguous mode of self-presentation that Freud's translator and colleague, Joan Riviere, termed masquerade. In her landmark 1929 article, "Womanliness as a Masquerade," Riviere unfolds the case history of a professionally successful woman who indulges in "inappropriate" flirtations with her male listeners. She does so, Riviere argues, in order to allay the castration anxieties her "masculine performance" provokes.[2] At the heart of the essay is Riviere's refusal to make any distinction between "genuine womanliness" and the masquerade. The bepainted Gwendolyn, whose girlish behavior and appearance are skillfully achieved and crucial to conjugal harmony, makes the same refusal. The second concept exemplified by this playlet is Luce Irigaray's more recent notion of mimicry as a provisional tactic "in which the woman deliberately assumes the feminine style and posture assigned to her within this discourse in order to uncover the mechanisms by which it exploits her" (220). Gwendolyn's performance has all the excessive hallmarks of such a strategy, but despite *consciously* purveying "woman," she nonetheless confines herself to the wearying cyclicity of a redundant burlesque. For the woman writer, such as Millay, a further question arises. If the role of woman itself entails a performance on demand, will the woman artist, who has a different sort of self-creation in mind, get a head start or inhabit a house divided?

This is a question Nancy Boyd openly considers. For instance, in "Madame a Tort!," a sculptor—once wholly absorbed in her work to the exclusion of all else—relates the one circumstance that she believes has kept her from artistic greatness. She recalls how, during the course of a sojourn in Paris, a blue-eyed woman in a mink coat "slipped into my palm one day the address of a beauty-parlor in the rue de Rivoli, and left me, smiling . . ." (163). The wares of this glamorous promoter (and promoter of glamour) are initially of little interest to the narrator, who, left to her own devices, is the least narcissistic of creatures. But finding herself in need of a quick, no-nonsense haircut, the one hygienic procedure to which she cannot attend herself, the narrator eventually drops in at the salon. Here she is met by a second emissary:

A black-eyed man with a small waist and smelling of violets appeared before me, wringing his hands. He placed a chair at my back and bowed me into it. Deftly but not without tenderness he wrapped me in a large white apron and tucked a towel into my collar. (165).

Thus confined, the narrator becomes the alarmed, but increasingly benumbed, recipient of a series of torturously complex beauty procedures, none of which she has requested. Whenever she protests, she is told simply, "Madame a tort!" (Madam is mistaken). Eventually she falls mute, unable to combat the battalion of androgynous, be-scented workers (the sexless minions of an absent sovereign?) who labor over her "as if I had been a half finished bust" (166).

This makeover—this creation of woman as an *objet d'art*—is clearly a violation, a rape: "I was helpless in his hands. I dared not move, for fear I should be branded. I sat fearfully still, and let him have his way" (171). It also takes on something of the flavor of an inquisition: "The odor of violets was all about me. A comb was being drawn through my hair savagely. Over an intense gas flame high up on the wall two pairs of curling-tongs were glowing red" (170). But what is she supposed to confess? That she was wrong to refuse the role of aesthetic object and her own potential for pleasure in the part? Whatever the answer, it is clear the violet-scented forces about her have had their way with her. Androgynous creatures combining patriarchal violence with a subtle appreciation of all things feminine, they compel her to envision her previously repressed aptitude for the masquerade.

The final step of this violation is the narrator's participation in her own redoing. When she wakes up back at her hotel, she discovers that the salon has delivered a hefty parcel, the bill for which has been automatically paid at the desk and added to her account. In a gesture of tacit surrender, she unwraps the articles and arranges them about her room. Finished, she catches sight of her own reflection in the glass: "No, there was no mistake. I was beautiful" (173). From that moment on, she is a convert—and a slave to the manifold rituals of her toilette. Occasionally, she feels a passing twinge of regret for her old life of sculpting and travel, but she has been relentlessly seduced into accepting a paralyzing regime of narcissistic self-creation which "holds its own bitter struggle" (174).

Nancy Boyd further explores the vicissitudes of the female artist in "The Implacable Aphrodite"—one of the *Distressing Dialogues* that is actually a dialogue, or playlet. In it, we meet "Miss Black, a graceful sculptress" who is serving nine o'clock tea (presumably this is the proper Bohemian tea hour) to Mr. White, "a man of parts, but badly assembled" (41). Throughout much of the script, Miss Black appears to be a consummate seductress, winning over the much-besought Mr. White through her apparent valorization of art over romance:

> *He* [*continuing*]: You have such an intrepid mind, I feel, so unblenched a vision. The petty concerns that make up the lives of other people, they are not your life. You see beyond their little disputes, their little aspirations, their little loves, into a world, a cosmos, where men and women can understand each other, can help each other, where the barriers of sex are like a mist in the air, dissipated with the dawn.
> *She* [*cosmically*]: It is true that for me there are no barriers. (42)

Not only does Miss Black's vocation lend her a mystique of transcendence, it serves to eroticize her as well. Soon one of her sculptures, a reclining nymph, catches Mr. White's eye: "Such subtle lines, such exquisite proportions. Who is she?" (43). Miss Black identifies her as Daphne fallen, but it turns out that Mr. White's primary interest is the model—the original of these enticing contours. After a stage direction for "an appreciable pause," Miss Black explains: "Why, you see, I *have* no model. They are difficult to get, and they are mostly so bad. I—am my own model. You notice the two long mirrors?—I place the stand between them, and work from my reflections" (44). Miss Black has collapsed the boundaries between viewer and object of the gaze, between artist and woman—boundaries that Mr. White has taken for granted and that, as we recall, her colleague in "Madame a Tort!" was unable to broach. If we are reading the sketch as a seduction, however, her achievement is reduced to a mere ploy, and the figure of the nymph seems planted, as though it has been deliberately left lying about to excite male libidos. Viewed from this angle, the sculpture is reduced to a prop in a high-class striptease.

But before sitting back and enjoying the show, Mr. White might profitably have consulted his Bulfinch's. Miss Black has identified the figure as Daphne: Daphne who fled from Apollo and begged to be transformed into another entity, Daphne who did not want to seduce anyone and who finally escaped altogether from the importunities of love. In permitting himself to be titillated by the statue, its model, and Miss Black herself, Mr. White assumes the role of Apollo, thwarted suitor. And, to his considerable chagrin, Miss Black, like Daphne before her, cuts short a budding romance. She is about to leave town, it turns out, cashing in on the freedom that, earlier in the evening, Mr. White had fervently agreed was absolutely essential to her work. But now, since they do not suit him, he finds her actions unnatural, grotesque. She is a "lying woman" (52)—or perhaps, in light of her refusal to play the part of woman as Mr. White understands it, she is lying to say that she is a woman at all. The sad part for Miss Black, though, is that she cannot cease being either a woman or an artist and unlike Daphne, she cannot turn into a tree. As the piece closes, she is restless, "running her jaded fingers through her hair" (53).

The heroines of "Madame a Tort!" and "The Implacable Aphrodite" represent for Millay the problem of coordinating a dual performance as woman and artist. As we have seen, the sculptor-protagonist of "Madame a Tort!" becomes the prisoner of femininity and, cast in its paralyzing mold, can no longer function as an artist. Miss Black remains productive; however, she channels a considerable portion of her energies into the masquerade, staging a performance for the man. Here, Millay wryly comments on the failure of femininity and the romantic conventions that engender it to provide Miss Black with a viable mode of communication about her situation and about "woman." While we can read her seductive mimicry as parody, within the realm of the playlet, seductiveness only signifies its face value—as bait for the man. Thus, to Miss Black's considerable annoyance, she finds herself reinscribing "woman" for the umpteenth time.

Miss Black is broadly drawn, but her saga is reminiscent of Millay's own reign as Greenwich Village femme fatale. This epoch has also been presented from what one might term Mr. White's point of view. In his 1929 *roman à clef*, *I Thought of Daisy*, Edmund Wilson creates a character, Rita Cavenaugh, who is a thinly veiled portrait of Millay. Wilson, who had been in love with Millay in the 1920s, ruefully recalls how Rita/Edna captivated men with her elfin beauty, while remaining essentially aloof from her pack of suitors, of which motley company he was soon a member in good standing.

From the start, however, Wilson's narrator feels ambivalent about Rita's style of self-presentation, the tone of which is set at their first meeting when Rita is persuaded to recite her poetry at the party they are both attending: "The effect was, at first, to embarrass me: it was a little as if a Shakespearian actor were suddenly, off the stage, to begin expressing private emotions with the intonations of the play" (12). Despite his qualms, the narrator finds himself seduced by the performance precisely because its staging intensifies "the uncounterfeitable force of sincerity" (12). His insights into the psychology of performance, though, are intermittent. What initiates catharsis in one scene triggers a mild paranoia in those that follow, for as time passes, the narrator begins to find himself increasingly ill at ease with what he views as Rita's habitual aura of artifice. Even her voice, the same voice that initially entranced him, becomes suspect:

While she had been speaking, I had been aware, for the first time since the earliest days of our acquaintance, of her acquired English accent. Not that she always spoke in this way: she had the accent in which she recited her poems and the accent of the Village gamin—nor did she hesitate to bite down on a hard up-country *r*, when some special situation—a sundae at the soda-fountain or a hammock on a porch—had suggested to her versatile spirit the role of a girl in a small town. . . . (99)

Rita's "versatile spirit" enables her to play "a girl in a small town," which is to say, she enacts her former self, until what was once a suffocating reality becomes a part she can assume at will. Moreover, according to the narrator, her performance as "princess and rake of the Village" (60) is also a means of triumphing over an abject and stultifying past: the "cursed indestructible dress of girlhood, too worn, too soiled, too small" (59). Whether intentionally or not, the narrator's metaphor links the struggles of Rita's small town past specifically to femininity, to a constraining girlhood and its depleted armoire.[3] Only as lauded woman poet and Bohemian aristocrat can Rita live down her past and accede to a plurality of roles she has been denied. Unlike the generic Mr. White, in his more detached moments, the narrator is wise enough to realize that Rita has a lot more to work out than the rudiments of the romance plot. In fact, as might be expected, all this working out makes her a remarkably poor candidate for long-term romantic involvement. As Wilson wryly comments in his tribute to Millay in *The Shores of Light*: "In any case, it was plain to me that proposals of marriage were not a source of great excitement" (764).

Partially in reaction to his frustration with Rita, the narrator turns his attention to another woman, the equally elusive but less mind-boggling Daisy. Through Daisy, whom he finally finagles into bed and imagines writing about at the close of the novel, the narrator feels he can come "naturally into contact with life" (220). She appears to offer a femininity shorn of duplicity: "I bent over Daisy—her head on the pillow had that look . . . of women in those moments when they have dropped off, along with their garments, all the ruses and resolutions with which they meet the world" (220). Daisy will be his enlivening muse, he continues to fantasize, carrying him, literarily speaking, far from the "impossible worlds" (220) Rita inhabits. Such a conclusion, though, is curiously at odds with what he has realized about Daisy earlier in the scene—namely, that his frequent reevaluations of her "nature" have been the product of his own shifting states of mind. An evening of pleasant sex, he rather rashly postulates, has changed all that: "I had outgrown those phases of myself of which my successive conceptions of Daisy had been merely the reflections in another" (219). The reader is more likely to believe that this last Daisy is but another reflection, this time of his postcoital, sanguine mood.

Although it was not Wilson's express purpose, *I Thought of Daisy* investigates the social construction of woman from a male perspective.[4] Perhaps it is Wilson's great intelligence (here I feel a bit like Miss Black buttering up Mr. White) that accounts for a further question implicit in his text: if women are constructed, who constructs them? The narrator loves both Rita and Daisy, but Rita remains adamantly in charge of her self-presentations, while the more passive Daisy permits men to see in her what they will. Ironically, the narrator, if not the novelist, seems to hold up Daisy as the "true" woman, as though the male-constructed version of femininity is what femininity is all about.

There is a poignant postscript to *I Thought of Daisy*, one that continues this representational debate. Shortly after Wilson sent Millay a draft of the novel in 1929, he lost track of her for many years. In the 1940s, they finally touched base again, but it was not until after her death that he received a letter she had written in 1929, which had been misdelivered and returned to sender:

If I had had it, I should have answered it as she asked me to do and might not so completely have lost touch with her for almost twenty years. I thought that she had been offended by a character that was partly derived from her or had so much disliked the book that she had not wanted to write me about it. I now find that she had made careful and copious notes and had good-naturedly undertaken to rewrite in what she thought a more appropriate vein the speeches assigned to the character partly based on herself. (*The Shores of Light*, 1961, 790–91)

However good-naturedly intended, Millay's gesture is telling, suggesting that, although she will not object to being cast in a part, she will continue to insist on artistic control over her scripts.

In this rewriting of the part of woman—of herself as woman— Millay, perhaps unconsciously, took a cue from one of her own

Nancy Boyd stories. In Nancy's longest piece, "The Seventh Stair," a melodramatic saga of a young woman, a kidnapped infant, and, naturally, a devoted suitor eager to right all wrongs via money, affection, and reiterations of "my poor child," one of the few un-hackneyed moments occurs when Jane, the heroine, stumbles on a manuscript written by her admirer:

"The author certainly has no knowledge of woman, whatever else he may know," she mused. . . . "No woman would flatten her nose against a window, any more than she'd wear cotton stockings when interviewing a theatrical manager. Listen to this, for Heaven's sake! Impossible!" she read a passage aloud.

" 'Of course, we women are different from you men,' said Clara. 'Men are unforgiving, but women forgive freely; it is their mother instinct.' A gentle look came into her mild blue eyes, and she clasped her hands upon her chest, her bosom filled with emotion."

"Bosom filled with sawdust!" said Jane. She noticed that some of the lines had been scratched out and written in again. He was evidently having a hard time with it. . . . "I could do a woman better than that myself," she said, and after a moment began to write, scarcely realizing what she was doing, revising and adding to the material suggested. (17)

One imagines that Millay's revisions of *I Thought of Daisy* might be a bit more biting, but here again, even if rather mildly expressed, are the themes of a woman's controlled self-presentation versus essentialistic myths about "woman." Indeed, as should be evident by now, a portion of Millay's project as Nancy Boyd was precisely to "do a woman better than that." But there's a snag. Boyd is an authority on how women play at being "woman," how they participate in a masquerade, a masquerade that can be undercut to the extent that, through mimicry, they direct their own command performances and deconstruct their origins. At the same time, how-ever, Nancy Boyd is a hack, a mere scribbler of potboilers and arch sketches for the women's magazines. It would seem as though mimicry is not worth much, after all, and thus, "to do a woman better than that" is a déclassé endeavor. Does Millay, like the sexless artist at the beginning of "Madame a Tort!," believe that, if she is a woman, the great artist must steer clear of gender? Certainly to the extent that she feared being typed as a "poetess," such a route must have been tempting. Tempting, but as Nancy Boyd, the dyspeptic dark angel at her ear, kept reminding her, impossible.

Millay's excess in the persona of Nancy Boyd and her segregation of Miss Boyd's work from her official oeuvre went hand in hand. In these brash tales, published separately from her "serious" poetry, Millay felt free to comment on the social construction that underlies any presentation of femininity, including her own. When Boyd does more than she needs to make a buck—when, like 'Toinette in "The White Peacock," she turns the *Ainslee's* potboiler or the *Vanity Fair* divertissement into a revelation of the hybrid that is woman and the "hash" the woman artist must serve up—she becomes a conduit for both mimicry's salutary playfulness and the unresolved dilemma of the masquerade.

## Notes

1. Although I argue for a progression from "sweet young thing" to self-conscious purveyor of femininity, I ought to clarify that the Nancy Boyd stories do not present this movement in an absolutely chronological fashion. "Mr. Dallas Larabee, Sinner" was actually one of Boyd's last *Ainslee's* pieces.

2. Like Millay, Riviere was born before the turn of the century and came to maturity after it. Stephen Heath has already drawn our attention to the historical context of Riviere's piece, arguing that, as an intellectual woman striving to carve a niche for herself in the male-dominated world of psychoanalysis, Riviere was in much the same bind as her female analysands (see Heath, "Joan Riviere"). The historical context of masquerade is also foregrounded in another pertinent article, Judith Fetterley's "Impersonating 'Little Women': The Radicalism of Alcott's *Behind a Mask*." Without reference to psychoanalysis, Fetterley comes up with essentially the same paradigm as Riviere: "*Behind a Mask* is Alcott's most radical text. It presents an incisive analysis of the economic situation of the white middle class woman in late 19th century society. It articulates a radical critique of the cultural constructs of 'femininity' and 'little womanhood,' exposing them as roles women must play, masks they must put on in order to survive" (2).

3. Wilson's scenario of female depletion is reminiscent of Freud's tracking of feminine types in his famous "Femininity" essay.

4. In his (unpaginated) foreword to the 1955 paperback reissue of *I Thought of Daisy*, Wilson explains that he had intended to write a Joycean or

Proustian "symphonic arrangement," in which specific characters dominate different sections of the novel. He adds that the Rita Cavenaugh character "upsets the scheme by attracting too much attention when she appears in the opening section. . . ."

# 11  *"Directions for Using the Empress"*

## *Millay's Supreme Fiction(s)*

### Sandra M. Gilbert

Above [Millay's] bed was a modern painting, all fractured geometrical planes that vaguely delineated a female figure, which the Millay girls called *Directions for Using the Empress*. . . . The picture [according to Norma Millay] was an abstract portrait of Vincent's mechanical dress form, the Empress, which gained and lost weight by an intricate system of adjusting nuts and screws.

—Edmund Wilson, *The Shores of Light*

"What is the essential nature of fully developed femininity? What is *das ewig Weibliche*?" asked the psychoanalyst Joan Riviere in an influential essay, "Womanliness as a Masquerade," which was published in 1929, and her answer implied, paradoxically, that the essence of what the nineteenth century had often called true womanliness was pure artifice. "The conception of womanliness as a mask," Riviere mused, "throws a little light on the enigma" of "fully developed femininity" (44).[1] Writing in London two years after the publication of *To the Lighthouse* and one year after the appearance of *Orlando*, this theorist—otherwise best known as a translator of Freud—was in a sense analyzing precisely the phenomenon Virginia Woolf had, in different ways, dramatized in both novels: the interrogation of sex roles necessitated by an age of surprisingly rapid sexchanges. For whether or not Riviere's speculations about the artifice of femininity were accurate, they were a product of just the history of social transformation that led to the disappearance of the woman who "naturally" knew how to be Mrs. Ramsay, the history that fostered the uncertainties of Lily Briscoe and Rose and Cam along with the indeterminacy of Orlando.

Even our current phrase "sex roles" may itself be seen as a consequence of that history. To be sure, the notion that "All the world's a stage / And all the men and women merely players" elaborates a metaphor that seems virtually timeless. Yet it is a relatively new idea that the categories "man" and "woman" may be as artificial as the parts of "schoolboy" or "lover" that these creatures play. In particular, for centuries ministers and physicians, philosophers and psychologists had presupposed the essentializing concept of "woman" that Riviere questioned when she suggested that the "ewig Weibliche" might be simply a mask or masquerade. Even Freud, despite his brilliant meditations on the difficult construction of "femininity," seems ultimately to have believed that there was such a quality as womanliness. When he asked, "What do women want?," he spoke, after all, in a context which implied that there were, ontologically, such beings as "women."[2]

However, as Susan Gubar and I argued in *Sexchanges* (the second volume of our three-part *No Man's Land: The Place of the Woman Writer in the Twentieth Century*), from the turn of the century onward sexologists had increasingly called attention to the artifice of gender, and no doubt as a consequence of this, from Riviere onward the very notion of femininity was put ever more radically in question. By the time Simone de Beauvoir wrote *The Second Sex* in the 1940s, she frequently defined all women as what I am calling "female female impersonators," implying a necessary disjunction between everywoman's self and the self-presentation western culture labels "feminine." In particular, de Beauvoir saw "femininity" as a function of costume and makeup. "Even if each woman dresses in conformity with her status," she declared,

a game is still being played. Artifice, like art, belongs to the realm of the imaginary. It is not only that girdle, brassiere, hair-dye, make-up disguise body and face; but that the least sophisticated of women, once she is 'dressed,' does not present *herself* to observation; she is, like . . . the actor on the stage, an agent through whom is suggested someone not there— that is, the character she represents, but is not. (502)

Perhaps unconsciously supporting de Beauvoir's point, Erving Goffman repeatedly cited such passages from *The Second Sex* throughout his influential 1959 study of social "impression-management" and "theatrical performance," *The Presentation of Self in Everyday Life*, without ever examining their gender implications. For the most part Goffman's "teams" of "players" were male: lawyers, diplomats, shoe salesmen. But when they were female, they were usually "women," implying that simply being a woman entailed a set of professional performative acts exactly equivalent to the theatrical activities involved in being a lawyer or a shoe salesman.[3]

In her insightful *Pornography and Silence: Culture's Revenge Against Nature*, Susan Griffin presents a view of women's role playing which while more polemical than Riviere's, Goffman's, or even de Beauvoir's, nevertheless addresses the same cultural phenomena the earlier theorists examined, at the same time suggesting parallels between female female impersonation and the long history of black mimicry (of, say, blacks "impersonating the white man's idea of a black slave") that Susan Gubar has discussed in connection with the Harlem Renaissance.[4] Woman's "false self," Griffin argues, "is the pornographic idea of the female. We have learned to impersonate her. Like the men and women living in the institution of slavery, we have become talented at seeming to be what we are not" (202).

In support of her claim, Griffin offers as paradigmatic examples of female female impersonation several anecdotes about Marilyn Monroe. According to Monroe's friend Simone Signoret, Griffin observes, the actress "rarely dressed anything like the self we know as 'Marilyn' " when she was not on camera and referred to "the costume required to create [her] illusory self as her 'Marilyn getup.' " Similarly, Griffin adds:

From another actress who was a friend of Monroe, we discover that Monroe even referred to this other personality as "her." Susan Strasberg writes that this famous "M. M." was "someone else . . . she became by shifting into another gear. It was deliberate." She tells us that once when she and Monroe walked with a friend through the streets of New York, Monroe turned to Strasberg and her friend and said, "Do you want me to be *her*?" Suddenly, she took on the "Marilyn" personality, and just as suddenly, strangers on the street began to recognize her. (204–5)

In the same vein, the French theorist Luce Irigaray has written about the "masquerade" of femininity, echoing Riviere's essay and proposing, as Griffin does, that such female female impersonation results from the fact that in patriarchal culture women are inevitably "exiled from themselves" (132–34).[5]

I am speculating here, however, that such self-exile, along with the impersonation it entails, may have been exacerbated by just the historical circumstances—the sexchanges and social changes—that have empowered such feminists as Griffin and Irigaray to study the artifice of "femininity." Certainly, as Woolf portrays her throughout much of *To the Lighthouse*, Mrs. Ramsay finds it "natural" to "be" the person her name delineates. Indeed, there is at least (from Woolf's point of view) a hypothetical continuity, rather than a disjunction, between the "wedge-shaped core of darkness" that this model mother imagines as her inmost self and the dark triangular shapes of the archetypal feminine that Lily Briscoe paints at the end of the novel and that Woolf herself depicted as early as *The Voyage Out*. But for Mrs. Ramsay's female descendants, newly aware of the arbitrariness of sex *roles*, there is no comparable continuity between inner feelings and outer mask, between consciousness and costume.

What are the literary consequences of such a discontinuity? Since fiction, by definition, entails feigning while poets have often tended to imply the confessional "sincerity" of the lyric speaker, we are likely to find the marks of the (female) masquerade more surprisingly inscribed in the lives and works of twentieth-century women poets than in female-authored novels or plays. Of course, no doubt because of the same heightened sense of social artifice that impelled Goffman to examine "impression-management" in the 1950s, modernist and postmodernist verse by both sexes has long called attention to the fictionality of every poem's supposed speaker. *Personae* was, after all, the title of Ezra Pound's third book (1909), as well as several later editions of his collected poems, and one of the newest words the New Critics introduced to readers was *persona*, meaning *mask* and intended to emphasize the gap between the writer in the world and the poet on the page.

Among the most crucial studies of modern poetry, moreover, was Richard Ellmann's classic *Yeats: The Man and the Masks* in 1948, whose title drew on a major Yeatsian trope to illuminate the significance of feigning—and its corollary, self-distancing—in the career of the Irish poet. And Yeats himself was obviously influenced by such key *fin de siècle* figures as Oscar Wilde and Max Beerbohm, both of whom half-seriously, half-ironically defended the advantages of cosmetology and costume. Nevertheless, despite pervasive attention to the artifice of poetic identity, a number of twentieth-century male artists laid claim to a masculinity that was both authentic and "ordinary" in their reaction against what they saw on the one hand as the feminization of the literary marketplace and against what they feared on the other hand was the effeminacy or inauthenticity of some of their male predecessors.

Among the most prominent of the male modernists, some guaranteed their manhood, along with the variety of performative possibilities it offered, by adopting stereotypically "male" roles which seem to have reflected not just economic but also psychological necessities. T. S. Eliot famously worked in a bank; William Carlos Williams was a physician; Wallace Stevens was, of course, an insurance lawyer.[6] The imperatives that drove them were perhaps most clearly formulated by Stevens, who mused early in his career, in a meditation entitled "Poetry and Manhood," that "those who say poetry is now the peculiar province of women say so because ideas about poetry are effeminate," with his antidote to this charge consisting in a list of "man-poets," including "Homer, Dante, Shakespeare, Milton, Keats, Browning, much of Tennyson" (26). That, in Stevens's opinion, true "man-poets" in the twentieth century were not—or at least *should* not—be impersonators, that they should be "naturally" and authentically "masculine," became plain in a letter he wrote to Harvey Breit in 1942. "It was only a few years ago when Joaquin Miller or Walt Whitman were considered to be approximations of a typical image [of the poet]," Stevens commented rather nervously.

But were they? Weren't they recognized by people of any sense at all as, personally, poseurs? They belong in the same category of eccentrics to which *queer-looking actors belong*. . . . The contemporary poet is simply a contemporary man who writes poetry. *He looks like anyone else, acts like anyone else, wears the same kind of clothes*, and certainly is not an incompetent. (415; emphasis added)

In contrast to this view, Stevens's female contemporaries seem to have done their best not to look "like anyone else." Because the "woman's part" has been in our century culturally redefined as a sort of specialized professional role that in its singularity balances a far greater range of specialized male roles, the woman poet may have at times felt a particular obligation to prepare a distinctively and artificially "feminine" face to "meet the faces that [she] meet[s]." Indeed, where for J. Alfred Prufrock such a preoccupation with costume (with, say, a "necktie rich and modest") becomes a sign of failure to achieve the authenticity implicit in a voicing of "an overwhelming question," for the woman poet a literal and figurative concern with clothing and makeup was often an enabling strategy that allowed her just the *being* in the world that it denied Eliot's unmanned speaker.[7]

Precisely, however, because this woman of letters, newly conscious of the artifice of her gender, "played" a public part that was unavailable to most of her ancestresses, she may have at times found herself far more radically estranged from her aesthetic persona than her male contemporaries were from theirs. On the one hand, therefore, she was often empowered by her estranged female female impersonation to produce poetry that commented on both the "feminine" and the "masculine" from the ironic perspective of the actress who knows, like Marilyn Monroe, that there is a radical gulf between "me" and "*her*." But on the other hand, because audiences—both readers and observers—frequently reified such a female artist in the "feminine" role she played, she herself was always in danger of being trapped behind the rigid mask of a self that she flaunted but despised as inauthentic.

In broadly comic terms, Dorothy Parker's "Waltz" (1933), one of that bleak humorist's most famous short stories, brilliantly fictionalizes both the advantages and disadvantages of female female impersonation. Stumbling around a dance floor with a man she dislikes, Parker's protagonist mouths "feminine" platitudes:

*"Why, thank you so much. I'd adore to. . . . Tired? I should say I'm not tired. I'd like to go on like this forever"*—while, in the privacy of her own mind, she viciously comments on both her partner and her "part"—"I don't want to dance with him. I don't want to dance with anybody," "I should say I'm not tired. I'm dead, that's all I am. . . . And the music is never going to stop playing, and we're going on like this, Double-Time Charlie and I, throughout eternity." (*Portable* 77, 81)[8]

Obviously, the hilarious tension between this unwilling dancer's words and her thoughts allows Parker, too, to analyze social rituals in which both author and heroine are engaged. Yet ultimately Parker can imagine no way out of the ballroom of gender for her speaker. After the music of the waltz has ceased, producing "in my ears . . . a silence like the sound of angel voices," the woman's partner offers to pay the orchestra to go on playing, and she is obliged to enthuse: *"Oh, that would be lovely, and look, do tell them to play this same thing. I'd simply adore to go on waltzing* (82)." Even while female female impersonation facilitates a dramatic critique of culture's central pas de deux, Parker implies, the costume of womanhood may inexorably dictate steps that are no joke.

"The Satin Dress" (1926), a poem Parker published some time before she produced "The Waltz," makes this point more explicitly and more grimly. The speaker of this ballad begins her stitchery with enthusiasm for what she imagines will be a liberating gown:

> Needle, needle, dip and dart,
> Thrusting up and down,
> Where's the man could ease a heart
> Like a satin gown?
> . . . . . . . . . . . . .
>
> Wantons go in bright brocade;
> Brides in organdie;
> Gingham's for the plighted maid;
> Satin's for the free!

But as the speaker sews, she realizes that the task of constructing her "bold" dress may be both interminable and fatal:

> Satin glows in candlelight—
> Satin's for the proud!
> They will say who watch at night,
> "What a fine shroud!"
>
> *(Portable* 125)[9]

The dress of the female female impersonator may free her into an exhilarating fictionality, this poem implies; yet it may also, finally, imprison and shroud her. For a poet, in particular, the artifice of the "feminine" threatened aesthetic reification even while it fostered creativity. The astute Parker, herself simultaneously empowered and oppressed by her own comic masquerade, would very likely have agreed with Louise Bogan's assertion that the role of charming, romantic public poet was, for early twentieth-century women, both a powerful part and a dangerous lot.

As I have argued elsewhere, Edna St. Vincent Millay (along with such other contemporaries as Elinor Wylie, H.D. and even Marianne Moore) was early reified, even fetishized, as a *woman* poet. Millay, wrote Joseph Collins in 1924,

is like a beautiful woman who has a varied, attractive wardrobe, and if one may judge from some of her appearances, she knows how to wear her clothes; but she does not always take the trouble to select discriminatingly or to put them on properly, or at least as effectively as she might easily do. (qtd. in Gilmore 2)

Similarly, the poet's erstwhile admirer Floyd Dell saw her as, variously, "a New England nun; a chorus girl on a holiday; the Botticelli Venus . . ." (qtd. in Churchill 264 and Gilmore 3).[10] And certainly, as I have also argued, she herself seems quite consciously to have posed as an apparently conventional femme fatale—at once a cheerful flapper and a weary princess—in order, both comically and seriously, to revise the contours of what had traditionally been seen as an ontological "femininity" that governed women's lives.[11] Her awareness of the artifice and even the duplicity entailed by her pose is of course insouciantly enacted in her early, popular *A Few Figs from Thistles*, the book that made her the "It-girl" of American poetry in 1922. But it is also dramatized with equal clarity not only in her letters home demanding "trailing" gowns for poetry readings but also by the fact that when she wrote many of the pieces in *A Few Figs* she was quite literally living a literary double life.

Millay began writing magazine sketches under the pseudonym "Nancy Boyd" shortly after she graduated from Vassar and moved to Greenwich Village. According to her sister Norma, she did this work "for a livelihood. . . . But foremost always was her poetry" (Norma Millay xxi–xxii). Yet the impudently skeptical perspective on "femininity" that "Nancy Boyd" expressed in popular pieces published in *Vanity Fair* and other stylish journals reflects significantly on the stance adopted by the poet called "Vincent" Millay. In particular, a number of the sketches that appeared in 1924 in "Nancy Boyd's" *Distressing Dialogues* and elsewhere focus on the artificial construction of the feminine, on the reification of woman's body, and therefore on the alienating disjunction between appearance and reality, mask and self, to which female flesh is subject.

For example, the famous Arnold Genthe photograph of a girlish and sylvan poet that had been a triumph for "Vincent" Millay was represented by "Nancy Boyd" as an absurdity. "Why is it that the girls of so many of our best families," inquired Millay's alter ego, "insist upon getting all safety-pinned up into several yards of mosquito-netting and standing about on somebody's golf-links while Arnold Genthe takes their photograph?" (*Dialogues*, 84). At the same time, in sketches entitled "Powder, Rouge and Lip-stick" and "Madame a Tort!", "Boyd" argued that, given cultural definitions of "femininity," a woman who abandoned apparently absurd strategies of self-presentation was as silly as one who did not. When the wife in the first sketch responds to her husband's insistence that she relinquish makeup, she appears in a "magnificent black and silver evening gown, above which rises a rather boyish neck, . . . sallow face with a pale mouth, a pink and gleaming nose, and no eyebrows whatsoever," explaining that now " 'I'm my own sweet, simple, natural, girlish self.' " At this, however, the man tells her that " 'You look like the very devil!' " (120) and forces her to make herself up again so that she is "scarlet-lipped, brilliant-eyed, enchanting" (121).

Similarly, in the second piece a woman sculptor who had been very unwillingly subjected to the ministrations of two Parisian beauty experts abandons her work and becomes "a slave to the most exacting of tyrants"—her mirror—when she discovers that it is her fate to be an art object, not an artist. "My skin was smoother and whiter than an infant's," she exults; "my cheeks were a delicate rose, my lips were carmine . . ." (*Dialogues*, 173). Again, in "Ships and Sealing-Wax," a revisionary dialogue between Alice (of *Alice in Wonderland*) and the loquacious walrus, the walrus's proposal that people should "stop talking . . . of sex" elicits from Alice a frantic search "in her vanity bag" for a "powdapuf." For the very "subject of sex" requires, according to "Boyd," that this storybook heroine "encrust her countenance with a thin layer of white lead" (273).

Makeup and making-up, masking and masquerading: for the comedienne that Edna Millay became when she was not presenting herself as "Vincent" (and sometimes when she was), these were crucial elements in the wonderland of "femininity." And though the woman who gained her greatest fame as a soulful, presumably sincere (and sometimes apparently sentimental) lyricist would seem to have had a very different attitude toward her own sexuality, one of the so-far uncollected "Boyd" pieces makes explicit the poet's sense that "Edna St. Vincent Millay" was just as fictive a construct as any other fainting heroine. In "Diary of an American Art Student in Paris," the supposed journal of a flighty flapper, "Boyd's" speaker visits a café where she is told that "the girl sitting at the next table was Edna St. Vincent Millay" and is surprised to find her "eating an enormous plate of sauerkraut and sausages. . . . Such a shock," she comments. "I have always imagined her so ethereal" (44).

Even without this sly confession of the distance between person and poet, however, the themes and forms of Millay's verses often suggest that she was hardly less ironic about gender imperatives than "Nancy Boyd" was. Indeed, although in such works as the sonnet cycle *Fatal Interview* Millay often frankly writes the poetry of passion with which her name has been consistently identified, a number of sonnets in *Fatal Interview*, along with many other texts in Millay's *Collected Poems*, radically undercut the aesthetic of heterosexual love, denying or deriding the emotional imperatives that would leave women drowned in desire.

To be sure, in *Fatal Interview* the flippancy of Millay's early *A*

*Few Figs* is translated into a rhetoric of greater dignity and hauteur. Yet even as she explores the nuances of passion, the poet balances assertions of power against confessions of vulnerability. In particular, at key intervals Millay sets into the sequence a group of sonnets that echo some of her earlier more sardonic poems in their emphasis on both the evanescence of love and the ultimate indifference, or at least the distance, of love's artificer, the supposedly impassioned woman poet. At the outset, sonnet II, "This beast that rends me in the sight of all," declares that "This love, this longing, this oblivious thing, . . . Will glut, will sicken, will be gone by spring," while sonnet VIII offers a witty and threatening revision of Marvell's "To His Coy Mistress:"

> Yet in an hour to come, disdainful dust,
> You shall be bowed and brought to bed with me.
>
> . . . . . . . . . . . . . . . . . .
> If not today, then later; if not here
> On the green grass, with sighing and delight,
> Then under it, all in good time, my dear,
> We shall be laid together in the night.[12]

Elaborating a vision of staunch New England women, sonnet XXXVI strikes a different but comparably triumphant (and hostile) note. "Hearing your words, and not a word among them / Tuned to my liking," the poet remembers the inexorable tides and weathers of Maine, and the shore-dwellers who survive onslaughts of harshness:

> There in the autumn when the men go forth
> With slapping skirts the island women stand
> In gardens stripped and scattered, peering north,
> With dahlia tubers dripping from the hand:
> The wind of their endurance, driving south,
> Flattened your words against your speaking mouth.

Moreover, perhaps the most famous sonnet in *Fatal Interview*— LII, "Oh, sleep forever in the Latmian cave,"—recounts the myth of Endymion and Diana to explain, by implication, the poet's bittersweet victories over her lover, *her* Endymion. Just as the human hero of the ancient myth is preserved "oblivious" in an eternal slumber by the moon goddess's power, so the nameless man to whom Millay addresses *Fatal Interview* is, as it were, embalmed alive in her poems, while she, like the moon, seems to "wanders mad." Yet as the work's couplet suggests, her apparent madness, like the moon's, is a sign of her divinity: ". . . she wanders mad, being all unfit / For mortal love, *that might not die of it*" (emphasis added). And indeed, sonnet XX, the most crucial aesthetic statement in the sequence, hints that this woman in her role as poet-artificer will not just survive love, she must and will transcend it. Resurrecting the Keatsian trope of the nightingale-artist as a personification of beauty, Millay proclaims her freedom from just those pressures of romance that would wound or drown the eroticized heroine:

> Beauty beyond all feathers that have flown
> Is free; you shall not hood her to your wrist,
> Nor sting her eyes, nor have her for your own
> In any fashion; beauty billed and kissed
> Is not your turtle; tread her like a dove—
> She loves you not; she never heard of love.

"I too beneath your moon, almighty Sex," a sonnet from the later *Huntsman, What Quarry?*, reviews and reappraises a notably modern—post-Havelock Ellis, post-Freud—love life with calm self-scrutiny and, in doing so, summarizes a key assumption that underlies even the most theatrical sufferings recorded in *Fatal Interview*. "Such as I am," the speaker boasts, "I have brought / To what it is, this tower" of art, and "*it is my own*" (emphasis added). For throughout all these frequently antiromantic poems about romance, Millay deliberately impersonates not so much a fatally afflicted heroine as a femme fatale whose adventures are energized by, and issue in, proud independence. But unlike the male-created femme fatale who haunted the nineteenth-century imagination—for instance, Keats's "Belle Dame Sans Merci" or Rider Haggard's *She who-must-be obeyed*—Millay's speaker is ironic about her triumphs: the masquerade of poetic form, as well as the double-consciousness of "Vincent"/"Nancy Boyd," facilitates a distancing of desire. And unlike the femme fatale envisioned by women writers at the turn of the century—Olive Schreiner's Lyndall, for example, or even Edith Wharton's Lily Bart—Millay-as-poetic-speaker surmounts the plots that would wound her.[13] For her, it is never fatal to be a femme fatale because she can always turn in detachment from the situation in which she is ostensibly entangled and because she can always deploy the vengeful arts of linguistic "making-up."

As if to flesh out her erotic sequences with further evidence of female self-possession, a number of Millay's narrative and dramatic poems explore further aspects of the sexual war of the words in which even as a romantic sonneteer this poet was so frequently engaged. For example "Rendezvous," in "Nancy Boyd's" tone of weary sarcasm, critiques the conventions of a stylized affair between an older woman and a younger man: "I wish you had not scrubbed—with pumice, I suppose— / The tobacco stains from your beautiful fingers. And I wish I did not feel like your mother." Similarly, "Armenonville" recounts a moment when the woman's alienated consciousness, inexorably "my own," disrupts the ritual dialogue of lovers:

> There swam across the lake, as I looked aside, avoiding
> Your eyes for a moment, there swam from under the pink
>     and red begonias,
> A small creature; I thought it was a water-rat. . . .
> . . . . . . . . . . . . . . . . . . . . . . .
> . . . and when suddenly I turned again to you,
> Aware that you were speaking, and perhaps had been speak-
>     ing for some time,
> I was aghast at my absence, for truly I did not know
> Whether you had been asking or telling.

The skeptical stance toward traditional notions of "femininity" implicit in these texts comes to the surface just as clearly in Millay's verses about and for women as it does in her dissections of the ideology of romance. In fact, this poet produced a range of poems which implicitly supports a point that de Beauvoir made about the "backstage" world of the "team" of women whom we are defining as female female impersonators:

What gives value to [private] relations among women is the truthfulness they imply. Confronting man woman is always play-acting; she lies when she makes believe that she accepts her status as the inessential other, she lies when she presents to him an imaginary personage through mimicry,

costumery, studied phrases. . . . With other women, a woman is behind
the scenes; she is polishing her equipment, but not in battle; she is getting
her costume together, preparing her make-up. . . . For some women, this
warm and frivolous intimacy is dearer than the serious pomp of relations
with men. (512–13)[14]

The Millay poems that express this "warm," if not "frivolous,"
intimacy with other women include her elegies for her Vassar friend
Dorothy Coleman and for Elinor Wylie, as well as the generalized
"To a Young Girl" and the more specifically personal "The courage
that my mother had." "To a Young Girl," especially, implies a
"backstage" female bonding in "impression-management" that is
intimately loving even while its strategy may seem as cynical as
those de Beauvoir describes. Beginning with a rhetorical question—
"Shall I despise you that your colourless tears / Made rainbows in
your lashes, and you forgot to weep?"—the speaker of the poem
goes on to prescribe the beauty made up, as it were, by at least an
impersonation of feminine feeling:

> I would not have you darken your lids with weeping,
> Beautiful eyes, but I would have you weep enough
> To wet the fingers of the hand held over the eye-lids,
> And stain a little the light frock's delicate stuff. [15]

More openly polemical, Millay's rousing feminist sonnet "To Inez
Milholland" begins as a paean to the glamorous, Vassar-educated
suffragist who was the first wife of Eugen Boissevain, later the
poet's own husband. "Read in Washington, November eighteenth,
1923 at the unveiling of a statue of three leaders in the cause of
Equal Rights for Women," this piece plays elegantly with rhetorical
negations ("Upon this marble bust that is not I / Lay the round,
formal wreath that is not fame") to move toward a sisterly affirma-
tion that is also expressed through an ironic prescription of what
should *not* be done: "Take up the song; forget the epitaph." At the
same time, through the odd tension between the poem's title ("To
Inez Milholland") and its use of the first person pronoun, this work
emphasizes both the political commonality of Milholland/Millay
and the public reification they share. For is "this marble bust that

is not I" not Inez or not Edna? And to which of these feminist female impersonators accrues the problematic "round, formal wreath that is not fame"?

If "To Inez Milholland" hints at a few of the dangers, or at least confusions, associated with the female masquerade as an aesthetic strategy, some of Millay's later poems examine these problems with greater frankness as they both analyze and enact the risks of costume. The speaker of "The Plaid Dress," for instance, reproaches herself with the "violent plaid / Of purple angers and red shames" that characterizes the metaphorical clothing in which she is attired, begging "Strong sun, that bleach / The curtains of my room, can you not render / Colourless this dress I wear?" By implication, the woman who cannot change the world must ultimately be maddened and demoralized by the futility of her own gestures, by "the yellow stripe / Of thin but valid treacheries . . . / The recurring checker of the serious breach of taste."

Even worse, immobilized in her female role, this woman—who is surely to be identified with the aging, disillusioned poet herself—realizes that she is now trapped in the costume she once elected, that like the apparently liberating frock in Parker's "Satin Dress," her gown has become "a fine shroud." Some fifteen years before she wrote "The Plaid Dress," Millay had depicted the protagonist of "An Ungrafted Tree" confronting a winter clothesline laden with "Garments, board-stiff, that galloped on the blast / Clashing like angel armies in a fray" and then, in the Eliotian cruelty of an April thaw, discovering a lost apron, emblem of an inescapable marriage, an inexorably recurring female role, "and the whole year to be lived through once more" (XI). Even more radically, however, the Millay of "The Plaid Dress" recognizes that she has in a sense *become* her dress:

> No more uncoloured than unmade,
> I fear, can be this garment that I may not doff;
> Confession does not strip it off,
> To send me homeward eased and bare;
>
> All through the formal, unoffending evening, under the clean
> Bright hair,

Lining the subtle gown . . . it is not seen,
But it is there.

(Millay's ellipsis)

To evoke a different metaphor, like the heroine of "To Inez Milhol-land," Millay-as-public-personality has been reified into a "marble bust that is not I" upon which readers "Lay the round, formal wreath that is not fame."

What exacerbated Millay's sense of reification and of notoriety—"not fame"—was, paradoxically, one of her most "sincere" endeavors: her propagandizing for the Allied cause during World War II, specifically her work for the Writers War Board and her composition of her hortatory collection *Make Bright the Arrows* (1940). Even as she struggled with these projects, which very likely issued from her long-standing rebellion against authoritarianism, she feared that she was producing "not poems, posters" and astutely articulated the effect such publications might have on her already fading public image. "How many more books of propaganda poetry . . . [my] reputation can withstand without falling under the weight of it, I do not know," she confided anxiously in a letter to an old friend, Charlotte Sills (*Letters*, 1952, 309, 311–12). That she was not wrong, moreover, is made clear—as Susan Schweik has observed—by the reception of these writings in middlebrow as well as highbrow circles. "Edna Makes Supreme Sacrifice," proclaimed a snide head-line in *Vice Versa*, and more explicitly, a *Time* reviewer of *Make Bright the Arrows* declared that "Millay lashes out at the warring world like a lady octopus caught in a whirlpool" (62). As Schweik also notes, "Millay went so far as to try to attribute to" these reviews what she tellingly called her "very *handsome* . . . nervous breakdown" (emphasis added) at the war's end, confessing to Edmund Wilson "that there is nothing on this earth which can so much get on the nerves of a good poet, as the writing of bad poetry. . . . [F]inally I cracked up under it" (*Letters*, 1952, 333).[16]

But in fact Wilson himself, along with Millay's biographers, re-ports that this artist had "cracked" repeatedly over the years—and arguably her breakdowns were consequences not just of the tension between public (speaker) and private (poet) fostered by wartime propagandizing but also of the periodic and quite literal breaking down of the machinery that kept public (poet) and private (self) in some sort of precarious equilibrium. Certainly the pain implicit in "The Plaid Dress," especially in the image of "this garment that I may not doff," would seem to suggest as much. At the same time, the notably feminine image of the *dress* through which Millay chooses to represent both her anxious self-analysis and her despairing sense of reification underlines yet again her sometimes exultant, sometimes ironic self-presentation as distinctively "feminine."

Two late verses, "Thanksgiving Dinner" and "The Fitting," indicate both the advantages and the disadvantages the poet experienced in dramatizing an apparently stereotypical femininity. In "Thanksgiving Dinner," she imagines a woman walking smilingly through the "broken garden," because she knows she can live, and feed her "love"—both her lover and her love for him—on "steaming, stolid winter roots." And in "The Fitting," she describes a session with a dressmaker in which the irony made possible through what I have been calling "female female impersonation" is emphasized by the distance between the speaker's thoughts of her lover and the activity of seamstresses who are "turning me, touching my secret body, doing what they were paid to do." If one occupies a "female" position with lucid detachment, these verses hint, one is free to celebrate the real values—nurturance, endurance—that the construction of "femininity" facilitates, even while, paradoxically, one comes to perceive the artifice of what are now called sex roles.

More darkly, however, "Thanksgiving Dinner" depicts the poet's garden as broken, frozen static—"Frozen are the ripe tomatoes, the red fruit and the hairy golden stem"—so that she must have recourse to "the woody fibres of the overgrown / Kohl-rabi . . . the spongy radish coarse and hot," and "what the squirrels may have left of the beechnuts and the acorns . . . "(Millay's ellipsis). And as the garden stiffens, dividing itself into a network of underground roots that only survive in darkness and a rigid wintry facade seen by the world, so the poet is definitively split into a two whose only virtue is that such doubleness might preclude the hardening of the divided pair—lady and octopus, woman and costume—into *one*, indeed into what *Time*'s hostile reviewer had called a "lady octopus."

Similarly, even while obliquely celebrating "my secret body,"

"The Fitting" dramatizes—and mourns—this split. The labors of the oppressed dressmaker in the poem, a "hardworking woman with a familiar and unknown face," illustrate both the difficulty and the pain associated with the constructed image through which the female female impersonator must speak (she "set her cold shears against me,—snip, snip; / Her knuckles gouged my breast"). And the speaker's response documents the self-exile experienced by such an impersonator ("My drooped eyes lifted to my guarded eyes in the glass, and glanced away as from someone they had never met").

Had this poet ever allowed herself to meet a self other than the one she felt it necessary to create in order to meet the faces that she met? Many of Millay's letters home—littered to the end with "cute" slang and baby talk—imply that the girlish mask of the flapper "Nancy Boyd" had inexorably invaded the body of the artist who asked only that her life be "my own." And that the "femininity" of this mask was itself problematic is suggested by what may be the etymology of the name "Nancy Boyd": according to Eric Partridge's *Dictionary of Slang*, a *Nancy boy* was in this period a colloquialism for "an effeminate man" or a "catamite," a derivation that intensifies the artifice of an already arduous masquerade (550).

Finally, then, John Crowe Ransom was not altogether mistaken in assuming that "this charming lady found it difficult . . . to come of age" (*The World's Body* 98). Artistically, the poet struggled persistently toward a maturity in which she could use the artifice of "femininity" without being used by it. Nevertheless, like her early nom de plume, Millay's youthful preoccupation with her "mechanical dress form, the Empress"—described by Edmund Wilson in my epigraph—may have been prophetic. And perhaps Wilson's own comment on the problem of the dress form was equally telling: "When we later learned that the inventor of the Empress had killed himself, we understood it perfectly" (*The Shores of Light*, 1961, 767n).

## Notes

1. For a fine discussion of the essay, see Heath, "Joan Riviere."
2. Among Freud's meditations on the construction of "femininity," see

"Some Psychological Consequences of the Anatomical Distinction Between the Sexes" and "Female Sexuality" in *Sexuality and the Psychology of Love*.

3. See Goffman, *The Presentation of Self*, 77–105; we are grateful to Lisa Jadwin for bringing the relevance of this text to our attention.

4. See Gilbert and Gubar, *Letters from the Front*, chapter 3.

5. See also Irigaray, on "mimicry": "One must assume the feminine role deliberately. Which means already to convert a form of subordination into an affirmation, and thus to begin to thwart it. . . . To play with mimesis is . . . for a woman, to try to recover the place of her exploitation by discourse, without allowing herself to be simply reduced to it" (*This Sex* 76).

6. To be sure, as Peter Ackroyd has revealed, Eliot had a penchant for wearing strange costumes and makeup (including lipstick and "green face powder") to certain literary parties. But as Ackroyd notes, "It is significant that the only people who noticed his make-up, and probably the only ones in whose company he wore it, were writers and artists; it is unlikely he powdered his face before going to the bank" (136), and of course as he settled definitively into his ultimate public role as publisher/editor/poet, he abandoned this youthful *jeu* in favor of strictly correct business attire.

7. For discussions of sexual anxiety in "The Love Song of J. Alfred Prufrock," see Gilbert and Gubar, *The War of the Words*, 31–32, 97–98.

8. Its first book publication, in 1933, was in *After Such Pleasures*, 97–106.

9. The poem's first book publication was in *Enough Rope*, 23. For a comparable poem with the same theme, see also "The Red Dress" (*Portable* 308).

10. I am grateful to Susan Gilmore for sharing with me her fine thesis entitled "To 'Last the Night': A New Look at the Poetry of Edna St. Vincent Millay."

11. See Gilbert, "Female Female Impersonator."

12. For a different reading of this poem, see Montefiore, *Feminism and Poetry*, 116–18.

13. On the femme fatale, see Gilbert and Gubar, *Sexchanges*, chapters 1, 2, and 4.

14. Interestingly, Goffman also cites this passage: see *The Presentation of Self*, 112–13.

15. For a different view of this poem, see Perlmutter, "A Doll's Heart," 175.

16. See also Schweik, *A Gulf So Deeply Cut*.

# 12  *"Posies of Sophistry"*
## *Impersonation and Authority in Millay's* Conversation at Midnight
### Susan Gilmore

Feminist critic Sandra M. Gilbert uses the term "female female impersonator" to describe the female speakers who populate much of Edna St. Vincent Millay's poetry ("Marianne Moore" 27). These are the speakers featured in such poems as "Daphne" (1920) and the sonnet beginning "Oh, oh, you will be sorry for that word!" (1923)—speakers who inhabit femininity as costume, asserting their ability to theatrically exploit and evade its roles at will. But what happens when a woman poet impersonates a man? My primary interest is not in drag, though Millay displayed a penchant for men's clothing and for her middle name "Vincent" as a nickname (Walker, *Masks Outrageous and Austere* 150). Instead, I examine the effects produced by Millay's choice of a chorus of male speakers for her staged political debate, *Conversation at Midnight*. This work's reception indicates what a woman writer may risk and gain by producing a reading of men reading woman. Millay's *Conversation at Midnight* subverts masculinist authoritative claims by exposing their dependence upon discursive representations of femininity, which are inherently unstable. Millay draws an equation between poetic form and sophistry, demonstrating that the same forms that can structure misogynistic arguments about gender serve equally well to effect these arguments' undoing.

In her 1937 verse drama, Millay foregoes a lyric female speaker for the voices of seven men engaged in an all-night bull session on topics ranging from the debate between communism and capitalism to religious faith, music, and even mushroom collecting. As its title suggests, not action but talk drives this play; the plot charts the slow boiling over of political and social rivalries at midnight's approach. A survey of the play's reviews (which were mixed to negative) reveals that in terms of both genre and gender, critics have viewed *Conversation at Midnight* as transgressive. Louis Untermeyer dismisses Millay's motives as presumptuous and unfathomable: "For some occult reason, she has decided to express herself like a man" (6). Millay's chief admirer and onetime suitor, Edmund Wilson, conflates poet and text, describing both as promiscuous, "in full dissolution" ("Give That Beat Again" 687).

Wilson's review reflects a conservative reaction to modernist experiment. Wilson traces the general decline of the "old strong beat of English verse," finding it "so broken, sprung, muted, loosened, that it might almost as well be abandoned altogether" (686). While he figures innovation as male aggression, Wilson appoints Millay the guardian of traditional forms. "And now Edna St. Vincent Millay," Wilson writes, "one of the sole surviving masters of English verse, seems to be going to pieces" (686). It is significant that Wilson sees not so much the verse as Millay herself going to pieces. What these reviews reveal is the critical Catch-22 facing Millay and her female contemporaries. Modernist aesthetics promote a rhetoric of absence and impersonality to describe the ideal relation between the writer and *his* work, yet critics demand the woman writer's presence and produce readings of *her* work that are stubbornly reductive. Thus, Wilson finds Millay incapable of "dissociation" (683), on the one hand, and, on the other, faults her for failing to cast herself in her work:

We keep listening instinctively through the chatter and chaff for the voice we are accustomer [*sic*] to hear. . . . And in the meantime, the dramatized points of view of Miss Millay's fictitious personalities never give rise to any conflict half so real as the conflicts within the poet herself, as she has expressed them directly in her own person. (684–85)

Millay's "E. St. V. M." (1920) problematizes reductive readings of women's work and questions the extent to which a persona might be the exclusive privilege of male writers. This ironic self-portrait, which Millay included in a letter to Wilson, parodies terms Millay's critics employ and anticipates the violence such catalogs threaten:

> Hair which she still devoutly trusts is red.
> Colorless eyes, employing
> A childish wonder
> To which they have no statistic
> Title.
> A large mouth,
> Lascivious,
> Aceticized by blasphemies.
> A long throat,
> Which will someday
> Be strangled.[1]

(*Letters*, 1952, 99)

"E. St. V. M" delineates the hazards of female female impersonation. As Luce Irigaray describes it, "To play with mimesis is thus, for a woman, to try to recover the place of her exploitation by discourse, without allowing herself to be simply reduced to it" (76). Millay's satiric catalog effectively beats Wilson at the business of portrait making; nonetheless it depicts the female speaker—her public persona—as one who can be read back into a silenced female body.

Through male impersonation, Millay finds one solution to the problem of the modernist persona as it mediates between desires for private identity and public authority. Male impersonation discourages reductive criticism by eliminating the female speakers with whom Millay is typically identified. But Millay's use of male speakers in a topical, highly politicized work should not be read as an attempt to "pass," that is, as an attempt to borrow male credibility. Male impersonation allows Millay to undermine her speakers' credibility in at least two ways: 1) it implies that "maleness," because imitable, is neither fixed nor natural; and 2) it exposes the material foundations that appeals to the natural would conceal. In this latter respect, Millay's experiments with male impersonation strike most directly at modernist claims: they reveal that authority constituted as the private yet impersonal mastery of the public relies on privilege, on access to settings in which the public and private are not so much divided spheres as one and the same. *Conversation at Midnight* locates and recovers the place of women's exploitation in the men's salon, an arena in which male public and political hegemony is privately enacted and secured. The play's one set—an elegantly appointed drawing room "surmounted by a huge mirror with an elaborate gilt frame" (xiv)—reflects the material and domestic underpinnings of patriarchal power. The homosocial gathering this setting hosts accrues power by literally excluding and figuratively objectifying women. Yet as the mirror's presence suggests, the tropes this gathering employs prove reflexive; Millay's male speakers ultimately find themselves to be the commodities around which their deals and debates center.

Poised between Millay's pacifist allegory, *Aria da Capo* (1920), and her pro-intervention, antifascism piece, *The Murder of Lidice* (1942), *Conversation at Midnight* expresses a transitional moment in Millay's personal politics and in America's political consciousness. The play's characters represent a cross section of types and economic interests. There is Merton, a sixty-eight-year-old stockbroker; John, a painter; Lucas, "a young man in the advertising business" (xi); and Anselmo, a Roman Catholic priest. Two other characters are satirically named: Carl, the communist poet, and Pygmalion, a short story writer and something of a dandy. Their host is Ricardo, a liberal agnostic of Italian aristocratic background. Though these characters vary in age, occupation, and political affiliation, all share membership in an elite educated class. The play's two working-class characters, Ricardo's butler, Metcalf, and Merton's chauffeur, Frank, appear only briefly, delineating economic disparities heightened by the Depression.

With the exception of Anselmo, these men's relationships turn around competitive one-upmanship and their mutual distrust of women.[2] The play begins with talk of the hunt and phallic boasting. "That was the year I killed five hundred quail," Merton reminisces. "I always carry my gun cocked" (1). As the topic shifts from raising hunting dogs to "raising" women (4), the violence and hazards of hunting (and the class status this hobby implies) become displaced onto woman as a sign for conspicuous consumption. The communist, Carl, figures woman as capitalism incarnate: women indulge in "sparrow-cuddling" as a fad between shopping trips for expensive gowns and beauty treatments; they are fickle "Marie Antoinettes" who will by and by send the birdbaths "to the Salvation Army" (5). The men's dialogue attempts to transpose all potential threats by and to the male body onto the bodies of women. If a woman can be a tyrant, a "Huntress" (5), and "a good shot" (8), she can also inevitably find herself, like her slang counterpart, a "bird" at the receiving end of the "cocked" gun.[3] The strangled neck of "E. St. V. M." disturbingly anticipates the threats of female decapitation and castration that abound in this *Conversation*. Merton's wife may fare no better than Carl's hapless Marie Antoinette: Merton claims his wife "damn near shot her foot off" (8) accompanying him on one expedition, and when she protects songbirds by springing his traps, Merton fumes, "I could have wrung / Her neck" (4).

The female body pervades ensuing topics as a sign for treacherous excess. Responding to Ricardo's defense of leisure as a necessary restorative, Carl proclaims: "Posies of sophistry, in a time of danger and despair, / To accompany the white orchids that the well-dressed woman will wear" (7). Carl equates the pretty talk of bourgeois men with the adornments of bourgeois women. But his analogy makes women capitalism's accessories in both senses of the word. The alliteration linking the "*w*ell-dressed *w*oman" with the "*w*hite orchid" she "*w*ill *w*ear" predicts the conflation of woman and corsage into ornamental object. Through the metonymic tropes Carl and his peers employ, women become simultaneously the bearers of capitalism's posies and the floral emblems of its accumulative excess. Yet despite their ability to objectify the female body through poetic tropes, the play's characters are unable to contain this body's danger as they perceive it. The "small / Quite unconcerned bejewelled hand," which the men invoke, via synecdoche, to malign the woman driver, signals what cannot be read: duplicitous feminine gestures the men "don't understand" (8).

As the discussion evolves, what is at stake emerges as the sanctity of high culture. Anselmo protests the heresy committed when "Vergil" becomes "a name in the advertisement of a cultured dressmaking house" (20). Though this complaint attempts to redraw the boundaries blurred when high culture collides with haute couture, when female subjects dress up in canonical clothes, Millay interrogates such charges of feminization as a male cultural elite's reactionary response to women's profitable literary production. Suzanne Clark finds a similar response to women's emergence "on the market" in modernism, which "gendered mass culture, identifying woman with the mass and regarding its productions as 'kitsch,' as 'camp,' and like advertising, as objects of critical disdain" (*Sentimental Modernism* 4). For their part, mass-cultural responses to Millay and her female contemporaries have tended to reinstall female production at the site of the domestic. A 1949 *Ladies' Home Journal* feature uses simile to read Millay's work back into the kitchen: "Polished as a sonnet . . . Light as a Lyric . . . Must be the kitchen for EDNA ST. VINCENT MILLAY" (Taber 56).[4]

John Crowe Ransom's characterization of Millay's audience as "Circles and Leagues of young ladies" ("The Poet as Woman" 76) indicates that modernism's New Critical proponents depicted Millay's popular success as emblematic of a peculiarly female brand of bourgeois consumerism. In *Conversation at Midnight*, however, Millay rejects claims that artists of either sex can position themselves outside the market. Lucas, the advertising man, laments his role as a purveyor of "red-hot, mother-love, body-odour, child-athlete, vitamines-C-and-D" (17) but distinguishes himself from the "boobs" (17) his advertising copy seduces: "Do you think I buy / The lousy stuff I am lyrical about from nine to five?—not I!" (18). Though Lucas would render his "cringing tribe" (17) of consumer dupes as a feminine or racial other, his remarks betray the anxiety that the lyric mode's speaking subject might relinquish his mastery in the service of "red-hot, mother-love"—that the "inviolable I" on which masculine autonomy is founded might not only be subsumed by mass production but might give voice to its own commodification. Millay's anxious speakers confront the lyric in a marketplace where form, like gender, has no stable referent and can be put on in an act of cultural drag.

One of Millay's satiric aims is to reveal the missing term in her male characters' ideological debates. Feminism as ideology surfaces rarely and, for the most part, obliquely in the dialogue. The men tend to renounce their feminist sympathies almost at inception,[5] and none adequately serves as a spokesman for Millay's lifelong commitment to women's rights. Despite her anthems to suffrage and equality, Millay found that public recognition of her work often insulted the principles it expressed. Millay's 1937 letter to the Secretary of New York University documents her protest at being excluded from a dinner for honorary degree recipients "that is, the male recipients" (*Letters*, 1952, 291). Published in the same year that this incident occurred, *Conversation at Midnight* documents in its very setting such exclusionary practices.

Only Ricardo musters a sustained analysis of women's oppression. His speech on woman's imprisonment within a domestic sphere (49–50) may explain why so many critics identify Ricardo as Millay's alter ego.[6] Nevertheless, by constructing his critique of domesticity as a fatalistic narrative, Ricardo fails to exempt himself from its oppressive practices. His speech portrays women as the victims of biological determinism—"The family circumstance / Is man's by choice, / Woman's by function" (49)—whereas in this play, Millay dramatizes the sources of female oppression as social and material.

Millay's male speakers and critics employ binary notions of gender and culture to preempt women's political and literary authority. To collapse such binarisms, Millay constitutes her male speakers' dialogues through both high and popular verse forms. *Conversation at Midnight* features blank verse soliloquies and intricate sonnets alongside parodic nursery rhymes. At times, Millay's free verse stanzas contain arguments for a more loosely and popularly defined poetics.[7] Elsewhere, Millay exploits formal verse to expose her male speakers' hypocrisies. Midway through the play, the men recite a litany of grievances against women. These complaints rehearse a series of sexist clichés; in the following exchange, for example, women are scattered and slovenly spendthrifts:

*Pygmalion:* And they leave lip-stick on cigarette-butts and napkins and all around your mouth and on your collar.
*Merton:* And when they buy something for 2.98 instead of 3 they think they've saved a dollar.

(49)

These protests against the sloppy incursions of the feminine into male territory (the telltale "lipstick" on the male collar and mouth) are themselves verbose. The couplets the men recite follow the rhyme scheme of a hymn but exceed even the hexameter's metrical demands.[8]

Millay presents stereotypical female speech as a fiction accessed strictly through the mediations of male poetic discourse. In a moment of peculiarly self-conscious babbling, Pygmalion renders female speech " 'As Ogden Nash might put it' " (47):

> And they're always saying, "Now don't interrupt me!" and always interrupting, and they can't let anything drop.
> And they insist on telling long stories, which they do very badly, because they never know what to leave out or where to stop.
>
> (48)

Pygmalion mimics Nash to mimic the perceived loquaciousness of women. Pygmalion's impersonation of a popular male writer of "light" verse to impersonate female speakers refutes easy equations of the feminine with the popular. Moreover, Millay's nested series of impersonations denaturalizes the feminine by rendering it the product of pastiche.

*Conversation at Midnight*'s pastiche of forms levels distinctions between high and popular culture by exposing the misogynistic tropes they share—tropes that unite the "two cultures" as the single province of male discourse. Not surprisingly, this formal heterogeneity unsettles Millay's critics. Edmund Wilson downplays intentionality and craftsmanship and prefers to ascribe Millay's erratic metrics and the play's collage of fragmented forms to the play's status as a reconstructed text ("Give That Beat Again" 682).[9] Wilson praises Millay's "new semi-verse medium" for a wittiness also found in her Nancy Boyd sketches; nonetheless, Wilson cautions readers that "Nancy Boyd is not Edna Millay" (685). Wilson's compulsion to shore up Millay's canon—to piece out the popular, politicized work from that of the "real" Millay—suggests that what these critics truly fear is the "going to pieces" of the high/mass culture divide that shores up male cultural hegemony.

The play's characters share the critics' fears that through contact with the popular as feminine, the masculine as culture is disintegrating. These fears inform a rare moment of consensus, in which the men agree that love and lyric verse as its medium have become feminized. Though each man's poetic "riff" on the subject reflects his character's ideological foibles, on the subject of women, Millay reveals these ideologies to be much less oppositional than they might initially seem. To the stockbroker, love is like an "exotic" outmoded currency that persists in circulating. Merton compares love to a merchant's sailing ship, "Battered to kindling," in his sonnet beginning "Lucas, Romantic Love is on the rocks" (52). Both Merton and Carl figure romantic love as ahistorical, inefficient, and, thus, an impediment to progress. Merton proclaims that love is

> A gallant ship; but shipping in our day
> Can't trust to winds to puff it where 'tis bid;
> We can't go on rounding the Cape that way—
> Where'd progress be, and coffee, if we did?
>
> (52)

Carl eschews Merton's colonialism but not his vision of masculine progress:

> We're about as through with this thing called Love as—
>     what?—
> Plumes in our helmets, powder on our hair.
> Love's lazy, won't keep step, is all the time
> Swooning into a dozen lilies, or under a yew,
> Or looking backward, and bursting into tears and rhyme;
> Holds everything up, just can't fit in, won't do.
>
> (52)

In this passage, Carl relies, once again, on the construct of the feminine as accessory. His comrades must shed the effeminate, materialist accoutrements of an archaic costume to facilitate his vision of social progress. In this scenario, as in the biblical story of Lot's wife and in the myth of Eurydice, to look backward—to feel nostalgia—is to be seduced by the feminine. Carl personifies romantic love as a melodramatic poetess—"tears and rhyme" spewing from the same effusive source. In Carl's communist utopia, the feminine is expendable and the lyric bodily reclaimed and reinvigorated by a society of men "with their sweat / Running like tears and making their chests all muddy" (66).

The expulsion of women from the conversational scene precipitates the emergence of the homoerotic as a category—a category that the men attempt to suppress through recourse to homophobic repartee and a renewed insistence on their heterosexuality. Pygmalion, the most overtly womanizing of the characters, gives and receives the most homophobic taunts. In questioning the intellect of Carl's "friendly, seated-about-the-fire man" and Carl's affinity for communism, Pygmalion charges Carl with being blindly "enamoured" of "the face of the beloved"—a face Pygmalion personifies as a Dionysian male "Babbling violence" and "frenzied from sacramental wine" (68). Later, Ricardo peremptorily rejects a drunken Pygmalion's overtures to dance ("Oh, *Dick!* Do you dance the tango?" "Yes. But not with you" [120]). In *Between Men: English Literature and Male Homosocial Desire*, Eve Sedgwick argues that "homophobia directed by men against men is misogynistic" (20).[10] Millay dramatizes not only the interactions of misogyny and homophobia within her men's salon but also this salon's underlying fear of the sexually indeterminate. It is as if male homosocial "circles and leagues" depend upon fixed yet rhetorically pliant notions of gender. Millay demonstrates that in reading women men read themselves; male identity becomes a poetic pose.

Millay's characterization of Pygmalion further destabilizes the gender binarisms his peers struggle to maintain. Though he is narcissistic and often blatantly misogynistic, in other ways Pygmalion is less like his mythic namesake than a Wildean aesthete. Millay presents him as a hedonist: he is "good looking, . . . very well-dressed, extremely attractive to women, gay, thoroughly disillusioned, making the most out of life for himself, not bothering to vote at all" (xii). Like Nancy Boyd and Millay's female rakes, Pygmalion emblematizes the virtues of style and artifice, of desire that is fickle rather than stable or essential. Moreover, the proximity of Millay's pseudonym to *Nancy boy*, slang for a homosexual or effeminate man, suggests that dandies and female female impersonators comparably disrupt essentializing claims.

Through Pygmalion, Millay overturns a series of binaries, substituting as positive attributes terms previously disparaged as feminine. Thus, while Pygmalion himself ridicules the feminine as excess in one instance, elsewhere he describes in positive terms the experience of art as pleasurable excess. Arguing for an unmediated relationship to music, Pygmalion describes himself listening at the concert hall "With my languorous eyelids shielded by my long white hand. . . ." (43; Millay's ellipsis). Millay does not encode the pleasurably attenuated body as a feminized one per se; however, Pygmalion is censured by his peers for stepping too far out of the heterosexual line. Thus, Pygmalion identifies only uneasily with the role of the hedonist as a passive consumer of pleasure and, like his peers, rejects it as an essentially feminized position.

As the play progresses, Millay's characters vaguely ascertain that they occupy masculine poses at the cost of self-fragmentation and, even, extinction. In the sonnet beginning "I can't make love to a woman I really respect" (51), Pygmalion's sexual double standards force him to choose between pleasure and "procreation." Millay employs a series of enjambed lines that exceed the sonnet's conventional pentameter to satirize Pygmalion's compulsions:

> I can't make love to a woman I really respect.
> It's an awfully personal thing, no matter what you say;
> It's a thing you can't share; and a woman you love, or re-
> spect,
> Why, she might be thinking, or something, and it gets in
> your way.
> Kind I always fall for, too, and that's the odd
> Thing about it; I *like* 'em brainy and aristocratic;
> But for—well—I want somebody who thinks I'm just about
> God,
> Or whose attitude toward me is more or less automatic.
>
> I've thought sometimes I'd marry; I'd like to have a son,
> I don't know why, I'd just like to have a kid,—
> Two, maybe, even three, but anyway one—
> But a woman wouldn't stand for me, be a fool if she did;

And it wouldn't be fair to her, either, if our embarrassed re-
lation
Were as rare as the elephant's, and solely for procreation.

(51)

Like most sonnets in the play, this example oscillates between the
two traditional forms: the closure of its Shakespearean rhyme
scheme and concluding couplet is undermined by its visual presenta-
tion as an octave and sestet with the Petrarchan form's accompa-
nying evocations of loss. Pygmalion "*like*[s] 'em brainy and aristo-
cratic" but only a "fool" would stand for him; a "fool" is the only
kind of woman he desires sexually, but the "fool" who could bear
Pygmalion would not be "woman" enough to bear his progeny.
Pygmalion's soliloquy on his unrequited, incompatible desires is
an exercise in sophistry propelled by the sonnet's form to a sterile
conclusion.

If sophistry renders these men's heterosexual relations sterile, it
renders their homosocial relations both fickle and explosive. Merton
laments the onset of "Unfilial and boorish times" (74), times he
characterizes as threatened by the extinction of high culture and
patriarchal etiquette—"our splendid heritage / In pawn-shop win-
dows!" (74). Pygmalion spells out the rules of patronage in terms
that reveal his circle's fragility:

> Suppose I liked your figure—let that stand,
> Just for the moment; no, I'll take that back—
> Suppose I liked your painting, spent the night
> Lauding it, heckling doubters, getting sore,
> And someone said you slam the things I write . . .
> I shouldn't like your painting any more.
>
> (10; Millay's ellipsis)

Pygmalion's cagey camp reveals a form of reciprocity verging on
violence. Indeed, by the conclusion of *Conversation at Midnight*,
the play's seven principal characters nearly come to blows. Recourse
to misogynistic jokes (as well as to ethnic and racial slurs and to
the liquor cabinet) fails to defuse ideological tensions or secure male
autonomy and solidarity.[11] Woman as sign circulates so ceaselessly
within the conversation that it ceases to mean at all. The female
body can bear posies as well as dirt (" 'I honour the dirt, if you

like,' Carl spoke from the door, / 'Because it is the dress my mother wore' " 66). These male speakers' ability to dress the female body in all the latest ideological fashions points to the ultimate contingency of metonymy as a trope. In revealing these contingencies, Millay underscores her characters' own susceptibility to objectification through patriarchal discourse. The analogical tropes Millay's speakers employ to inscribe the female body render the male body equally subject to discursive manipulation and violation.

The play's characters attempt to deny the possibility of male objectification through their persistent portrayals of the victimized female body. According to their arguments, to occupy a feminine position is to ruin and be ruined: Pygmalion implores his peers to "let the poor benighted bitched-up country go to hell in peace" (58). Similarly, the men attempt to figure politics as gendering and engendering exclusively through the feminized body: Pygmalion casts Carl as "the bride of Socialism" "penetrated by Socialism" and bulging with "Revolution" (70).

Yet Carl names Merton "the father" (70) responsible for his impregnation, and ultimately, political conflict finds expression in the dialogue as male aggression against male bodies.[12] Carl likens Ricardo's liberalism to a "dreaded germ" that must be "warred upon" for threatening "the workers of the Soviet republic" with contagion: "Shall a man with a virulent and highly infectious disease / Be at large in the community?" (92–93). John describes his loss of innocence—the destruction of his belief in man's "essential goodness" by the unchivalrous incursions of a second emerging war—in terms of rape:

> . . . I *knew*
> No nation would attack the undefended, the disarmed,—
> But now, having been defiled, I do not trust
> So far.
>
> (37)

According to Pygmalion, the taking of political "vows" is a gesture akin to being sodomized:

> . . . The Marxian mind,
> Repulsing the advances of Faith from the front, is buggered
> By Faith from behind.
>
> (92)

My intent here is not to portray homosexuality as essentially sadistic nor is it to suggest that this is a view Millay herself would endorse. These characters do not so much recognize as conceal the homoerotic within metaphors of political and heterosexual violation. However, it is only by the revelation of the homoerotic at the locus of homosocial power that the patriarchal signification of women can be exposed as a series of misogynistic displacements. Millay reveals that the political solidarity of this men's circle depends upon homophobic and misogynistic tropes that ultimately prove corrosive.

It is impossible to conclude a discussion of *Conversation at Midnight* without further considering its status as a drama and the levels of impersonation this genre facilitates. But this play's potential as a fluid medium (as opposed to a textual artifact) has generally been overlooked. Although in her foreword Millay urges readers "to think of *Conversation at Midnight* in terms of the theatre" (viii), the play was not produced publicly until 1961. It enjoyed an extended run in Los Angeles but only a brief tryout in New York in 1964. Though *New York Times* reviewer Howard Taubman praised the play's abundance of "talk that sings and soars, rages and strikes fire" and the "sense and sensibility" of its language, Taubman dismissed the play as "talk, not drama" (27). Nevertheless, this genre should not seem such a novelty today with the cult popularity of such all-talk vehicles as the intellectual buddy movie *My Dinner with Andre*.

Both of the 1960s' productions of *Conversation at Midnight* were staged by Robert Gist and featured all-male casts. Another possible staging—one that would foreground the performative status of gender as the play presents it—might take its cue from Eve Merriam's feminist vaudeville *The Club. Conversation at Midnight* prefigures and is similar in conceit to *The Club*, in which women in drag impersonate a group of turn-of-the-century dandies enjoying an evening of vintage jokes, songs, skits, cigars, and, of course, debate.

Like Millay's characters, this gathering of men attempts to adhere through misogynistic discourse and, as in *Conversation at Midnight*, such discourse fails to prevent the rivalries of Merriam's club-goers from coming to blows.

An all-female staging of *Conversation at Midnight* would not only enact gender as a drama of impersonation but would reject as false the choice between political presence and artistic distance. Beyond its cross-casting, the production I am proposing would differ from Gist's productions in another important way. Gist omitted the text's scattered narrative interjections. While this omission might be dramatically expedient, it erases the presence of the narrator—one whose omniscience gives the play a kind of satiric leverage.[13] I would reintroduce this role, for the narrator occupies the position of female voyeur in this drama, eavesdropping on a scene of elite male power and pretension. The narrator could be costumed in either male or female dress, but an actor bearing a faint resemblance to Millay would assert another register of satire in a piece that speaks so directly to its own reception and that refutes impersonality as neither possible nor desirable. Early in the play, Ricardo claims that "to speak well is to speak with authority" (23). In dramatizing patriarchal discourse as sophistry, Millay creates a space for her own literary and political authority.

## Notes

1. The poem continues.

2. Millay describes Anselmo as a feminized figure, "more sensuous than ascetic" with features that are "delicately cut and of extreme refinement" (xiii). On occasion, Anselmo defends women's disparaged hobbies as his own, taking up their marginal status. (See, for example, the discussion on bird watching, 5–6). Not surprisingly, Anselmo leaves the party early, less than halfway through the play.

3. The satiric force of this hunting discussion depends, in part, on the implicit punning: birds are metonymically and analogically aligned with the female while the cock in "cocked" is coded as male. Indeed, "songbirds" (4) suggests the lyric female poet so frequently romanticized as such in nineteenth- and early twentieth-century criticism. Millay's assertion of this figure here suggests that this conversation contests not so much who may shoot as who may sing.

4. To readers of "the magazine women believe in," Taber presents Millay's formal prowess as a lesson in household economy: "She wanted it [the kitchen] streamlined, functional (a sonnet has only fourteen lines, never an extra one)" (185).

5. See Lucas on women drivers (8–9).

6. That Wilson ("Give That Beat Again" 684) and numerous reviewers privilege Ricardo's views may reflect their own political preferences more than Millay's. Millay hardly endorses Ricardo and employs Carl to satirize his indecision as a "silk-lined Liberal" (111).

7. See Carl's defense of common beauty, "Beautiful as a dandelion-blossom, golden in the green grass, / This life can be" (90).

8. Here Millay rejects stereotypes surrounding female speech by deliberately thwarting metrical conventions. Implicitly, this gesture also rejects her critics' insistence on the need for female poets to rein in their emotions through recourse to strict verse forms such as the sonnet. Debra Fried provides an excellent critique of criticism that assigns to form the role of "corset" in Millay's work ("Andromeda" 6). Fried argues that Millay's sonnets reflect not a submission to form but a conscious staging of its relation to poetic agency: "The question of whether writing in an established lyric genre is an act of taking command or of being commanded is one upon which Millay's sonnets reflect" (3).

9. In the preface, Millay describes rewriting the play from memory after the original manuscript was destroyed by a fire. She also indicates that the play's "differences in metrical style" and the variety of verse forms it contains "are an aspect of the book as first planned" (vii–viii).

10. My use of the terms *homoerotic* and *homosocial* relies on Sedgwick's hypothesis of "the potential unbrokenness of a continuum between homosocial and homosexual—a continuum whose visibility, for men, in our society, is radically disrupted" (1–2). I also share with Sedgwick her rejection of the assumption that "patriarchal power is primarily or necessarily homosexual (as distinct from homosocial), or that male homosexual desire has a primary or necessary relationship to misogyny" (20).

11. The conversation is replete with bigotry including quips about a "darkey" in a "hen-house" (24) and "The Menace of the Jews" (57).

12. *Conversation at Midnight*'s vision of male-on-male aggression brings it closer to *Aria da Capo*, with its murderous shepherds, than *The Murder of Lidice*, with its emphasis on fascism as the male rapist of the feminine domestic.

13. For example, see the narrator's aside regarding Merton's antisemitism, 57.

*Works Cited*
*Contributors*
*Index*

# Works Cited

Ackroyd, Peter. *T. S. Eliot: A Life.* New York: Simon, 1984.

Amory, Cleveland, and Frederic Bradlee, eds. *Vanity Fair: Selections from America's Most Memorable Magazine.* New York: Viking, 1960.

Atkins, Elizabeth. *Edna St. Vincent Millay and Her Times.* Chicago: U of Chicago P, 1936.

Atwood, Margaret. "The Female Body." *The Female Body: Figures, Styles, Speculations.* Ed. Laurence Goldstein. Ann Arbor: U of Michigan P, 1991. 1–5.

Bakhtin, Mikhail. *The Dialogic Imagination: Four Essays by M. M. Bakhtin.* Ed. Michael Holquist. Trans. Caryl Emerson and Michael Holquist. Austin: U of Texas P, 1981.

Barber, C. L. "An Essay on the Sonnets." *Elizabethan Poetry: Modern Essays in Criticism.* Ed. Paul J. Alpers. New York: Galaxy, 1967. 299–320.

———. "From Ritual to Comedy: An Examination of *Henry IV*." *Shakespeare: Modern Essays in Criticism.* Rev. ed. Ed. Leonard F. Dean. New York: Oxford UP, 1968. 144–66.

Barker, Francis. *The Tremulous Private Body: Essays on Subjection.* London: Methuen, 1984.

Baudelaire, Charles. *Les Fleurs du Mal.* Trans. Richard Howard. Boston: Godine, 1983.

———. *The Flowers of Evil.* Trans. George Dillon and Edna St. Vincent Millay. Preface by Edna St. Vincent Millay. New York: Harper, 1936.

Baudrillard, Jean. *Cool Memories.* Trans. Chris Turner. New York: Verso, 1990.

———. *Simulations.* Trans. Paul Foss, Paul Patton, and Philip Bleitchman. New York: Semiotext(e), 1983.

Belsey, Catherine. "Love and Death in 'To His Coy Mistress.'" *Post-Structuralist Readings of English Poetry.* Ed. Richard Machin and Christopher Norris. Cambridge: Cambridge UP, 1987.

Benet, William Rose. *The Reader's Encyclopedia.* New York: Crowell, 1965.

Bennett, Paula. *My Life a Loaded Gun: Female Creativity and Feminist Poetics.* Boston: Beacon, 1986.

Berger, John. *Ways of Seeing*. New York: Penguin, 1972.

Bergson, Henri. "Time as Lived Duration." *The Human Experience of Time: The Development of its Philosophic Meaning*. Ed. Charles Sherover. New York: New York UP, 1975. 218–38.

Bersani, Leo. *Baudelaire and Freud*. Berkeley: U of California P, 1977.

Bordo, Susan. " 'Material Girl': The Effacements of Postmodern Culture." Goldstein 106–30.

Boyd, Nancy [Edna St. Vincent Millay]. "Diary of An American Art Student in Paris." *Vanity Fair* 7.3 (Mar. 1919):44.

———. *Distressing Dialogues*. New York: Harper, 1924.

———. "The Door." *Ainslee's* 43.6 (July 1919): 130–41.

———. "The Implacable Aphrodite." *Distressing Dialogues*. 41–53.

———. "Madame a Tort!" *Distressing Dialogues*. 163–74.

———. "Mr. Dallas Larabee, Sinner." *Ainslee's* 46.2 (Oct. 1920): 80–89.

———. "Powder, Rouge and Lip-stick." *Distressing Dialogues*. 111–22.

———. "The Seventh Stair." *Ainslee's* 44.3 (Oct. 1919): 1–56.

———. "The White Peacock." *Ainslee's* 44.6 (Jan. 1920): 97–104.

Brittin, Norma. *Edna St. Vincent Millay*. Rev. ed. Boston: Twayne, 1982.

Brooks, Cleanth. "Edna Millay's Maturity." *Southwest Review* 20 (Jan. 1935): 1–5.

Brown, Dorothy. *Setting a Course: American Women in the 1920s*. Boston: Twayne, 1987.

Butler, Judith. *Gender Trouble: Feminism and the Subversion of Identity*. New York: Routledge, 1990.

Cadava, Eduardo, Peter Connor, and Jean-Luc Nancy, eds. *Who Comes After the Subject?* New York: Routledge, 1991.

*The Chapbook: A Monthly Miscellany*. Ed. Harold Monro. Especially issues 13 (July 1920), 14 (Aug. 1920), 19 (Jan. 1921), 36 (Apr. 1923).

Chodorow, Nancy. "Family Structure and Feminine Personality." *Woman, Culture, and Society*. Ed. M. Z. Rosaldo and L. Lamphere. Stanford: Stanford UP, 1974. 43–66.

Churchill, Alan. *The Improper Bohemians*. New York: Dutton, 1959.

Ciardi, John. "Edna St. Vincent Millay: A Figure of Passionate Living." *Saturday Review of Literature* 11 Nov. 1950: 8ff.

Cixous, Hélène. "Fiction and Its Phantoms." *New Literary History* 7 (1975): 525–48.

Clark, Suzanne. *Sentimental Modernism: Women Writers and the Revolution of the Word*. Bloomington: Indiana UP, 1991.

———. "The Unwarranted Discourse: Sentimental Community, Modernist Women, and the Case of Millay." *Genre* 20 (Summer 1987): 133–52.

Clément, Catherine. *Opera, or the Undoing of Women*. Trans. Betsy Wing. Minneapolis: U Minnesota P, 1988.

Coleridge, Samuel T. *On the Principles of Genial Criticism Concerning the Fine Arts.* Bristol, 1814.

Collins, Joseph. "Gallantry and Our Women Writers." *Taking the Literary Pulse: Psychological Studies of Life and Letters.* New York: Doran, 1924.

Cox, C. B., and A. E. Dyson. *Modern Poetry: Studies in Practical Criticism.* London: Edward Arnold, 1963.

Daniel, Samuel. *Delia.* 1592. Menston, England: Scholar, 1969.

Dash, Joan. *A Life of One's Own.* New York: Harper, 1973.

D'Aulaire, Edgar Parin, and Ingri D'Aulaire. *D'Aulaire's Book of Greek Myths.* New York: Doubleday, 1962.

De Beauvoir, Simone. *The Second Sex.* Trans. H. M. Parshley. New York: Bantam, 1961.

Debord, Guy. *Comments on* The Society of the Spectacle. Trans. Malcolm Imrie. New York: Verso, 1990.

———. *Society of the Spectacle.* 1967. Exeter: Rebel Press, 1987.

De Lauretis, Teresa. *Technologies of Gender: Essays on Theory, Film, and Fiction.* Bloomington: Indiana UP, 1987.

Deutsch, Babette. "Three Women Poets." *Shadowland* 7 (Dec. 1922): 51, 71, 75.

Eagleton, Terry. *The Ideology of the Aesthetic.* Oxford: Basil Blackwell, 1990.

Eliot, T. S. *The Complete Poems and Plays.* New York: Harcourt, 1962.

———. *The Complete Poems and Plays, 1909–1950.* New York: Harcourt, 1971.

———. *Four Quartets.* New York: Harcourt, 1971.

———. *Selected Essays.* New York: Harcourt, 1978.

———. "Tradition and the Individual Talent." *Selected Essays of T. S. Eliot.* New York: Harcourt, 1964.

Ellman, Richard. *Yeats: The Man and the Masks.* 1948. New York: Norton, 1978.

Ellman, Richard, and Robert O'Clair, eds. *Modern Poems: A Norton Introduction.* 2d ed. New York: Norton, 1989.

Eysteinsson, Astradur. *The Concept of Modernism.* Ithaca: Cornell UP, 1990.

Farr, Judith. "Elinor Wylie, Edna St. Vincent Millay, and the Elizabethan Sonnet Tradition." *Poetic Traditions of the English Renaissance.* Ed. Maynard Mack and George deForest Lord. New Haven: Yale UP, 1982. 287–305.

Fetterley, Judith. "Impersonating 'Little Women': The Radicalism of Alcott's *Behind a Mask.*" *Women's Studies* 10 (1983): 1–14.

Fineman, Joel. *Shakespeare's Perjured Eye.* Berkeley: U of California P, 1986.

Foucault, Michel. *The Archaeology of Knowledge and the Discourse on Language.* Trans. A. M. Sheridan Smith. New York: Pantheon, 1972.

Frank, Elizabeth. "A Doll's House: The Girl in the Poetry of Edna St.

Vincent Millay and Louise Bogan." *Critical Essays on Louise Bogan.* Ed. Martha Collins. Boston: Hall, 1984. 128–48.

Freud, Sigmund. *The Ego and the Id.* Trans. Joan Riviere and James Strachey. New York: Norton, 1962.

———. "Femininity," *New Introductory Lectures on Psychoanalysis.* Trans. James Strachey. New York: Norton, 1961. 112–35.

———. *Sexuality and the Psychology of Love.* New York: Collier, 1963.

———. "The Uncanny." *Standard Edition of the Complete Psychological Works.* Vol. 17. Ed. and trans. James Strachey. London: Hogarth, 1953. 217–52.

Fried, Debra. "Andromeda Unbound: Gender and Genre in Millay's Sonnets." *Twentieth Century Literature* 32.1 (1986): 1–22.

———. "Edna St. Vincent Millay." *Modern American Women Writers.* Ed. Elaine Showalter et al. New York: Scribners, 1991. 287–302.

Garvin, Paul, ed. *A Prague School Reader on Esthetics, Literary Structure, and Style.* Washington: Georgetown UP, 1964.

Gilbert, Sandra M. "Female Female Impersonator: Millay and the Theatre of Personality." *Critical Essays on Edna St. Vincent Millay.* Ed. William Thesing. New York: Hall, 1993. 293–312.

———. "Marianne Moore as Female Female Impersonator." *Marianne Moore: The Art of a Modernist.* Ed. Joseph Parisi. Ann Arbor: UMI, 1990. 27–46.

Gilbert, Sandra M., and Susan Gubar. *Letters from the Front.* New Haven: Yale UP, 1993. Vol. 3 of *No Man's Land: The Place of the Woman Writer in the Twentieth Century.* 3 vols.

———, eds. *The Norton Anthology of Literature by Women: The Tradition in English.* New York: Norton, 1985.

———. *Sexchanges.* New Haven: Yale UP, 1989. Vol. 2 of *No Man's Land: The Place of the Woman Writer in the Twentieth Century.* 3 vols.

———. *The War of the Words.* New Haven: Yale UP, 1988. Vol. 1 of *No Man's Land: The Place of the Woman Writer in the Twentieth Century.* 3 vols.

Gilligan, Carol. *In a Different Voice: Psychological Theories and Women's Development.* Cambridge: Harvard UP, 1982.

Gilmore, Susan. "To 'Last the Night': A New Look at the Poetry of Edna St. Vincent Millay." Honors Thesis. Brown University, 1985.

Goffman, Erving. *The Presentation of Self in Everyday Life.* New York: Doubleday, 1959.

Goldstein, Laurence, ed. *The Female Body: Figures, Styles, Speculations.* Ann Arbor: U of Michigan P, 19 91.

Gould, Jean. *The Poet and Her Book: A Biography of Edna St. Vincent Millay.* New York: Dodd, 1969.

Graves, Robert. *The Greek Myths.* Vol. 1. Baltimore: Penguin, 1955.

Griffin, Susan. *Pornography and Silence: Culture's Revenge Against Nature.* New York: Harper, 1981.

Gurko, Miriam. *Restless Spirit: The Life of Edna St. Vincent Millay.* New York: Crowell, 1962.

Hamilton, Edith. *Mythology: Timeless Tales of Gods and Heroes.* New York: NAL, 1942.

Hardy, Barbara. *The Advantage of Lyric: Essays on Feeling in Poetry.* Bloomington: Indiana UP, 1977.

H.D. [Hilda Doolittle]. *Hermetic Definition.* New York : New Directions, 1972.

Heath, Stephen. "Joan Riviere and the Masquerade." *Formations of Fantasy.* Ed. Victor Burgin, James Donald, and Cora Kaplan. London: Methuen, 1986. 45–61.

Heilbrun, Carolyn G. *Writing a Woman's Life.* New York: Norton, 1988.

Hughes, Robert. *The Shock of the New.* Rev. ed. New York: Knopf, 1990.

Irigaray, Luce. *This Sex Which Is Not One.* 1977. Trans. Catherine Porter with Carolyn Burke. Ithaca: Cornell UP, 1985.

James, Henry. *The Portrait of a Lady.* New York: Oxford UP, 1981.

Jenkins, William D. "Housewifery and Motherhood: The Question of Role Change in the Progressive Era." *Woman's Being, Woman's Place.* Ed. Mary Kelly. Boston: Hall, 1979. 142–54.

Jones, Phyllis M. "Amatory Sonnet Sequences and the Female Perspective of Elinor Wylie and Edna St. Vincent Millay." *Women's Studies* 10 (1983): 41–61.

Kaiser, Jo Ellen Green. "Fashioning an Instrument of Power: Eliot, Pound, H.D., and the Institutionalization of Literary Studies." Diss. U of California, Berkeley, 1992.

Kant, Immanuel. *Critique of Judgment.* Trans. Werner S. Pluhar. Indianapolis: Hackett, 1987.

———. *Critique of Pure Reason.* Trans. Norman Kemp Smith. New York: St. Martin's, 1965.

———. "Observations on the Feeling of the Beautiful and Sublime." *Literary Criticism and Theory.* Ed. Robert Con Davis and Laurie Finke. White Plains, NY: Longman, 1989. 394–405.

Klemans, Patricia A., " 'Being Born A Woman': A New Look at Edna St. Vincent Millay." *Colby Library Quarterly* 15 (Mar. 1979): 7–18.

Kraditor, Aileen S. *The Ideas of the Woman Suffrage Movement, 1890–1920.* New York: Columbia UP 1965.

Kreymborg, Alfred. *A History of American Poetry.* New York: Tudor, 1934.

Kristeva, Julia. "The Adolescent Novel." *Abjection, Melancholia, and Love: The Work of Julia Kristeva.* Ed. John Fletcher and Andrew Benjamin. London: Routledge, 1990. 8–23.

———. *Black Sun.* Trans. Leon Roudiez. New York: Columbia UP, 1989.

———. *The Powers of Horror: An Essay on Abjection.* Trans. Leon Roudiez. New York: Columbia UP, 1982.

———. *Revolution in Poetic Language.* Trans. Margaret Waller. New York: Columbia UP, 1984.

———. "The Speaking Subject Is Not Innocent." Trans. Chris Miller. *Freedom and Interpretation.* Ed. Barbara Johnson. New York: Basic, 1993. 147–74.

———. "Women's Time." *The Kristeva Reader.* Ed. Toril Moi. New York: Columbia UP, 1986. 187–213.

Lawrence, D. H. "Edgar Allan Poe." *Studies in Classic American Literature: Selected Literary Criticism.* Ed. Anthony Beal. New York: Viking, 1966. 330–46.

Lloyd-Smith, Allan Gardner. *Uncanny American Fiction: Medusa's Face.* New York: St. Martin's, 1989.

Longenbach, James. *Modernist Poetics of History: Pound, Eliot, and the Sense of the Past.* Princeton:Princeton UP, 1987.

McGuirk, Kevin. "Philoctetes Radicalized: 'Twenty-One Love Poems' and the Lyric Career of Adrienne Rich." *Contemporary Literature* 34 (1993): 61–87.

Mariani, Paul. *William Carlos Williams: A New World Naked.* New York: Norton, 1981.

Marvell, Andrew. *The Poems.* Vol. 1 of *The Poems and Letters of Andrew Marvell.* Ed. H. M. Margoliouth. Revised by Pierre Legouis and E. E. Duncan Jones. Oxford: Oxford UP, 1971.

Mermin, Dorothy. *Elizabeth Barrett Browning: The Origins of a New Poetry.* Chicago: U of Chicago P, 1989.

Merriam, Eve. *The Club: A Musical Diversion.* Musical direction and arrangement by Alexandra Ivanoff. New York: French, 1977.

Meyerhoff, Hans. *Time in Literature.* Berkeley: U of California P, 1955.

Millay, Edna St. Vincent. *Aria da Capo.* New York: Harper, 1920.

———. *The Ballad of the Harp-Weaver.* Illus. by Beth Peck. New York: Philomel, 1991.

———. "The Barrel." *Vanity Fair* 18.5 (July 1922): 35–36.

———. *The Buck in the Snow and Other Poems.* New York: Harper, 1928.

———. *Collected Poems.* Ed. Norma Millay. New York: Harper, 1956.

———. *Collected Sonnets.* Rev. and expanded ed. New York: Harper, 1988.

———. *Conversation at Midnight.* New York: Harper, 1937.

———. *Edna St. Vincent Millay: Letters.* Ed. Allan Ross MacDougall. 1952. Camden, ME: Down East, 1982.

———. *Edna St. Vincent Milay: Selected Poems.* Ed. Colin Falck. Manchester, England: Carcanet/New York: Harper: 1991.

———. *Fatal Interview.* New York: Harper, 1931.

———. *A Few Figs from Thistles*. New York: Mitchell Kennerley, 1920. Enlarged ed., 1922.

———. *The Harp-Weaver and Other Poems*. New York: Harper, 1923.

———. *Huntsman, What Quarry?* New York: Harper, 1939.

———. *The Lamp and the Bell*. New York: Harper, 1921.

———. Letter to George Dillon. 25 Dec. 1935. Richard Eberhart. "Seven Letters of Millay on the Publishing of *The Flowers of Evil*." *Tamarack* 2 (Winter 1982–83): 5–15.

———. *Make Bright the Arrows*. New York: Harper, 1940.

———. *Mine the Harvest*. New York: Harper, 1945.

———. *The Murder of Lidice*. New York: Harper, 1942.

———. *Renascence and Other Poems*. New York: Mitchell Kennerley, 1917.

———. *Second April*. New York: Mitchell Kennerley, 1921.

———. *Wine from These Grapes*. New York: Harper, 1934.

Millay, Norma. Introduction. *Collected Lyrics*. By Edna St. Vincent Millay. 1943. New York: Harper, 1981. xxi–xxii.

Miller, D. A. *Narrative and Its Discontents: Problems of Closure in the Traditional Novel*. Princeton: Princeton UP, 1981.

Miller, Jean Baker. *Toward a New Psychology of Women*. Boston: Beacon, 1976.

Miller, Nancy K. *Subject to Change: Reading Feminist Writing*. New York: Columbia UP, 1988.

Montefiore, Jan. *Feminism and Poetry: Language, Experience, Identity in Women's Writing*. London: Pandora, 1987.

Mulvey, Laura. "Visual Text and Narrative Cinema." Warhol and Herndl 432–42.

Nierman, Judith. *Edna St. Vincent Millay: A Reference Guide*. Boston: Hall, 1977.

Parker, Dorothy. *After Such Pleasures*. New York: Viking, 1933.

———. *Enough Rope*. New York: Liverright, 1926.

———. *The Portable Dorothy Parker*. New York: Viking, 1944.

Parker, Patricia. *Literary Fat Ladies: Rhetoric, Gender, Property*. London: Methuen, 1987.

Partridge, Eric. *A Dictionary of Slang and Unconventional English from the Fifteenth Century to the Present Day*. 5th ed. New York: Macmillan, 1961.

Patton, John. "Edna St. Vincent Millay." *The Heath Anthology of American Literature*. Vol. 2. Gen. ed. Paul Lauter. 1154–56.

———. "Edna St. Vincent Millay as a Verse Dramatist." Diss. U of Colorado, Boulder, 1962.

Perlmutter, Elizabeth P. "A Doll's Heart: The Girl in the Poetry of Edna St. Vincent Millay and Louise Bogan." *Twentieth Century Literature* 23.2 (2 May 1977): 157–79.

Poulet, Georges. *Studies in Human Time*. New York: Harper, 1959.

Pound, Ezra. *Literary Essays of Ezra Pound.* Ed. by T. S. Eliot. New York: New Directions, 1935.

———. *Selected Letters of Ezra Pound, 1907–1941.* Ed. D. D. Paige. New York: New Directions, 1971.

*Princeton Encyclopedia of Poetry and Poetics.* Ed. Alex Preminger et al. Enlarged ed. Princeton: Princeton UP, 1974.

Quinones, Ricardo. *The Renaissance Discovery of Time.* Cambridge: Harvard UP, 1972.

Rabine, Leslie W. *Reading the Romantic Heroine: Text, History, Ideology.* Ann Arbor: U of Michigan P, 1985.

Radway, Janice. *Reading the Romance: Women, Patriarchy, and Popular Culture.* Chapel Hill: North Carolina UP, 1984.

Ransom, John Crowe. *The New Criticism.* Norfolk, CT: New Directions, 1940.

———. "The Poet as Woman." *Southern Review* 2 (Spring 1937): 783–806. Rpt. in *The World's Body.* 76–110.

———. *The World's Body.* New York: Scribner's, 1938.

Rich, Adrienne. *On Lies, Secrets, and Silence: Selected Prose, 1966–1978.* New York: Norton, 1979.

———. "Twenty-One Love Poems." *The Dream of a Common Language: Poems, 1974–1977.* New York: Norton, 1978.

Richards, I. A. *Principles of Literary Criticism.* New York: Harcourt, 1925.

Riviere, Joan. "Womanliness as a Masquerade." *Formations of Fantasy.* Ed. Victor Burgin, James Donald, and Cora Kaplan. London: Methuen, 1986. 35–44.

Ronsard, Pierre de. "Sonnets pour Hélène." *Poésies Choisies II.* Ed. Paul Maury. Paris: Librairie Larousse, 1933.

Rosenthal, M. L. *The Modern Poets: A Critical Introduction.* New York: Oxford, 1960.

Rossetti, Dante Gabriel. *The House of Life. The Norton Anthology of English Literature.* 6th ed. Vol. 2. New York: Norton, 1993. 1467.

Rothman, Sheila M. *Woman's Proper Place: A History of Changing Ideals and Practices, 1870 to the Present.* New York: Basic, 1978.

Schweik, Susan. *A Gulf So Deeply Cut: American Women Poets and the Second World War.* Madison: U of Wisconsin P, 1991.

Sedgwick, Eve Kosofsky. *Between Men: English Literature and Male Homosocial Desire.* New York: Columbia UP, 1985.

Shakespeare, William. Sonnet 73. *The Complete Signet Classic Shakespeare.* Gen. ed. Sylvan Barnet. New York: Harcourt, 1972.

Shapiro, Karl. "Edna St. Vincent Millay's *Collected Poems.*" *Prairie Schooner* 31 (Spring 1957): 13.

Silverman, Kaja. *The Acoustic Mirror: The Female Voice in Psychoanalysis and Cinema.* Bloomington: Indiana UP, 1988.

Stanbrough, Jane. "Edna St. Vincent Millay and the Language of Vulnera-

bility." *Shakespeare's Sisters: Feminist Essays on Women Poets.* Ed. Sandra
M. Gilbert and Susan Gubar. Bloomington: Indiana UP, 1979. 183–99.

Stevens, Wallace. *The Letters of Wallace Stevens.* Ed. Holly Stevens. New
York: Knopf, 1981.

Stout, Janis P. "Fretting Not: Multiple Traditions of the Sonnet in the
Twentieth Century." *Concerning Poetry* 18. 1, 2 (1985): 21–35.

Taber, Gladys. "Poet's Kitchen." *Ladies' Home Journal* Feb. 1949: 55–56+.

Tate, Allen. "Miss Millay's Sonnets: A Review of *Fatal Interview.*" *New
Republic* 6 May 1931: 335.

Taubman, Howard. "Theater: Work of a Poet; *Conversation* by Edna St.
Vincent Millay." Rev. of *Conversation at Midnight,* by Edna St. Vincent
Millay. *New York Times* 13 Nov. 1964: 27.

Thesing, William, ed. *Critical Essays on Edna St. Vincent Millay.* New York:
Hall, 1993.

Twitchell, James B. *The Living Dead: A Study of the Vampire in Romantic
Literature.* Durham, NC: Duke UP, 1981.

Untermeyer, Louis. "Seven Men Talking." Rev. of *Conversation at Mid-
night,* by Edna St. Vincent Millay. *Saturday Review of Literature* 24 July
1937: 6.

Walker, Cheryl. *Masks Outrageous and Austere: Culture, Psyche, and Persona
in Modern Women Poets.* Bloomington: Indiana UP, 1991.

———. *The Nightingale's Burden: Women Poets and American Culture Before
1900.* Bloomington: Indiana UP, 1982.

Warhol, Robyn R., and Diane Herndl, eds. *Feminisms: An Anthology of
Literary Theory and Criticism.* New Brunswick: Rutgers UP, 1991.

Williams, John. *English Renaissance Poetry.* New York:Anchor, 1963.

Williams, William Carlos. *The Autobiography of William Carlos Williams.*
New York: New Directions, 1951.

Wilson, Edmund. "Give That Beat Again." Rev. of *Conversation at Mid-
night,* by Edna St. Vincent Millay. *New Republic* 28 July 1937: 338–40.
Rpt. in *The Shores of Light.* 1952. 681–87.

———. *I Thought of Daisy.* Baltimore: Penguin, 1963.

———. *The Shores of Light: A Literary Chronicle of the Twenties and Thirties.*
New York: Farrar, 1952. New York: Vintage, 1961.

Wroth, Mary. *Pamphilia to Amphilanthus.* Ed. G. F. Waller. Salzburg Stud-
ies in English Literature Ser. 64. Salzburg, Aus.: U of Salzburg, 1977.

Yeats, William Butler. *Collected Poems.* New York: Macmillan, 1956.

Yost, Karl. *A Bibliography of the Works of Edna St. Vincent Millay.* New
York: Burt Franklin, 1937.

# Contributors

*Suzanne Clark* is an associate professor of English at the University of Oregon. She is the author of articles on women writers and feminist criticism, including an interview with Julia Kristeva, cultural criticism, the sentimental, rhetoric and pedagogy, and a book, *Sentimental Modernism: Women Writers and the Revolution of the Word*. Currently, she is working on a book about academic freedom, community, and Cold War literature.

*Diane P. Freedman* is an assistant professor of English at the University of New Hampshire and is the author of *An Alchemy of Genres: Cross-Genre Writing by American Feminist Poet-Critics* and the coeditor of *The Intimate Critique: Autobiographical Literary Criticism* as well as the forthcoming *Nexus: Writings on Location*. Her critical articles, personal essays, and poetry have appeared in such publications as *College Literature*; *The Bucknell Review*; *Anxious Power: Reading, Writing, and Ambivalence in Narrative by Women*; *Constructing and Reconstructing Gender: The Links among Communication, Language, and Gender*; *Crazyquilt*; *Sou'wester*; *Wind*; and *Permafrost*.

*Sandra M. Gilbert,* a professor of English at the University of California at Davis and a prolific critic, is also a poet and the author of several collaborative works with Susan Gubar, including a recent multivolume work entitled *No Man's Land: The Place of the Woman Writer in the Twentieth Century*. Gilbert is the editor of the Ad Feminam series at Southern Illinois University Press.

*Susan Gilmore* will receive her Ph.D. from Cornell University. Her dissertation, entitled " 'Not Quite a Lady': Mina Loy, Edna St. Vincent Millay, H.D., Gwendolyn Brooks, and the Poetics of Impersonation," focuses on the ways in which twentieth-century women poets appropriate and critique a modernist aesthetic of impersonality. Her article, "Anagram and Imposture in the Work of Mina Loy," will appear in the critical anthology *Mina Loy: Woman and Poet*. She received her M.F.A. in poetry from Cornell University and is an associate editor for *Epoch* magazine.

*Stacy Carson Hubbard* is an assistant professor of English at the State University of New York at Buffalo. She has published articles on Gwendolyn Brooks, Marianne Moore, and Gertrude Stein and is currently completing a book on twentieth-century American women's poetry.

*Robert Johnson* is an associate professor of English at Midwestern State University in Wichita Falls. His recently published work includes a short story in the *Seattle Review*, an article on gender in *Proteus*, and articles on popular criticism in the *St. Louis Journalism Review* and the *CEA Critic*.

*Jo Ellen Green Kaiser* is an assistant professor of English at the University of Kentucky. She is currently working on a book-length study, "Edna St. Vincent Millay and the Spaces of Modernity," which traces the intersection of Millay and modernism. She has written several articles on Millay, the most recent of which will appear in a special World War II issue of *Food and Foodways*.

*Marilyn May Lombardi*, an associate professor of English at the University of North Carolina at Greensboro, is the author of *The Body and the Song: Elizabeth Bishop's Poetics* and the editor of *Elizabeth Bishop: The Geography of Gender*. Her recent articles on Bishop and Mary Shelley have appeared in *Twentieth Century Literature* and *Papers on Language and Literature*.

*Lisa Myers* teaches at the University of Pennsylvania. She is at work on a book, tentatively entitled "Embodied Voices: Gender, Authority, and Self-Presentation in Modern Poetry." It focuses on negotiations between and among public and private audiences in the work of Millay, Eliot, Moore, and Stevens.

*Holly Peppe*, former professor and director of the English Language and Literature Institute at the American College of Rome, Italy, holds degrees from Brown University and the University of New Hampshire. Her doctoral dissertation, focusing on Millay's literary reputation and sonnet sequences, provides an alternative evaluation of the poet's contributions to American literature and culture. Together with Millay's literary executor, Elizabeth Barnett, she edited Norma Millay's introduction to Millay's *Collected Sonnets*. She currently serves as President and CEO of the Millay Society. She is also the Director of External Affairs at ORBIS International, a global health care organization based in New York City.

*Ernest J. Smith* is an assistant professor of English at the University of Central Florida. His Ph.D. is from New York University. He is the author of *"The Imaged Word": The Infrastructure of Hart Crane's White Buildings* and is currently at work on a study of John Berryman and Sylvia Plath.

*Cheryl Walker*, Armour Professor of English at Scripps College, is the author of *The Nightingale's Burden: Women Poets and American Culture Before 1900* and *Masks Outrageous and Austere: Culture, Psyche, and Persona in Modern Women Poets*. She has edited *American Women Poets of the Nineteenth Century: An Anthology*.

*Deborah Woodard* wrote her dissertation on issues of self-presentation and the romance plot in the texts of Millay and other early twentieth-century women lyricists and received her Ph.D. from the University of Washington in 1993. She has completed a poetry manuscript entitled *Hawker of Tulips* and is the author of a chapbook, *The Book of Riddles*. Her poetry also appears in several journals including *The Antioch Review*, *Carolina Quarterly*, *How(ever)*, and *Willow Springs*.

# Index